College Physics

College Physics

Clarence E. Bennett
Professor of Physics
University of Maine

Sixth Edition

BARNES & NOBLE BOOKS
A DIVISION OF HARPER & ROW, PUBLISHERS
New York, Hagerstown, San Francisco, London

L.C. catalogue card number: 67-16622

ISBN: 0-06-460021-1

Manufactured in the United States of America

88 89 90 20 19 18 17

PREFACE

It is the purpose of this outline to summarize the essential features of first-year college physics in a manner as logical as possible and consistent with the mathematical background ordinarily assumed in generally accepted texts of college grade. The subject matter is divided, for convenience, in the customary manner, into the classical branches of Mechanics, Properties of Matter and Sound, Heat, Electricity and Magnetism, Atomic and Nuclear Physics, and Light; yet considerable stress is laid upon the unity of the subject as a whole.

Previous editions of this outline have proved helpful to students studying the subject in college courses along with some textbook as well as to others, including that large body of secondary school instructors who appreciate a condensed summary of the material ordinarily presented in college courses for their own easy reference.

For the college teacher who realizes that the completely satisfactory physics textbook has not yet been written, but who has felt obliged to select one from the many which are excellent in parts, and use it exclusively, this outline may also serve a useful purpose. It can be used as a foundation for a lecture course to be supplemented by a text for amplification, but one which need not be followed exclusively. It is felt that this procedure may help the student to acquire the proper perspective on the whole subject, which he so often fails to get in the first-year course.

The requirements of the elementary student have been kept constantly in mind in the preparation of this outline and, therefore, advanced students of the subject should be lenient in their criticisms that certain developments are incomplete or that certain statements are not unequivocally precise or correct.

The present edition of this outline of physics is a complete revision of the earlier editions. Numerous rearrangements have been made and some new material has been added. In recognition of the widespread adoption of M.K.S. units by textbook authors, although the practice is far from universal, increased emphasis has been placed on them in this edition. In so far as practicable both M.K.S. and C.G.S. units are used. The calculus is also introduced in this edition somewhat cautiously.

The sections on the electric current and magnetism have been completely rewritten, placing far less emphasis than formerly on the concept of the magnetic pole. Moreover, the treatment of atomic, and particularly nuclear, physics has been appreciably extended.

The author wishes to take this opportunity to thank those friends who have been kind enough to forward suggestions to him.

C. E. B.

Orono, Maine

Table of Contents

Part I: Mechanics

1 Introduction 1
2 Statics: Study of Forces in Equilibrium 7
3 Dynamics of Translatory Motion: Study of Forces Not in Equilibrium 14
4 Work and Energy. Machines 24
5 Dynamics of Rotary Motion: Study of Torques Not in Equilibrium 30
6 Special Dynamical Considerations of Mass Points and Rigid Bodies 36

Part II: Properties of Matter and Sound

7 Statics of Elasticity and Mechanics of Fluids 45
8 Wave Motion and Sound 55

Part III: Heat

9 Nature of Heat and Temperature 67
10 Calorimetry and Thermal Properties of Substances 74
11 Heat Transfer and Thermodynamics 79

Part IV: Electricity and Magnetism

12 Nature of Electricity and Electrostatics 87
13 Electric Currents (Steady) 98
14 Magnetism and the Magnetic Effects of Currents 112
15 Electromagnetic Induction, Oscillations, and Waves 127
16 Gaseous Conduction, the Electron, and the Nuclear Atom 138

Part V: Light

17 The Nature of Light: Its Propagation and Measurement 153
18 Geometric Optics: Mirrors, Lenses, and Other Optical Instruments 161
19 Optical Phenomena: Physical Optics 171

Appendixes

I Glossary of Terms and Definitions 183
II Laws and Principles 198
III Table of Analogies Between Translatory and Rotary Motion 204
IV Supplementary Questions and Problems 205
V Physical Constants 225
VI The Metric System 228
VII Vapor Pressures of Water 229
VIII Four-Place Logarithms 230
IX Natural Sines and Tangents 234
X Periodic Chart of the Elements 235

Index 237

ABOUT THE AUTHOR

For a number of years Professor Clarence E. Bennett was head of the Department of Physics at the University of Maine. Previously he was a member of the faculty at Brown University and at the Massachusetts Institute of Technology. He holds the Ph.D. degree from Brown University.

A fellow of the American Association for the Advancement of Science and of the American Physical Society, and a member of the American Association of Physics Teachers, the Optical Society of America, and the American Society for Engineering Education, he has contributed articles to scientific journals and is the author of the College Outlines *Physics Problems* and *Physics without Mathematics,* and of the standard textbook, *First-Year College Physics.*

HINTS ON HOW TO STUDY PHYSICS

Good study habits are essential to the most effective use of this Outline and of any supplementary text. It is suggested that the student locate in the Outline the material assigned for study in connection with his lecture course for a given class meeting. The *reference table* on pages ix–xvii will be found useful for this purpose. He should then read carefully both the Outline and the text presentation of the material, noting that different wording often helps to clarify the same topic. The first reading should be done very slowly, and with pencil in hand to underline important statements as well as to make marginal notes in both Outline and text. Terseness is considered a virtue in physics texts, and so such material usually requires time for reflection.

It is also essential for the student to master all definitions of terms, utilizing the *glossary* on pages 183–197 and the *summary of laws and principles* on pages 198–203. Very often the definitions are in the form of equations; a complete grasp of the defining equations makes the mathematical manipulations required in problem solving seem more obvious than when the relationships are merely memorized as formulas.

After the student has reread the text until he feels that he really understands the subject at hand, and not before, he should look to the *questions and problems* at the ends of chapters and on pages 205–222, as opportunities to test his grasp. Too often students feel that the main job is to get the problems solved with only such occasional references to the text as may be necessary. But this is a very short-sighted view. Usually this procedure requires more time in the long run, since problem-solving time is greatly reduced when the student has a prior understanding of the situation.

Detailed instructions for the solving of problems are given on pages 12–13, 19–20, 33–34, 49–50, and 108. It is felt that these instructions are more helpful than a display of solved problems could possibly be, since watching one problem being solved does not guarantee success with the next one. On the other hand, the method of attack, based upon an understanding of the subject matter, is common to many problems.

NOTE: For further suggestions on efficient study, consult *An Outline of Best Methods of Study*, by Samuel Smith, *et al.*, in the College Outline Series. *Physics without Mathematics*, a more elementary treatment of the subject, and *Physics Problems*, a detailed work on problem solving, both College Outlines by Clarence E. Bennett, may also be helpful.

College Physics

1: Introduction

DEFINITION OF PHYSICS

Physics is the study of the physical world considered as a whole. Although it is usually subdivided for convenience into branches such as Mechanics, Properties of Matter, Sound, Heat, Electricity and Magnetism, Atomic and Nuclear Physics, and Light, these subdivisions do not exist separately. This is becausc of the interrelations of the concepts involved. Thus these subdivisions are not and cannot be sharply defined. For some purposes it is better to disregard these classical divisions and divide physics into two very broad divisions, experimental and theoretical physics. This procedure, however, is not customarily followed in elementary expositions of the subject, and so the present outline will develop the subject in the more conventional manner; yet considerable stress will be laid upon the unity of the whole subject.

LANGUAGE OF PHYSICS

The language of physics is to a certain extent the language of mathematics. This is because mathematics affords analytical and symbolical methods of making logical deductions from fundamental postulates. Such postulates, under the name of natural laws, form the fundamental building blocks upon which the whole science of physics can be built in a logical manner. It follows that the manner of presentation of the subject is restricted by the amount of mathematical familiarity credited to the student. For this reason certain compromises between logical development and pedagogical expediency are usually to be found in elementary college textbooks, because seldom can more mathematics than algebra, geometry, and trigonometry be taken for granted as part of the reader's equipment. Increasingly, the calculus is being introduced into the first-year physics course. Therefore certain references to the calculus will be made in this outline. It must be constantly borne in mind that what constitutes an explanation of any new phenomenon varies with the reader's viewpoint, whence it is necessary that the language used be suitable to specific requirements even though it may not always express a development in the most logical manner.

FUNDAMENTAL CONCEPTS OF PHYSICS

The study of elementary physics on the college level is largely a study of physical concepts, some easily grasped and others not so easily understood by the beginner. These concepts are introduced one by one into the study either by direct definition or by derivation from simpler concepts. Thus certain concepts are considered more fundamental than others which are derived from them.

Most of the concepts of physics are so completely interwoven and connected with one another by mathematical relationships that only a very few are fundamental in the sense that they are what they are by mere definition. The whole study of forces and motions, usually referred to as mechanics, is readily reduced to a logical consideration of the interrelations of three such fundamental quantities capable of intuitive definition only. These three are *length, time,* and *mass,* although at the outset of the study it is convenient to add the concept of *force* to this category. In reality, however, force is not completely independent of the others, but there is good reason to believe that certain definitions, such as the dynamical definition of force, can be appreciated only after a working vocabulary has been established.

Length. Length (distance between two points) is usually expressed as the number of times an arbitrarily chosen unit of length subdivides the distance in question. The metric standard of length is the *meter,* which is subdivided into 100 centimeters and 1000 millimeters, etc. It is by international agreement the distance between two scratches on a platinum-iridium bar kept near Paris. The English standard is the *yard,* subdivided into 3 feet or 36 inches. It is the distance between two scratches on a bar kept in London. The *centimeter* and the *foot* are the working units in the two systems respectively. The use of the meter as a working standard, instead of the centimeter, has become increasingly popular, however. One inch is equivalent to 2.54 centimeters.

Time. Time is a measure of duration. It is expressed in units of which the mean solar second is the adopted standard in scientific and engineering work. The mean solar second is 1/86400 of a mean solar day, the latter being the time required for the earth to rotate once on its axis, averaged over the entire year, and measured with respect to the sun.

Mass. Mass is a measure of inertia, which is understood to be a property of matter by virtue of which resistance is offered to change of motion. The metric unit of mass is the inertia of a block of platinum kept near Paris and called the kilogram, said to be equivalent to 1000 *grams.* The English unit of mass is the inertia of a block of platinum kept in London and called the *pound.* One pound is equivalent to approximately 454 grams, or .454 kg.

Force. Until the vocabulary of motion is established, force can be defined intuitively as a push or a pull which tends to produce change of motion and is exemplified by the force of gravity, which is called weight. Engineers adopt as units of force the weights of the units of mass at standard locations, and designate them by *pound weight* and *kilogram weight* in their respective systems. In such usage force displaces mass as a fundamental concept.

EXAMPLES OF SIGNIFICANT DERIVED PRELIMINARY CONCEPTS OF PHYSICS*

Average Velocity. Average velocity ($\bar{v}$) is expressed by dividing a length by time, $\bar{v} = \frac{L}{t}$. *Note:* The use of symbols enables physical relationships to be expressed as mathematical equations. Since the choice of symbols is arbitrary it should be obvious that formulas should not be simply "memorized."

Work. Work is the product of force times the distance through which the point of application is moved in the direction in which the force acts. This is the same as the product of a displacement by that part of a force which points in the same direction. (Fig. 1, p. 4.) $W = FD \cos \theta$.

Note: This relationship holds only for a constant force. For a variable force the methods of the calculus are required, as will be shown on p. 24.

Work is commonly expressed in foot-pounds. The metric unit of work is the *erg*, which is equal to one dyne-cm.**

*These concepts are to be discussed in detail later on.

**See p. 18 for definition of dyne.

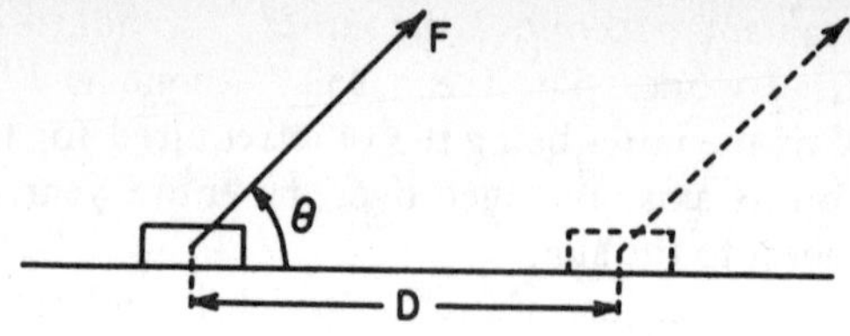

Fig. 1—Work W = FD cos θ

Power. Power is the time-rate at which work is done. $P = \frac{W}{t}$. The horsepower is 550 ft.-lbs. per second, or 33,000 ft.-lbs. per minute.

Energy. Energy is the capacity to do work and is acquired by a body as a result of having work done on it. Energy is *potential* if it is dependent upon position or shape. Energy is *kinetic* if it is dependent upon motion.

Energy and work are expressed in the same units.

The concept of energy is important because of the *law of the conservation of energy,* which states: Energy can be transformed, but in no process can energy be created or destroyed.*

Review Questions

(1) How many grams are equivalent to one pound?
(2) Express 76 cm. in mm.; in inches.
(3) Express 150 lbs. in grams; in kilograms.
(4) How much work would be done against gravity in moving a 50-lb. body 100 ft. at constant speed on a horizontal frictionless surface?
(5) Make a list of processes in which energy is transformed. Which of these deal with kinetic energy?

*See pp. 24–27 for a more complete discussion of energy.

Part I: Mechanics

2: Statics: Study of Forces in Equilibrium

Comment: This material would be presented in completely logical courses only after a complete discussion of motion, including the motion of a rigid body as well as the motion of a mass point, had been undertaken. Yet pedagogically this material is thought by some to be more readily handled first, since it requires fewer new concepts than the study of motion. This procedure also makes possible the development of mechanics around the different kinds of motion, of which statics is the simplest of all—being the consideration of no motion at all. Also this procedure parallels the historical development of the subject. Incidentally, the material of this chapter is so arranged that, except for the brief discussion of vectors, the whole chapter may be postponed to follow Chapter V without changing the continuity of the study.

FORCES

General Nature of a Force. A force is a push or a pull which tends to produce change of motion. Forces require a study of motion for their complete understanding, but a study of forces in equilibrium, i.e., acting upon bodies experiencing no change of motion, can be made independently of a study of motion.

Types of Forces. All forces are either *contact* or *field* forces, depending upon whether they act directly by contact or appear to act at a distance. In the latter case the force is attributed to the location of whatever it acts upon, i.e., the gravitational, the electrical, or the magnetic field. These concepts will be discussed later.

Weight (w) is the force of gravity, i.e., the pull of the earth on a body. *Friction* (f) is a tangential force between two contact surfaces. It is proportional to the normal (perpendicular) force (N) pressing the surfaces together, and the nature (n) of the surfaces when the velocity (v) is constant. (Fig. 2.) $f = nN$. n (coefficient

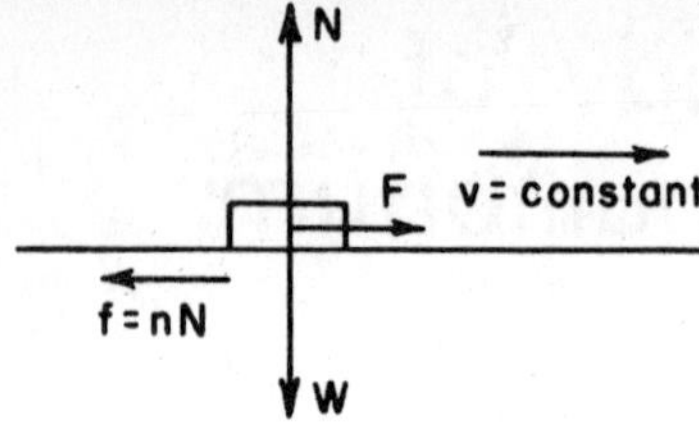

Fig. 2—Friction force f

of friction) = $\frac{f}{N}$. The coefficient of moving friction is usually less than the coefficient of static friction.

Vector Nature of a Force. Quantities which require a specification of direction as well as magnitude are called *vector quantities.* Quantities which require a specification of magnitude only are called *scalar quantities.* Forces are vector quantities (but not all vector quantities are forces). Vectors are represented by arrows, drawn to scale, to indicate direction and magnitude. The arrowhead indicates the sense of the vector.

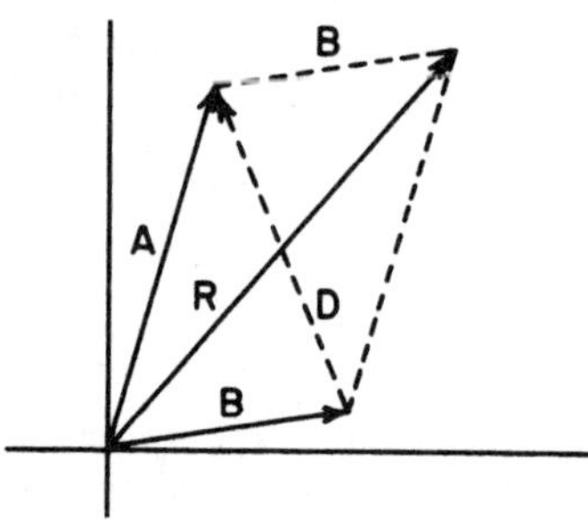

Fig. 3—Vector R is the *resultant* of vectors A and B. Vectors A and B are *component* vectors of vector R. D is the vector difference between B and A.

Vectors are *compounded* (added) by geometrical considerations. The *resultant* of two vector quantities is given both in magnitude and direction by the diagonal of a parallelogram of which the two vectors are adjacent sides. (Fig. 3.) If the second vector is laid off from the head end of the first, the line joining the tail end of the first to the head end of the second is also the resultant vector.

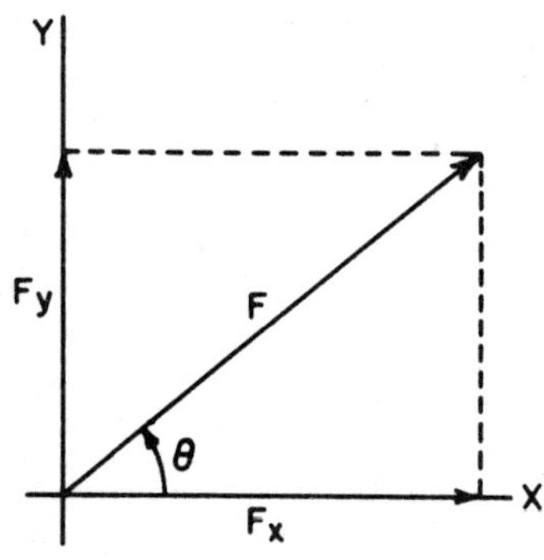

Fig. 4—x- and y-components of vector F. $F_x = F \cos \theta$; $F_y = F \sin \theta$.

Vectors can be *resolved* into *component* vectors, of which there may be any number so long as the vector sum of the components is the vector in question. The component of a vector in any direction is found by determining the projection of the vector in the direction in question, i.e., by dropping from the head end of the vector a line perpendicular to a line passing through the tail end of the vector and pointing in the direction in question. Components taken in the conventional x- and y-mathematical directions, which, of course, are mutually perpendicular, are called rectangular components and are designated as x- and y-components, respectively (Fig. 4). Such components are significant in that the sum of the squares of their magnitudes equals the square of the magnitude of the resultant. They are also simply represented by trigonometric functions. If a vector such as a force F (Fig. 4) makes an angle θ with the x-axis, then $F_x = F \cos \theta$, and $F_y = F \sin \theta$, and the direction of the force vector is given by $\tan \theta = \frac{F_y}{F_x}$.

Special cases of vector-compounding are:

(a) If F_1 and F_2 are equal and point the same way, $F_1 + F_2 = 2F_1 = 2F_2$ in the same direction.

(b) If F_1 and F_2 are equal in magnitude but opposed in direction, $F_1 + F_2 = 0$.

(c) If F_1 is equal to F_2 but makes an angle of 120° with it, $F_1 + F_2 = F_1 = F_2$ in a direction 60° from each.

(d) If F_1 and F_2 are equal but make 90° with each other, $F_1 + F_2 = \sqrt{2}F_1 = \sqrt{2}F_2$ in a direction 45° from each.

In the case of x- and y-components (usually referred to as *rectangular components*) the x-component of the resultant is the sum of the x-components of the component vectors, and similarly the y-component of the resultant is the sum of the y-components of the component vectors. (Fig. 5.)

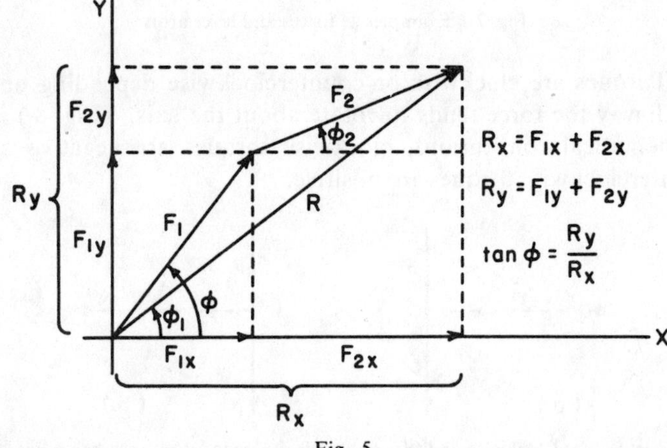

Fig. 5

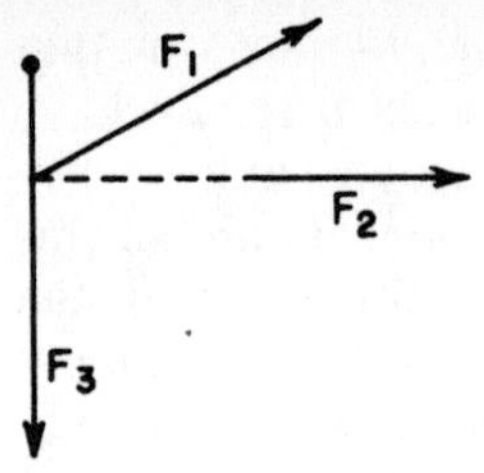

Fig. 6—Concurrent forces

$$R_x = F_{1x} + F_{2x} + F_{3x} + \cdots$$
$$R_y = F_{1y} + F_{2y} + F_{3y} + \cdots$$
$$R = \sqrt{R_x^2 + R_y^2}.$$

Concurrent and Coplanar Forces. If the lines of action of a set of forces pass through a point, the forces are said to be *concurrent.* (Fig. 6.) Forces lying in one plane are said to be *coplanar.*

CONCEPT OF TORQUE (Moment of Force)

By *experience* it is learned that forces not only tend to produce *translatory motion,* i.e., motion such that all straight lines maintain their direction unaltered, but also tend to produce *rotation* if some point is fixed so as to constitute an axis. Also, the effectiveness of a force to produce rotation is greater the farther the line of action of the force is from the axis. *Torque,* or *moment of force,* is defined as the product of *force* times *lever arm*, the latter being the perpendicular distance from the axis to the line of action of the force. (Fig. 7.)

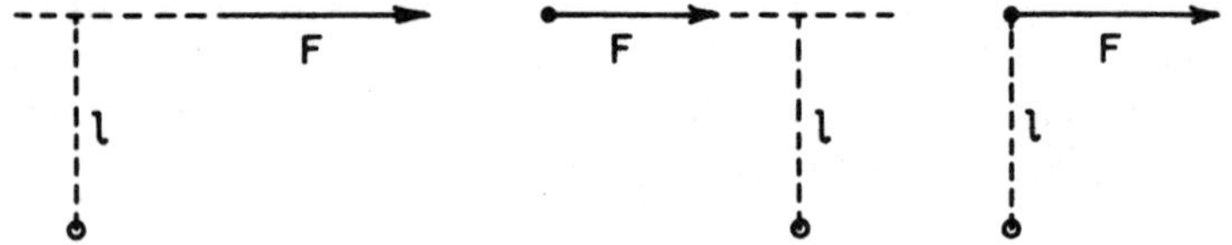

Fig. 7—Examples of forces and lever arms

Torques are clockwise or counterclockwise depending upon which way the force tends to rotate about the axis. (Fig. 8.) By mathematical conventions, clockwise torques are negative and counterclockwise torques are positive.

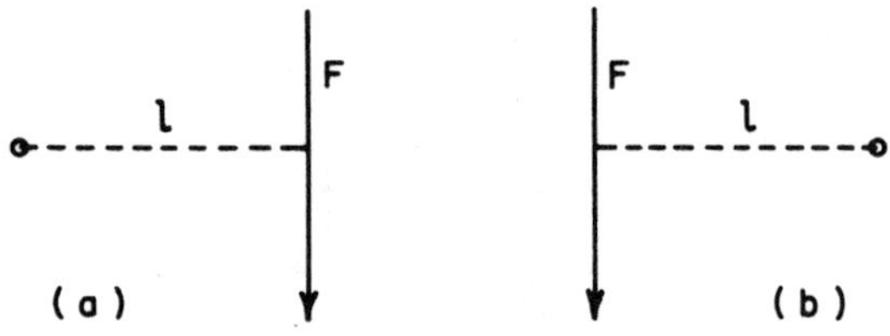

Fig. 8—(a) Clockwise and (b) counterclockwise torques, each being Fxl

For parallel forces the location of the line of action of the resultant of a number of forces should be specified with respect to some axis. For ordinary bodies the forces due to gravity acting upon individual points of the body can be treated as a set of parallel forces acting through a point called the *center of gravity*. Two equal and opposite parallel forces separated by a distance l (Fig. 9) constitute a *couple*. The product Fl is called the *moment of the couple.*

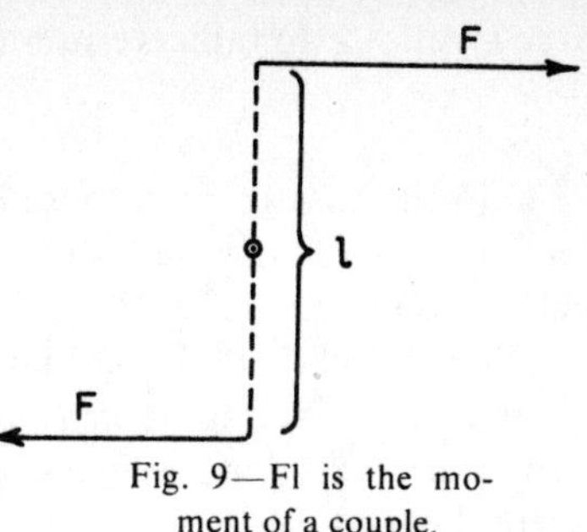

Fig. 9—Fl is the moment of a couple.

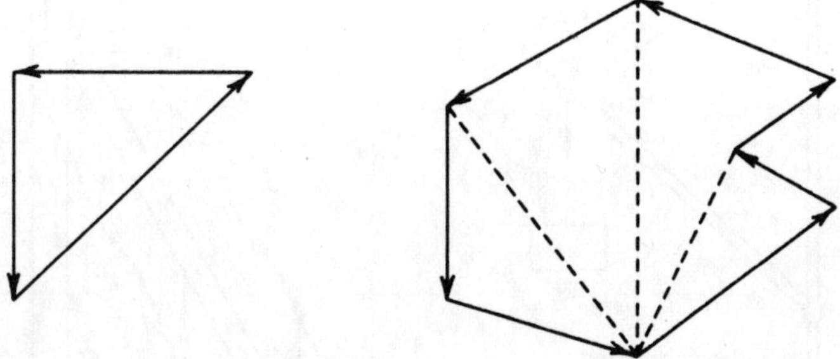
Fig. 10—Concurrent forces in equilibrium must form closed polygons.

CONDITIONS OF EQUILIBRIUM

It can be shown that all motions can be resolved into translations and rotations. Hence it can be concluded that a body is in equilibrium, i.e., undergoing no change in motion, if all tendencies toward translation, and all tendencies toward rotation about any axis, are reduced to zero.

First Condition of Equilibrium (concerns Translation). The vector sum of all the forces acting *upon* a body must equal zero. For concurrent forces this is not only a necessary condition but a sufficient condition, because concurrent forces cannot produce rotation about the point of intersection.

In terms of rectangular components, the algebraic sum of the x- and the y-components are separately equal to zero, i.e., using the symbol Σ to indicate summation:

$$\Sigma F_x = 0;\ \Sigma F_y = 0.$$

In the case of only three concurrent forces, the vectors must form a closed triangle. For more than three, they must form a closed polygon. (Fig. 10, p. 11).

Second Condition of Equilibrium (concerns Rotation). For coplanar forces acting upon a body the sum of all torques (L) taken about *any* axis perpendicular to the plane of the forces must equal zero; i.e., $\Sigma L = 0$.

Procedure for Solving Problems Involving Coplanar Forces in Equilibrium (Statics). (See Fig. 11 and Fig. 12.)

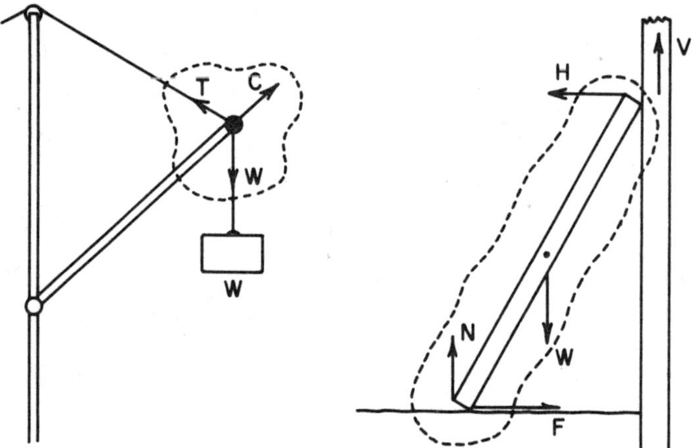

Fig. 11—Crane problem. (Point through which forces act is isolated.)

Fig. 12—Ladder problem. (Whole ladder is isolated.)

(1) Draw a diagram indicating the given quantities.
(2) Isolate the body or member of particular interest (the point of intersection, if the forces are concurrent).
(3) Indicate and label *all* forces acting *on* the isolated body. It is to be noticed that for each force acting *on* the body there is a corresponding force exerted *by* the body upon some other body. These are to be neglected.
(4) Tabulate separately the x-components and the y-components of these forces.
(5) Set the algebraic sum of the x-components equal to zero and

the algebraic sum of the y-components also equal to zero, thereby obtaining two independent equations.

(6) Tabulate separately the clockwise and the counterclockwise torques exerted by each force about some conveniently chosen axis, indicating the latter as positive and the former as negative.

(7) Set the algebraic sum of these torques equal to zero, thereby obtaining a third equation.

(8) Solve the three independent simultaneous equations thus obtained for the unknown quantities, making use of any other known relations such as $F = nN$ in the case of a friction force. It is usually desirable to solve the equations for the unknown quantity, expressing the result algebraically before inserting numerical values. This procedure generally leads to a minimum amount of arithmetic which is readily handled by simple slide rule operations.

Note: The above procedure is readily generalized to include forces not in a single plane, by considering x-, y-, and z-components separately. However, this extension is not usually considered in the first-year course.

Review Questions

(1) What is meant by a vector quantity?
(2) Define the coefficient of static friction.
(3) Give the x- and y-components of a vector of magnitude 100 units, making an angle of 30° with the x-axis.
(4) What is the lever arm of a torque? What is a moment of force?
(5) State the two conditions of equilibrium of a set of coplanar forces.
(6) A 50-lb. body is supported by two ropes which make an angle of 120° with each other. What is the tension in each rope?
(7) A uniform ladder leaning against a smooth wall makes an angle of 60° with the ground. If the ladder is 10 ft. long and weighs 60 lbs., what is the vertical thrust of the ground? What is the horizontal push of the wall? What is the coefficient of friction between the ladder and the ground, assuming the ladder to be just on the point of slipping?

3: Dynamics of Translatory Motion: Study of Forces Not in Equilibrium

Comment: *Dynamics* deals with bodies in motion both translatory and rotary. The geometrical study of motion in the abstract is called *Kinematics* and, as such, properly precedes the formal study of Dynamics. In this outline Dynamics will be subdivided into three parts as follows: Dynamics of Translatory Motion; Dynamics of Rotary Motion; and Special Dynamical Considerations. Each part will be prefaced by suitable kinematical considerations.

KINEMATICS OF TRANSLATORY MOTION

Elementary Concepts.

Position refers to the definite location of a body or a point in space by reference to some origin of coordinates. Position (P) on a line is determined by one coordinate (x); in a plane, by two (x, y); and in space, by three coordinates (x, y, z). (Fig. 13.)

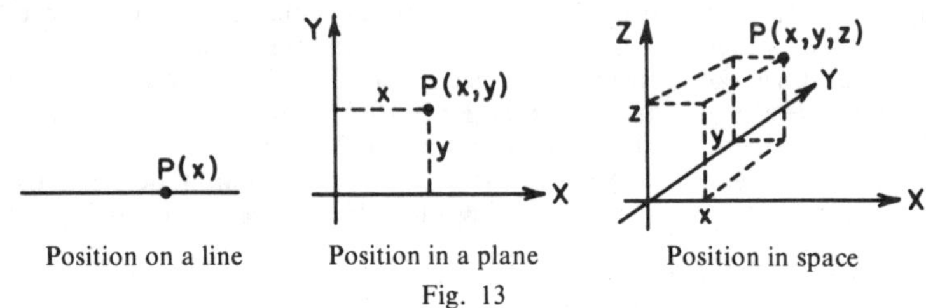

Position on a line   Position in a plane   Position in space

Fig. 13

Displacement (s) refers to a change of position (Fig. 14) and is a vector quantity (direction fully as significant as magnitude). Displacement is not to be confused with distance travelled.

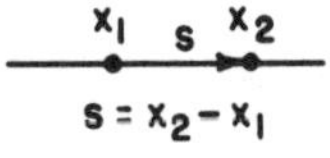

x_1 s x_2

$s = x_2 - x_1$

Fig. 14

Velocity (v) is the time-rate of change of position; i.e., it is the time-rate of displacement. Velocity is also a vector quantity. *Speed* refers to the magnitude of a velocity.

(a) *Average velocity* ($\bar{v}$) is the total displacement divided by the time required to make the displacement. $\bar{v} = \frac{s}{t}$. (Average quantities are usually indicated by a bar over the symbol.

(b) For *instantaneous velocity,* $v = \frac{\Delta s}{\Delta t}$, where Δt is an extremely short interval of time differing from zero by a negligible amount. *Note:* If Δt is taken small enough, $\bar{v}$ for the interval coincides with the actual value of v at each instant.

It should be noted that Newton invented the calculus to describe kinematical concepts. Thus, in calculus notation,

$$v = \lim_{\Delta t \to 0} \frac{\Delta s}{\Delta t} = \frac{ds}{dt}.$$

This also means that $s = \int v\, dt$.

Acceleration (a) is the time-rate of change of velocity. It is also a vector quantity. *Note:* Velocity can change in *direction* or *magnitude* or *both.*

(a) *Average acceleration* $\bar{a} = \frac{v - v_0}{t}$.

(b) *Instantaneous acceleration* $a = \frac{\Delta v}{\Delta t}$ as $\Delta t \to 0$.

Also $a = \frac{dv}{dt} = \frac{d^2s}{dt^2}$, and $v = \int a\, dt$. The relations which follow, however, hold whether they are derived by the use of the calculus or by simpler mathematical methods. The calculus simply makes the concepts more meaningful. One does not have to use calculus to use the relations correctly in problems.

Note: The quantities v and a are subject to a convention of signs. Directions upward or toward the right are usually taken to be positive, whence the acceleration of gravity is usually considered as negative.

Types of Translatory Motion.

Uniform motion (having constant velocity) is necessarily straight-line motion. $s = vt$ since $v = \bar{v}$ in this case. Rest ($v = 0$) is a special case of uniform motion. (Fig. 15, p. 16.)

In *uniformly accelerated motion,* velocity is not constant but changing uniformly. Since velocity can change in magnitude and

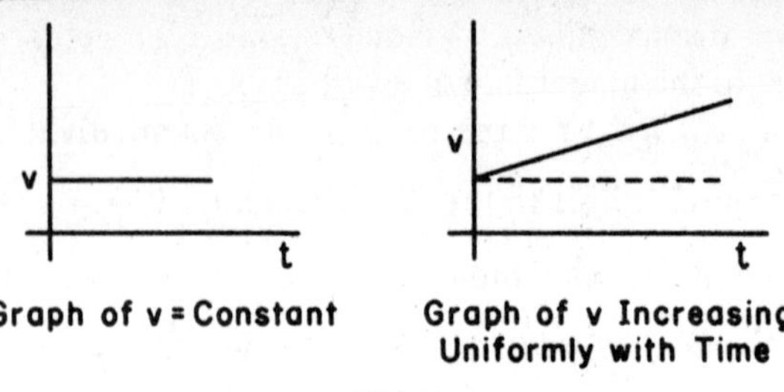

Fig. 15

direction, two special cases arise.

(a) The case of uniform change in *magnitude* only of v is called uniformly accelerated *linear* motion (where v_0 is the initial velocity).

$$v = v_0 + at$$
$$s = v_0 t + \tfrac{1}{2} at^2$$
$$v^2 = v_0^2 + 2as$$

Illustrated by freely falling bodies.

(b) The case of uniform change in *direction* only of v is called uniform *curvilinear* motion or translatory motion in a circle (not rotation).

$$a_c = \frac{v^2}{r}$$

a_c is directed toward the center of the circle. (Fig. 16.)

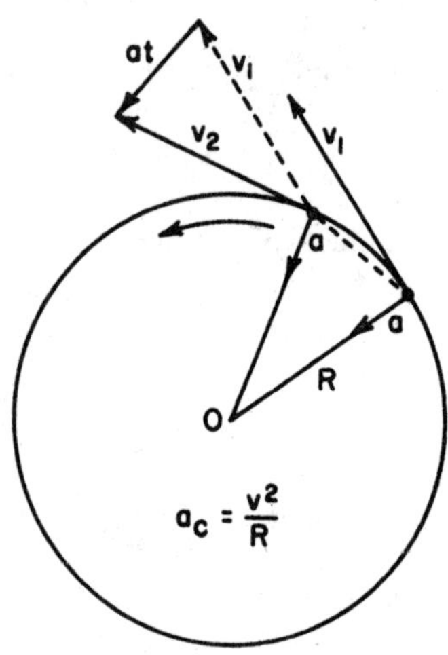

Fig. 16 — Uniform curvilinear motion. Speed constant but direction of velocity is continually changing.

Motions more complicated than uniformly accelerated motions are usually treated as *special motions* and are reserved for special consideration in a later section.

TRANSLATIONAL DYNAMICS PROPER (Matter undergoing a change in motion as a result of the action of forces)

Newton's Three Laws of Motion. These laws are to be accepted without derivation as the basis for a logical development of the principles of mechanics. These laws are subject to experimental proof only.

(1) A body at rest or moving with uniform velocity continues so to move forever unless a force acts upon it.

(2) If a force is applied to a body, the body acquires an acceleration in the direction in which the force acts and proportional in magnitude to it.

(3) To every force there is an equal and opposite reaction-force.

Comment: Law 2 is really a corollary to law 1 and together they point out that it is not a question of supplying a force to maintain a constant linear motion, but that a force is required to prevent it, once it is started.

Interpretation of Newton's Second Law. There are several experimental relations between force and motion:

(a) For different forces acting upon the same mass, different accelerations are produced which are proportional to the forces, i.e., $\left[\frac{F_1}{F_2} = \frac{a_1}{a_2}\right]$ for constant m.

(b) For different masses to acquire equal accelerations by different forces, the forces must be proportional to the masses; i.e., $\left[\frac{F_1}{F_2} = \frac{m_1}{m_2}\right]$ for constant a.

(c) Equal forces acting upon different masses produce different accelerations that are proportional to the masses; i.e., $\left[\frac{a_1}{a_2} = \frac{m_2}{m_1}\right]$ for constant F.

The preceding facts are best expressed by the relation F = kma which, by the use of consistent units, becomes the mathematical statement of Newton's second law, one of the most fundamental relations in elementary mechanics.

Dynamical Units. The preceding equation is usually simplified by such a choice of units as will make k equal to unity. Since acceleration has the dimensions of length per unit time per unit time, and thus is expressed in feet per second per second in English units, or centimeters per second per second in the centimeter-gram-second (C.G.S.) metric units, or meters per second per second in the meter-kilogram-second (M.K.S.) metric units, k can be made equal to unity by a proper choice of force and mass units. The obvious requirement is that *unit force* must give *unit acceleration* to *unit mass.* In scientific work the standard pound and the standard gram are usually accepted as fundamental units of mass in their corresponding systems, leaving it necessary to specify the force unit. Since it is a well-known fact that the force of gravity gives unit mass an acceleration of approximately 32 ft. per sec. per sec. or 980 cm. per sec. per sec., it is obvious that the unit of force must be approximately $^1/_{32}$ of the weight of a pound mass, or approximately $^1/_{980}$ of the weight of a gram mass, thus making force a derived quantity. The former is called a *poundal* and the latter a *dyne.* The unit of force which is required to give one kilogram of mass an acceleration of 1 meter per second is called the *newton.* Systems thus specified are called *Absolute Systems.*

In engineering work, on the other hand, the pound and the gram are usually taken to specify the weight of (i.e., the force of gravity upon) the standard pound and the standard gram respectively. Therefore, if k is to equal unity the unit of mass in the English system has to be approximately 32 times the pound mass and is called the *slug,* and the unit mass in the metric system has to be approximately 980 times the standard gram. This latter unit is not usually named. In this usage force becomes a fundamental quantity in physics, and mass a derived quantity, a point of view which is not acceptable to physicists because of the absolute nature of mass, and because of the fact that weight (force) varies with locality corresponding to local variations in the acceleration of gravity (g). It must not be implied, however, that the engineering system is fundamentally incorrect, because in using this system a standard value of g is recognized. These engineering systems of units are usually referred to as *Gravitational Systems.* In English units, standard g = 32.174 ft./sec.^{2}, which becomes the numerical conversion factor between the units of mass in the two systems (Gravitational and Absolute).

In pre-engineering physics it is customary to use the Gravitational System when English units are used, i.e., to express *force* (weight) in *pounds*, and *mass* in *slugs*, in which case the units are called *British Engineering Units*. When metric units are used, however, it is customary to use the Absolute System, i.e., to express *force* in *dynes* and *mass* in *grams*, or to express force in *newtons* and mass in *kilograms*. In this connection it must be clearly borne in mind that *weight* is a *force* and is, therefore, related to mass by Newton's second law W = mg (g is the acceleration of gravity; usually sufficiently approximated by 32.2 ft. per sec. per sec., or 980 cm. per sec. per sec., or 9.8 meters per sec. per sec.). Engineers frequently attempt to avoid confusion by developing relations in mechanics in terms of w (weight) rather than in terms of m (mass), as more commonly done by physicists. This procedure is, of course, quite proper if correctly done. It is, however, absolutely necessary that all units be consistent with Newton's law, which is accepted as a law of nature.

$$F = MA$$

(when the following units are used because k is then equal to unity.)

Throughout this outline it will hereafter be assumed that units are always chosen so as to make k equal to unity, whence it will always be proper to write F = MA.

SYSTEM	FORCE	MASS	ACCELERATION
English Absolute	poundal	pound	ft./sec.^{2}
British Engineering*	pound	slug (32.2 lb.)	ft./sec.^{2}
Metric Absolute*	dyne	gram	cm./sec.^{2}
French Engineering	gram	980 gram	cm./sec.^{2}
M.K.S. System	newton	kilogram	m./sec.^{2}

The M.K.S. system of units is becoming increasingly popular, but has not yet completely replaced the ones starred above in engineering work. In this system the meter and the kilogram are not only the fundamental units; they are the working standards as well. The chief advantages of this system lie in the electrical rather than in the mechanical field.

Problem Procedure in Translatory Dynamics.

Draw a diagram and represent *all forces* acting *upon* a body or an isolated portion of a body as in statics.

---

*These two systems are more commonly used in college physics courses than the others.

If all the forces in question do not act along a single line, tabulate separately the x- and the y-components of these forces, considering the x direction as the direction of motion and the y direction as the direction perpendicular to it if the motion happens to be in a single direction. *Note:* Frequently it is desirable to consider separately the forces acting upon isolated parts of a body rather than the forces acting upon the body as a whole.

Set the algebraic sum of the forces, or their components along the direction of motion, equal to the product of the mass of the body upon which they act (or the isolated part of it in question) times the acceleration of it in the same direction; i.e., set $\Sigma F_x = ma_x$. Do the same for the y-components; i.e., set $\Sigma F_y = ma_y$, noting that $a = 0$ in the direction $\perp$ to the direction of motion when the motion is restricted to one direction. (Obviously this is the same procedure followed in statics where $\Sigma F_x = 0$ and $\Sigma F_y = 0$, merely because statics deals with the special case where $a_x = a_y = 0$.)

Solve the equation or equations thus obtained for the unknown quantities, noting that for motion in one direction an independent equation results from such a force analysis upon each and every isolated portion of the body considered. Of course, if the motion is not along a single straight line, independent equations result from such an analysis along each of the x-, y-, and also z-axes.

When all the forces acting upon a body of known mass are constant forces of known value, the preceding analysis will give the resulting constant accelerations; whereupon the kinematic relations connecting v, v_0, s, a, and t (previously discussed) all hold true, in each separate direction respectively.

Caution: The foregoing method of force analysis, making use of the fact that Net F = ma, is absolutely reliable if care is exercised in the use of units. The safest procedure is to always express dynamical and kinematical quantities in terms of their fundamental units as previously discussed. Otherwise units must be indicated in every equation and treated like algebraic quantities in every mathematical manipulation, i.e., multiplied, divided, etc., to give the proper units for the answer. When fundamental units are used throughout, it is known in advance that the answer will be expressed in the fundamental units for the quantity in question.

Centripetal and Centrifugal Forces. When a body moves with constant *speed* in a circle (uniform curvilinear motion) it has an acceleration $a = \frac{v^2}{r}$ (as shown before); whence a force must be acting upon it if the body has any mass at all. Therefore, since $F = ma$, $F = \frac{mv^2}{r}$ and points toward the center of the circular path. This force is called *centripetal force.* Centripetal force should not be thought of as a specific force acting upon a body when a force diagram is being set up, but rather as the "ma" or inertia force to which the sum of the tangible radial forces is set equal, when "a" is a central acceleration and has the value $\frac{v^2}{r}$. The reaction to a centripetal force is called a *centrifugal force* and does not act upon the body in question revolving in a circle, but is a force exerted by this body upon some other body.

Projectile Motion. When a body is projected from a gun its motion usually has two components, one horizontal and the other vertical. These motions can be considered independently. The horizontal one is of the uniform variety (see p. 15), whereas the vertical motion is that of a freely falling body, if air resistance is neglected. Thus the horizontal (or x-component of) velocity is constant [i.e., equals the original x-component (v_{ox}) of velocity] and the y-component (v_y) can be calculated since $v_y = v_{oy} - gt$. These two components give the resultant velocity (v) at any point in the trajectory by $v = \sqrt{v_x^2 + v_y^2}$. Similarly formulae for the rise (Y), the time of flight, and the range (R) can be developed by treating the components of the motion separately and then compounding by the Pythagorean theorem. The important thing to note is $v_y = 0$ at the top of the path, wherefore the half-time of flight is given by the relation $t = \frac{v_{oy}}{g} = \frac{v_o \sin \theta}{g}$ (Fig. 17). Therefore $R = v_{ox}(2t) = \frac{2v_o^2 \cos \theta \sin \theta}{g}$, if air resistance is neglected.

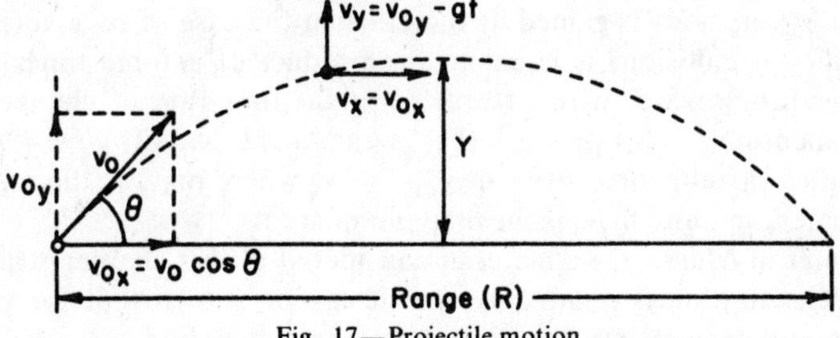

Fig. 17—Projectile motion

Momentum and Impulse. *Momentum* is defined as the product of mass times velocity (mv). It is a vector quantity. It is distinctly a dynamical rather than a kinematical quantity and is sometimes referred to as a quantity of motion (implying matter in motion as contrasted with motion in the abstract). Newton's second law as actually stated by him defined force as proportional to the time-rate of change of momentum rather than proportional to mass times acceleration; but if mass is assumed constant (extremely high velocity considerations neglected) and the proportionality constant is made equal to unity by the proper choice of units as indicated on p. 19, the two expressions are identical; thus: $F = \frac{\Delta (mv)}{\Delta t}$ becomes $m \times \frac{\Delta v}{\Delta t} = ma$ when $\Delta t \rightarrow o$. In the calculus notation, $F = \frac{d}{dt}(mv)$. If m is constant, $F = m\frac{dv}{dt} = ma$.

The *conservation of momentum* follows from Newton's third law: a body can exert a force upon a second body only if the second body exerts an equal and oppositely directed force upon the first body. If two bodies so acting upon one another, as in a collision, are isolated so that no external forces (such as friction) act upon them, it can be shown that the total momentum of such a system remains constant. This means that in a collision the total momentum of the whole system before the collision equals the total momentum after the collision, providing the system is isolated as described. In such situations due consideration must be given to the directions of the momentum components since they are vector quantities. The law of the conservation of momentum is a restatement of Newton's first law as applied to a whole system.

The change of momentum suffered by a single body (what is lost by one body is gained by the other in the case of two isolated bodies in collision) is equal to the product of a force times the time during which it acts (force being the time-rate of change of momentum). This product (Ft) is called the *impulse of a force.* For a constant force $Ft = m_1v_1 - m_0v_0$ where m_0v_0 is the initial momentum, and m_1v_1 is the final momentum.

Center of Mass. The material considered in this chapter strictly applies to a mass point only, but it can be shown that for purposes of translation, the mass of an extended body can be assumed to be concentrated in a point called the *center of mass.* Therefore, whenever reference has been made to a body in motion, the body is to be thought of as replaced by a point of equivalent mass located at the body's center of mass. This procedure is justified since only translatory motion has been dealt with. In other words, forces which tend to produce only translational motion can be considered to act at the center of mass of a body.

Review Questions

(1) What is the difference between average velocity and instantaneous velocity?
(2) From fundamental definitions, show that for uniformly accelerated linear motion $v = v_0 + at$; $s = v_0t + \frac{1}{2}at^2$; $v^2 = v_0^2 + 2as$.
(3) How can a body have a constant speed and also an acceleration?
(4) What are Newton's three laws of motion?
(5) What is a slug? a dyne? a pound of force? a newton?
(6) A block is acted upon by a horizontal force of 10 lbs. If it is supported by a table which exerts a frictional force of 1 lb., and if it has a mass of 0.5 slug, what acceleration does it acquire?
(7) The same body of the preceding problem is dragged along the same table by a cord which passes over a pulley at the edge of the table to a suspended body which weighs 8 lbs. What is the tension in the cord, and the acceleration of the two bodies? (Assume g = 32 ft./sec.^{2}) *Ans.* T = 5.7 lbs. A = 9.3 ft./sec.^{2} approx.
(8) A projectile is fired at an angle of 45° to the horizontal with a velocity 1,000 ft. per second. How long will it continue to rise? How high will it rise? Where will it strike the level ground?

4: Work and Energy. Machines

CONCEPTS OF WORK AND ENERGY

Definition of Work. As indicated on p. 3, work is a technical concept. If while a body is being displaced, a force acts upon it, and if the force acts in the same direction as the displacement, then the product of the force and the displacement is defined as the *work* done *on* the body. If the force acts in a direction other than that of the displacement, the component of the one in the direction of the other is required. Thus

$$W = F \cos \theta \, s = Fs \cos \theta$$

where F is a constant force, s is the displacement, and θ is the angle between their directions. If the force is a variable one, the quantity $dw = f \cos \theta \, ds$ is defined as the *increment of work* corresponding to an *increment of displacement*, ds, whereupon

$$W = \int_{s_1}^{s_2} f \cos \theta \, ds.$$

Work is not a vector, but a *scalar* quantity.

It should be pointed out that work is an entirely different concept from torque, yet each is the product of a force and a length.

$$W = F \cos \theta \, s \text{ (work)}; \; L = F \sin \theta \, l \text{ (torque)}$$
$$= F l \sin \theta \text{ (force} \times \text{lever arm)}$$

where θ is the angle between F and s, or F and l. $F \cos \theta$ is parallel to s, whereas F is perpendicular to $l \sin \theta$ (lever arm). Work may be expressed in ft.-lbs, but torque is said to be in lbs.-ft.

Definition of Energy. When a body has the capacity to do work, it is said to have *energy*. Energy due to position is called *potential* energy and energy due to motion is called *kinetic* energy.

Conservation of Energy. Energy is a useful concept because of the *law of the conservation of energy*, a law fully as important as Newton's laws of force and motion. Hence the method of energy analysis is suggested for many problems in mechanics instead of the force analysis discussed in the preceding chapter. *In no ordinary mechanical process can energy be created or destroyed.* Its total amount in the universe is to be considered constant.

The Relation of Energy to Translatory Motion.

Work-Energy Theorem: Since energy is the capacity to do work, and work is the product of a force times the displacement it produces in the direction in which the force acts ($W = Fs\cos\theta$), and since $F = ma$ (in the direction of F), and since (s) can be expressed in terms of (v) when (a) is constant, as follows: $v^2 = v_0^2 + 2as$, it follows that $W = mas = \frac{mv^2}{2} - \frac{mv_0^2}{2}$. The quantity $\frac{mv^2}{2}$ is called *kinetic energy* and the foregoing is an important theorem which, stated in words, says that the *work done on a body equals the gain in the kinetic energy of the body.*

Kinetic energy, qualitatively defined above as the energy due to motion, is thus quantitatively defined by the relation

$$K.E. = \tfrac{1}{2}mv^2.$$

Potential energy, defined qualitatively above as energy due to position, is more properly defined as the capacity of a body to do work as a result of work having been previously done upon the body against conservative forces, such that if the body is restored to its initial potition all this work is completely undone. Since gravity is a conservative force and a body is endowed with potentail energy by elevating it, potential energy is often referred to as $P.E. = mgh$. It must be clearly pointed out, however, that energy of position is not synonymous with energy of elevation. Forces which can do work on a body are of two kinds:

(a) *Conservative forces,* which are dependent upon position only: for which the net work they do on a body is zero when the body is moved around a closed path and brought back to its starting point. (Examples: gravity and elastic forces. Also electric and magnetic forces to be discussed later.)

(b) *Dissipative forces* (such as friction), for which the foregoing is not true.

Energy Method of Treating Problems in Mechanics: The law of conservation of energy requires that for a conservative mechanical system the sum of its kinetic energy and its potential energy remain constant. This means that, in the absence of friction-like dissipative forces, losses in potential energy are accounted for by increases in kinetic energy. A method of treating problems in mechanics, especially those problems in which time does not enter explicitly, is thus afforded. Since potential energy is dependent upon some point or base of reference, it is a relative rather than an absolute quantity, and any convenient reference base can be chosen in particular problems. With respect to this base level, a body's energy is sometimes all potential and later all kinetic.

(a) Example: Swinging simple pendulum. (Fig. 18.) P.E. (at top of swing) = K.E. (at bottom of swing). $mgh = \frac{1}{2} mv^2$.

(b) Example of energy considerations combined with momentum considerations: Ballistic pendulum. (Fig. 19.) A bullet of

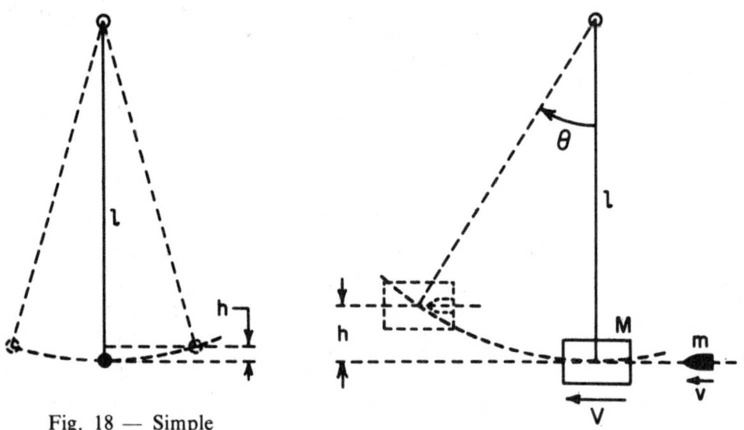

Fig. 18 — Simple pendulum

Fig. 19—Ballistic pendulum

mass (m) is fired into a massive block of mass (M) supported like a pendulum. The velocity (v) of the bullet is determined as follows:

$$mv = (M + m) V; \text{ where } (M + m) gh = \frac{M + m}{2} V^2 .$$

$$\therefore v = \frac{M + m}{m} \sqrt{2gh.}$$

(c) Example of a block sliding down an incline starting from rest. Find the velocity at the bottom.

By force considerations; $m g \sin \alpha = ma$; $v^2 = v_0^2 + 2as$; etc.

∴ v can be computed. But by energy considerations;

$$mgh = \frac{mv^2}{2}.$$

$\therefore v = \sqrt{2gh}$ directly.

Summary. General conclusions about energy:

(a) Energy is always associated with mass (inertia).
(b) For conservative forces K.E. + P.E. = constant.
(c) Concept of equilibrium in terms of energy.
  1. For unstable equilibrium P.E. is a maximum.
  2. For stable equilibrium P.E. is a minimum.
  3. For neutral equilibrium P.E. is a constant.

PRINCIPLE OF VIRTUAL WORK AND THE LAW OF MACHINES

Principle of Virtual Work. Considering a set of forccs acting upon a body which is in equilibrium, the law of the conservation of energy requires that the work done *on the body* by some of these forces must be balanced by the work done *by the body* against the rest of these forces if the body undergoes any displacement however small. This means that the *net* work done on a body by a set of forces in equilibrium must be zero for any arbitrary displacement. Since real forces would not remain in equilibrium except at the equilibrium position, the displacement suggested above must be imaginary, or virtual. This *principle of virtual work* can well be considered the condition for equilibrium.

Law of Machines. As a result of the foregoing principle, it becomes possible to understand how *machines* transmit and multiply forces which act upon bodies even when no real displacements are produced. In all such cases the work done (real or virtual) *by* the machine must equal the work done (real or virtual) *on* the machine.

Mechanical advantage is the ratio of the force exerted by the machine to the force applied to the machine. Mechanical advantage is accomplished by a sacrifice of distance thus: If $F_1d_1 = F_2d_2$ (work on = work done by), where F is the force applied to the machine, and which displaces its point of application a distance d_1, then $\frac{F_1}{F_2} = \frac{d_2}{d_1}$. Hence for a perfect (100% efficient) machine the ratio of distances (sometimes called the *theoretical mechanical advantage*) is equal to the inverse of the ratio of the corresponding forces (the *real mechanical advantage*). Thus a small force multiplied by a large displacement is equivalent to a large force multiplied by a small displacement, and vice versa.

Efficiency of a machine is the ratio of the actual work done by the machine, to the actual work done on the machine, the two quantities differing by the work done in overcoming friction. This is the same as the ratio of the actual to the theoretical mechanical advantage.

Examples of machines:

(a) *Lever.* The law of the lever, that the force applied *to* the lever times its lever arm equals the force exerted *by* the lever times its lever arm, follows directly from the preceding considerations. (Fig. 20.)

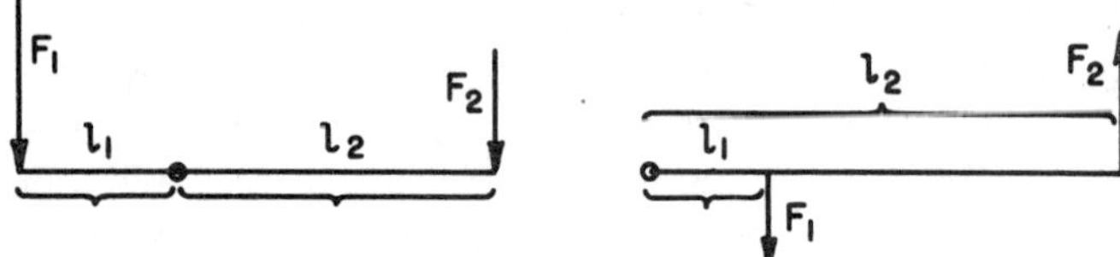

Fig. 20—Examples of levers

(b) *Pulley.* The movable pulley has mechanical advantage (M.A.) by virtue of the fact that the cord running over the pulley travels farther than the pulley during a displacement, whence the pulley itself can exert a force greater than the force applied to it via the cord. The theoretical mechanical advantage of a pulley or a block of pulleys is equal to the number of free cords running to the movable pulley or pulleys. A fixed pulley affords no gain in mechanical advantage yet it may provide a convenience. (Fig. 21.) The mechanical advantage of a fixed pulley is unity.

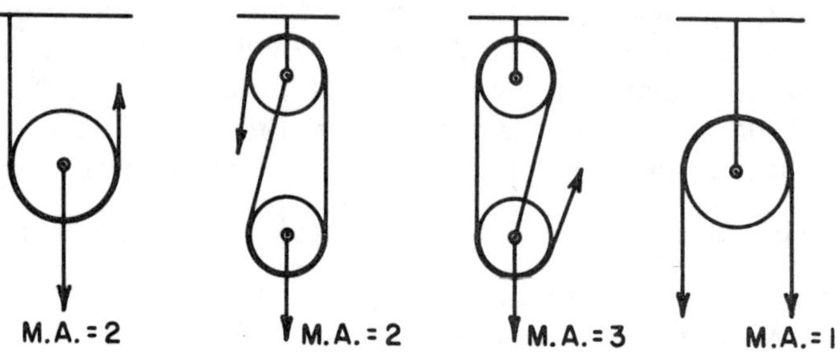

Fig. 21—Examples of pulleys

(c) *Wheel and Axle.* It can be shown that the theoretical M.A. of a wheel and axle is the ratio of the radius of the wheel to the radius of the axle. (Fig. 22.)

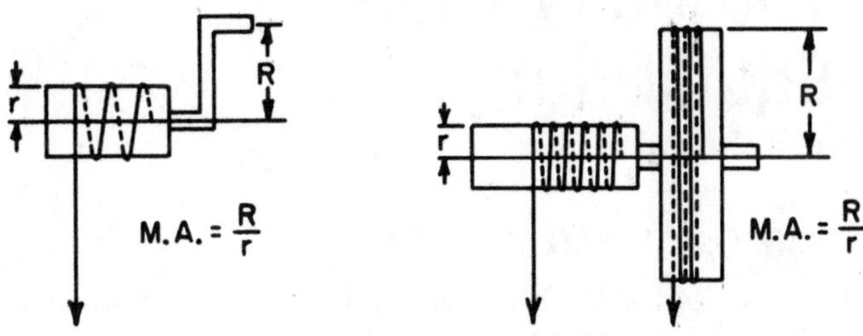

Fig. 22—Examples of wheel and axle

(d) *Inclined Plane.* Because the length of the incline exceeds the height through which a load is raised by an inclined plane, such a device has a theoretical M.A. exactly equal to the ratio of these distances. (Fig. 23.) The *wedge* and *screw* are modifications of the inclined plane.

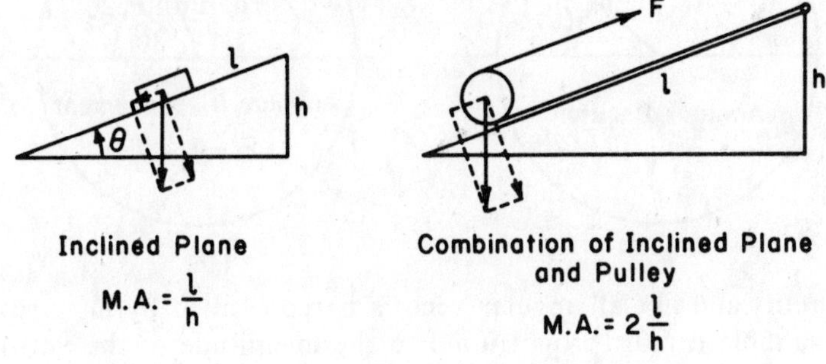

Fig. 23

Review Questions

(1) What is the maximum velocity of a pendulum bob which rises 6 inches above the lowest point of its swing?

(2) What velocity would a sled acquire at the foot of a frictionless slide 30 ft. high? How far would it travel along a horizontal surface at the foot of the slide before coming to rest if the coefficient of friction is $^1/_5$? *Ans.* 150 ft.

(3) Make a list of different types of machines and express the theoretical mechanical advantage of each.

5: Dynamics of Rotary Motion: Study of Torques Not in Equilibrium

KINEMATICS OF ROTARY MOTION

Angular Concepts and Their Translational Analogues. *Angular position* (θ) is determined by a circular coordinate referred to a fixed radius. (Fig. 24.)

Angular displacement (ϕ) is analogous to linear displacement (s). $s = r\phi$. See Fig. 25. ϕ is measured in *radians* where a radian is $\frac{1}{2\pi}$th of a complete circle. Angular displacement is a vector

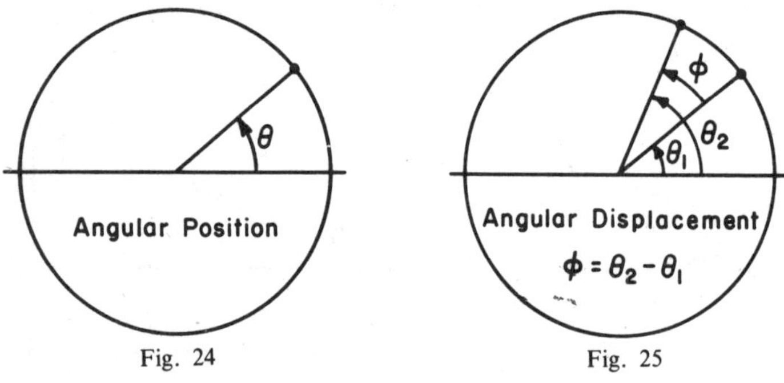

Fig. 24 Fig. 25

quantity and like all angular vectors is represented by an arrow of suitable length (proportional to the magnitude of the vector quantity) and pointing in such a way (arbitrarily agreed upon) as to indicate the direction of advance of a right-handed screw.

Angular velocity (ω) is the time-rate of angular displacement (ϕ). It is also a vector quantity. (ω ⇔ v.)

(a) *Average angular velocity* ($\overline{\omega}$ analogous to $\overline{v}$):

$$\overline{\omega} = \frac{\phi}{t} \Leftrightarrow \overline{v} = \frac{s}{t};\ \overline{v} = r\overline{\omega}.$$

(b) *Instantaneous angular velocity:*

$$\omega = \frac{\Delta\phi}{\Delta t} \text{ as } \Delta t \rightarrow 0 \Leftrightarrow v = \frac{\Delta s}{\Delta t} \text{ as } \Delta t \rightarrow 0; \ (v = r\omega).$$

$$\omega = \frac{d\phi}{dt} \Leftrightarrow v = \frac{ds}{dt}.$$

Angular acceleration (α) is the time-rate of change of angular velocity (ω). It is also a vector quantity. ($\alpha \Leftrightarrow a$.)

(a) *Average angular acceleration* $\bar{\alpha} = \dfrac{\omega - \omega_0}{t}$ analogous to $\bar{a} = \dfrac{v - v_0}{t}$; $\bar{a} = r\bar{\alpha}$.

(b) *Instantaneous angular acceleration* $\alpha = \dfrac{\Delta\omega}{\Delta t}$ as $\Delta t \rightarrow 0 \Leftrightarrow a = \dfrac{\Delta v}{\Delta t}$ as $\Delta t \rightarrow 0$; $a = r\alpha$. $\alpha = \dfrac{d\omega}{dt} \Leftrightarrow a = \dfrac{dv}{dt}$.

Types of Rotary Motion. In *uniform rotary motion,* ω = constant, or $\alpha = 0$. In *uniformly accelerated rotary motion,* $\omega \neq$ constant. If α results from uniform changes in the magnitude only of ω, then:

$$\begin{array}{lcl} \omega = \omega_0 + \alpha t & \Leftrightarrow & v = v_0 + at \\ \phi = \omega_0 t + \frac{1}{2}\alpha t^2 & \Leftrightarrow & s = v_0 t + \frac{1}{2}at^2 \\ \omega^2 = \omega_0^2 + 2\alpha\phi & \Leftrightarrow & v^2 = v_0^2 + 2as \end{array}$$

When the direction only of ω changes, a type of motion called *precession* results for which the direction of the acceleration is perpendicular to the direction of the angular velocity. See p. 35.

ROTATIONAL DYNAMICS PROPER

Note: Newton's laws (p. 17) apply equally well to rotary motion as to linear motion. The student is urged to write them down substituting torque for force and angular quantities for linear quantities.

Concept of Moment of Inertia. Moment of inertia (I) in rotation is analogous to mass (m) in translation. It is the sum of the products of each mass particle of a body multiplied by the square of its respective distance from the axis of rotation. $I = \Sigma mr^2 = \int r^2 dm$, where dm is the mathematical representation for an infinitesimal amount of mass. It differs for different axes of rotation. (Fig. 26, p. 32.)

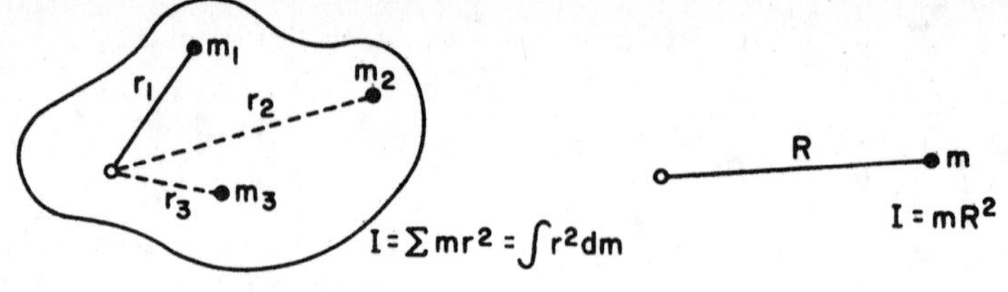

Fig. 26

Moment of inertia (I) can be calculated by mathematical methods for a homogeneous symmetrical body rotating about a specific axis, but values of I for such bodies, referred to specific axes, are usually taken from tables prepared for purposes of rotational calculations. See Fig. 27.

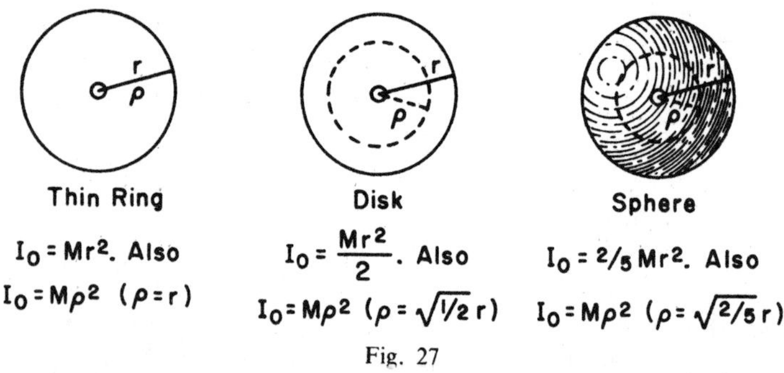

Fig. 27

By reference to Newton's second law, moment of inertia (I) bears the same relation to torque (L) and angular acceleration (α) which mass (m) bears to force (F) and linear acceleration (a). Net $L = I\alpha$ ⇔ Net $F = ma$. (This relation also serves to define I operationally.)

Significance of I is further brought out by considerations of kinetic energy. For each particle of mass (m) of which a body rotating about an axis is constituted:

$$\text{K.E.} = \tfrac{1}{2}mv^2 = \tfrac{1}{2}mr^2\omega^2 = \tfrac{1}{2}(mr^2)\,\omega^2.$$

And, for the whole body of mass $M = m_1 + m_2 + m_3 + \cdots = \Sigma m$, K.E. $= \tfrac{1}{2}(\Sigma mr^2)\,\omega^2 = \tfrac{1}{2}I\,\omega^2$.

Since $I = \Sigma mr^2$, it can be thought of as the product of the sum of all the mass particles (the total mass M of a body) multiplied by the square of some sort of average r, whence the concept of *radius of gyration* (ρ) is suggested. It is defined as that distance from the axis of rotation at which the whole mass of the body can be assumed concentrated for purposes of rotation. $I = M\rho^2$ always. For an infinitely thin ring, ρ, with respect to the center of the ring, coincides with r, the radius, since all of the mass is *actually* concentrated at this distance from the center.

Values for I_0 with respect to an axis through the center of mass are given by (Fig. 27):

$$\text{Ring: } I_0 = Mr^2, \text{ where } M = \Sigma m.$$
$$\text{Disk: } I_0 = \tfrac{1}{2} Mr^2.$$
$$\text{Sphere: } I_0 = \tfrac{2}{5} Mr^2.$$
$$\text{Thin uniform rod: } I_0 = \tfrac{1}{12} ML^2 \perp \text{ to its length (L).}$$

Moment of inertia with respect to an axis parallel to an axis through the center of mass and separated from it by a distance a is given by $I = I_0 + ma^2$.

Problem Procedure in Rotary Motion. If the motion is pure rotation about some axis, the net sum of all the torques (clockwise and counterclockwise) can be set equal to the product of the moment of inertia about that axis times the angular acceleration about that same axis. This procedure is the same as that followed in statics where $\Sigma L = 0$ merely because statics deals with the case of $\alpha = 0$ as well as $a = 0$.

Any motion of a body can be considered as made up of a translatory motion of its center of mass and a rotation about its center of mass, whence a definite problem procedure is suggested:

(1) Set the net sum of the forces acting on a body equal to ma for the whole body, or any isolated part of it, taking x- and y-components when necessary.

(2) Set the net sum of all torques about some axis equal to $I\alpha$ about that axis.

(3) Make use of the fact that $a = r\alpha$.

(4) Solve the simultaneous equations thus obtained for the unknown quantities making use of all other known relations.

An alternate procedure is sometimes followed for problems involving rolling. The point of contact between the rolling body and the surface on which it rolls is referred to as the *instantaneous axis*. About this instantaneous axis (which, of course, is continuously changing) the motion is all rotation without any translation. With respect to it, the first method above is applicable.

The moment of inertia about the instantaneous axis usually has to be calculated from the formula $I = I_0 + ma^2$.

Energy Considerations for Rotation. In rotation, work can be done by a torque acting through an angular displacement thus: $W = L\phi = Fs$ since $L = Fr$ for a constant force F, and $\phi = \frac{s}{r}$. (Note that F acts ⊥ to r in every torque.)

The work-energy theorem requires that the *total* work done on a body (work of translation plus work of rotation) equal the total gain in kinetic energy. K.E. of translation of the center of mass $= \frac{1}{2} mv_0^2$ and K.E. of rotation about the center of mass $= \frac{1}{2} I\omega^2$.

In the case of rolling, note that the work done in rotation about the center of mass by friction is just equal to the work lost in overcoming friction in the translation of the center of mass.

Energy method of treating problems: As before, when conservative forces are considered or when no energy is dissipated by friction (case of rolling just discussed above), the sum of the potential energy and the kinetic energy (i.e., that of translation of the center of mass plus that of rotation about the center of mass) remains constant. Frequently then, it is useful to note that $mgh = \frac{1}{2} m v_0^2 + \frac{1}{2} I_0 \omega^2$. (Fig. 28.)

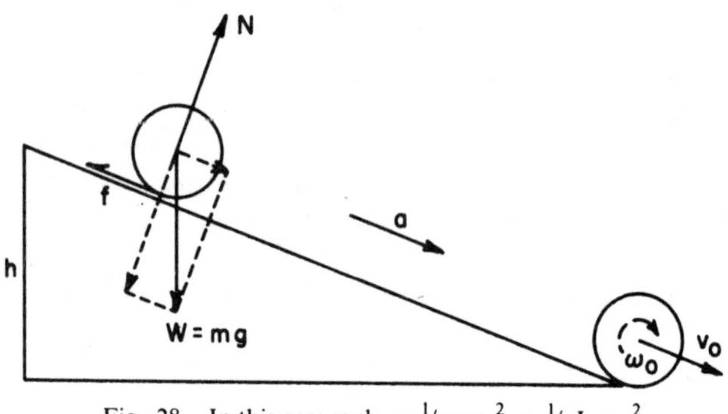

Fig. 28—In this case $mgh = \frac{1}{2} mv_0^2 + \frac{1}{2} I_0 \omega_0^2$

In the event that the motion is considered to be all rotation about the instantaneous axis, $mgh = \frac{1}{2} I\omega^2$ where $I = I_0 + mh^2$.

Angular Momentum. Angular momentum ($I\omega$), a vector quantity, is analogous to linear momentum (mv).

In the absence of external torques the angular momentum of

an isolated system remains constant; i.e., angular momentum is conserved. $I_1\omega_1 = I_2\omega_2$ (Newton's first law applied to the rotation of a whole system).

Example 1. A body on a frictionless, fixed-axis, rotating platform can have its angular speed controlled by variations of its radius of gyration.

Example 2. A gyroscope tends to maintain its axis in a fixed direction.

As the net force acting on a body is its time-rate of change of linear momentum, the net torque acting upon a body can be defined as the time-rate of change of the angular momentum of the body (Newton's second law applied to rotation).

Precession of Tops. When a torque acts upon a body rotating with velocity ω, in such a way as to appear to rotate the axis of ω about an axis $\perp$ to the ω-axis, the result is rotary motion about an axis perpendicular to each of the other two axes. (Fig. 29.) This motion is called *precession* and is analogous to curvilinear translatory motion.

It can be shown that $L = I\omega p$, where L is the torque, I is the moment of inertia, and p is the precessional velocity. Therefore $p = \frac{L}{I\omega}$.

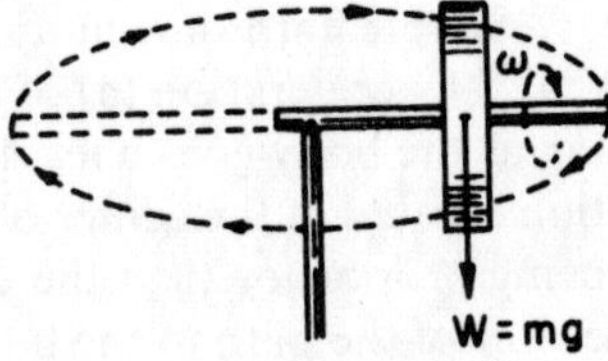

Fig. 29—Precession

Review Questions

(1) Show, by analogy to translation, that for uniformly accelerated rotary motion, $\omega = \omega_0 + \alpha t$; $\phi = \omega_0 t + \frac{1}{2}\alpha t^2$; $\omega^2 = \omega_0^2 + 2\alpha\phi$.

(2) What is meant by moment of inertia? radius of gyration?

(3) How long will it take for a wheel of 2 slugs mass rotating at 600 R.P.M. to come to rest at a uniform rate if the mass is all assumed to be in the rim of radius 2 ft., and the retarding frictional torque amounts to 16 lbs.-ft.? *Ans.* 31.4 sec.

(4) How much work is done in the preceding problem?

(5) What linear velocity will a uniform cylinder acquire rolling from rest down an incline from a 1.5-ft. elevation? *Ans.* 8 ft./sec.

6: Special Dynamical Considerations of Mass Points and Rigid Bodies

PERIODIC MOTIONS

Motions that are repeated in equal intervals of time are called *periodic* motions. All such motions are conveniently classified as *translatory* or *rotary* periodic motions.

Simple Harmonic Motion. The most important translatory periodic motion is a vibratory to-and-fro motion called *simple harmonic motion* exemplified by the bouncing of a bob suspended from a vertical stretched spring.

Simple harmonic motion (S.H.M.) is *linear* and of such a type that the acceleration (a) of the vibrating body is constantly changing as the body goes back and forth through an equilibrium position located at the center of the path of the motion, the magnitude being proportional to the *displacement* (x) (the distance from the center of the path to the body's position at a given time), and oppositely directed. Analytically, the criterion for S.H.M. is $a = -cx$ (c, constant). Such a motion is difficult to analyze by direct mathematical methods, i.e., the calculus is required, but it can be handled readily in the following manner (Fig. 30).

Relation between S.H.M. and Curvilinear Motion. If a mass point revolves with constant angular velocity (ω) in a circular path, the projection of the particle's motion upon a diameter of the circle satisfies the criterion for simple harmonic motion. Therefore, it is very convenient to *imagine* a *circle of reference* associated with every S.H.M. and to think of the S.H.M. as the projection, on a diameter of this circle, of a uniform curvilinear motion. (Fig. 30.)

Kinematical Concepts in S.H.M. (Refer to Fig. 30.) *Displacement* (x) is the distance measured outward from the equilibrium position (center of the circle of reference) to the position of the particle performing the S.H.M.

Amplitude (r) is the maximum value which the displacement can have. It is one-half the over-all length of the path of the

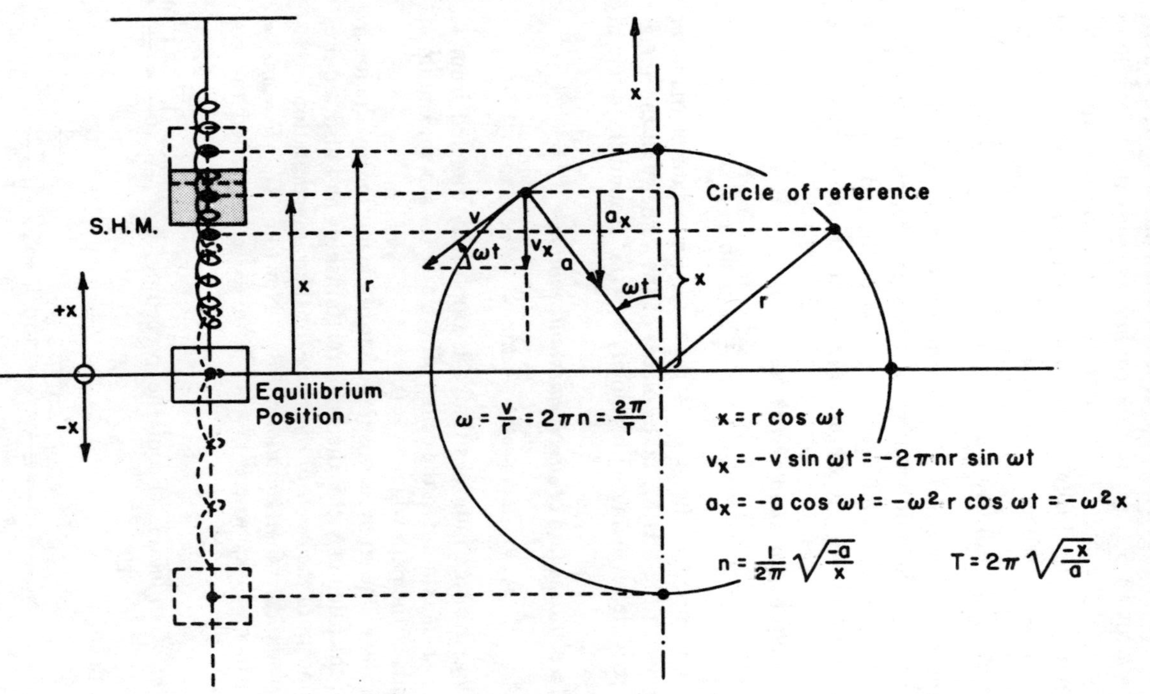

Fig. 30—Simple harmonic motion (along the vertical x-axis)

motion and corresponds to the radius of the circle of reference (Fig. 30). $x = r \cos \omega t$, when ωt is the angle made by the *x-axis, along which the S.H.M. is here considered,* with the line joining the center of the circle to the imaginary particle performing the imaginary counterclockwise curvilinear motion, in the time (t) measured with respect to the time when the imaginary particle was crossing the positive x-axis. $\omega = \frac{v}{r} = 2\pi n = \frac{2\pi}{T}$ where n is the *frequency* of the S.H.M. (the number of complete vibrations per second, or the number of revolutions per second made by the imaginary particle), and T is the *period* of the motion (the time required for a complete vibration) equal to the reciprocal of the frequency.

Velocity (v_x) *of simple harmonic motion:*

$$v_x = -v \sin \omega t = -2\pi n r \sin \omega t.$$

It is the component along the x-diameter (or whatever diameter along which the S.H.M. takes place) of the velocity of the imaginary particle revolving with velocity $v = r\omega$ around the circle of reference.

Acceleration (a_x) *of simple harmonic motion:*

$$a_x = -a \cos \omega t = -\omega^2 x = -4\pi^2 n^2 x.$$

The negative sign indicates that a is oppositely directed from x. *Note:* v is maximum at the center where $a = 0$. a is maximum at the ends of the path where $v = 0$.

Note: The analysis of simple harmonic motion by the methods of the calculus yields the same relationships and also requires the concept of the *circle of reference* for their interpretation.

Dynamical Considerations. By Newton II, $F = ma = -4\pi^2 n^2 mx = -kx$ where $k = 4\pi^2 n^2 m = \omega^2 m$ (called the *coefficient of stiffness*). From the preceding, $n = \frac{1}{2\pi}\sqrt{\frac{k}{m}} = \frac{1}{T}$.

Also, since

$$k = \frac{-F}{x},\ n = \frac{1}{2\pi}\sqrt{\frac{-a}{x}} \text{ and } T = 2\pi\sqrt{\frac{-x}{a}}.$$

Example: It can be shown that the motion of a simple pendulum approximates simple harmonic motion for vibrations of very small amplitude, for which the motion is practically linear. For such a simple pendulum $T = 2\pi\sqrt{\frac{L}{g}}$.

It will be shown later that all elastic forces tend to produce simple harmonic motion. This is why, in Fig. 30, a mass bob suspended from a coiled spring is drawn to represent S.H.M. See Hooke's law, p. 45.

Energy Considerations for S.H.M. Kinetic energy of S.H.M.: K.E. $= \frac{1}{2}mv_x^2$. Since a force which produces simple harmonic motion is a conservative force (because it is dependent upon position alone, thus: $F = -kx$), there is also a potential energy P.E. $= \frac{kx^2}{2}$ (on the average). Also $\frac{1}{2}\ mv_x^2 + \frac{kx^2}{2} =$ constant.

Note: When $v = 0$, $x =$ maximum; energy all potential. When $x = 0$, $v =$ maximum; energy all kinetic.

Rotary Harmonic Motion. Rotary harmonic motion (R.H.M.) is characterized by the angular acceleration (α) being proportional to the angular displacement (ϕ). (Fig. 31.) I.e., $\alpha = -c'\phi$, where c′ is constant. The motion of a mass point performing R.H.M. is the same as S.H.M. except that the motion takes place along the arc of a circle instead of along a straight line.

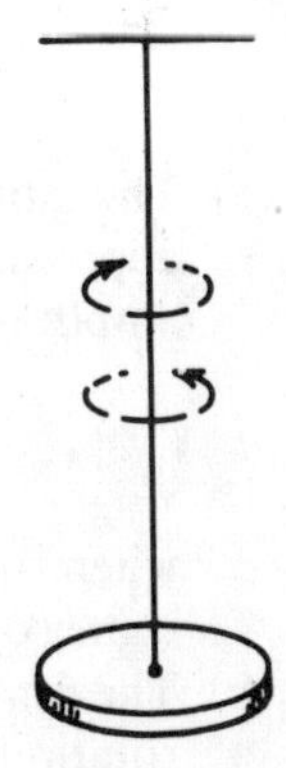

Fig. 31—Rotary harmonic motion

The dynamical relations for rotary harmonic motion can be written down by analogy to simple harmonic motion; thus $L = -k'\phi \Leftrightarrow F = -kx$. $k' =$ coefficient of torsional stiffness; $k =$ coefficient of stiffness; furthermore $k' = 4\pi^2 n'^2 I \Leftrightarrow k = 4\pi^2 n^2 m$.

$n' = \frac{1}{2\pi}\sqrt{\frac{k'}{I}} = \frac{1}{2\pi}\sqrt{\frac{L}{I\phi}} = \frac{1}{2\pi}\sqrt{\frac{-\alpha}{\phi}}$ for R.H.M. compared

with $n = \frac{1}{2\pi}\sqrt{\frac{k}{m}} = \frac{1}{2\pi}\sqrt{\frac{F}{mx}} = \frac{1}{2\pi}\sqrt{\frac{-a}{x}}$ for S.H.M.

It should be noted that whereas in this outline *simple harmonic* motion has been defined by the relation $a = -cx$, and *rotary harmonic* motion has been defined by the relation $\alpha = -c'\phi$, these expressions are but special cases of a general relationship which states that *acceleration* is *negatively* proportional to *dis-*

placement. Consequently, mathematicians often do not distinguish between the two special cases and call both motions *simple harmonic.*

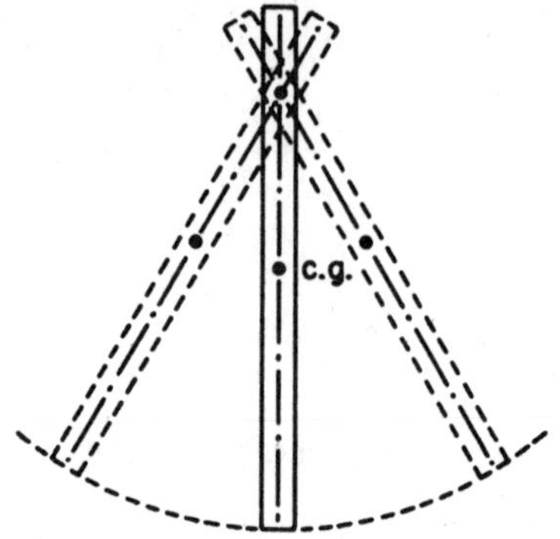

Fig. 32—Compound pendulum

(a) The motion of the compound (physical) pendulum (Fig. 32) approximates rotary harmonic motion for small angular amplitudes.

$$T = 2\pi \sqrt{\frac{-\phi}{\alpha}} = 2\pi \sqrt{\frac{I}{mgh}}$$

where h is the distance between the axis of rotation and the center of gravity (cg.). Recall $I = I_0 + mh^2$.

(b) The center of oscillation is a point separated from the axis of rotation by a distance such that if all the mass of the pendulum were concentrated at this distance from the axis in the form of a simple pendulum, it would have the same period of oscillation. This distance is known as the length of the equivalent simple pendulum. The *center of oscillation,* and the *center of suspension* from which it is determined, may be interchanged without changing the period. Also, the center of oscillation is the *center of percussion,* or the point where the body may be struck without jar.

PLANETARY MOTION AND GRAVITATION

Kepler's Laws of Planetary Motion.

(1) The planets move in ellipses, which are very nearly circular, with the sun at one focus.

(2) The radius vector from the sun to a planet sweeps out equal areas in equal times.

(3) The squares of the periods of revolution of the planets are proportional to the cubes of their greatest distances from the sun.

Newton's Law of Gravitation. From the foregoing laws of Kepler, Newton showed that each planet and the sun attract each other, as do all mass particles in the universe, by a force proportional to the product of their masses and inversely as the squares of their distance apart. I.e., $F = -G \frac{Mm}{R^2}$ where M and m are the masses of the sun and the planet respectively, and R is the distance of separation. G is a constant, the gravitation constant, found by careful measurement to be 6.66×10^{-8} in C.G.S. units. This law can be justified by observations on the motion of the moon.

By applying this law of mutual attraction between all particles of matter in the universe, the masses of the earth, sun, and other astronomical bodies can be calculated with considerable precision. (Mass of earth = 5.97×10^{27} grams.)

The force of attraction between a body of mass M and a body of *unit mass* (m = 1) is called the *gravitational field intensity* due to mass M at the place where the unit mass (m) is located.

The product of the gravitational field intensity multiplied by the distance a unit of mass is moved in the direction of the gravitational field is called the difference in *gravitational potential* between the end point and the initial point of the displacement. It is equal to the work done on the unit mass in moving it from the initial to the final position.

REVIEW QUESTIONS

(1) What is meant by simple harmonic motion?
(2) What are the relations for displacement, velocity, and acceleration in S.H.M.?
(3) What will be the period of a simple pendulum 64 ft. long?
(4) What is the basis for the claim that the mass of the earth is 5.97×10^{27} grams?

Part II: Properties of Matter and Sound (Mechanics of Deformable Bodies)

7: Statics of Elasticity and Mechanics of Fluids

Comment: Up to this point all bodies have been treated as if they were equivalent to mass points (centers of mass) if not actually mass points, or as if their masses were distributed throughout them in a perfectly definite manner such that the distance between any two mass points remained constant. This latter condition characterizes a body as *rigid.* It is now proposed to study the mechanics of *deformable* bodies for which the distance between mass points within a body may be changed by the application of forces. All matter is characterized by a relative tendency to recover from distortion which may be a change of shape or of volume or both. This property is called *elasticity* and by virtue of it all matter is subdivided for convenience into *solids* and *fluids* depending upon the extent to which it is displayed. Fluids yield so readily to forces tending to change their shape that they are said to have no rigidity, but actually the distinction is only relative. Fluids are further subdivided into two groups, *liquids* and *gases,* depending upon whether or not they display a free surface. Also liquids, although offering practically no resistance to change of shape, do offer considerable resistance to change of volume, whereas gases yield very readily to either change.

ELASTIC CONCEPTS AND PROPERTIES

Stresses and Strains. When a substance is deformed in any way, internal mutual forces called *stresses* are developed between adjacent parts of the substance. These forces tend to restore the substance to its equilibrium condition. Quantitatively, a *stress* is such a force per unit area of surface upon which it acts. When a substance or a body is deformed, the fractional deformation is called a *strain.*

Hooke's Law. Within the elastic limit, the ratio of stress to strain is observed to be constant, i.e., $F = kx$ for a simple stretched string, where k is the coefficient of stiffness as defined on p. 38.

The constant is also called an *elastic modulus,* of which several different types are commonly considered.

Young's Modulus (Y): For longitudinal deformation (simple stretch or longitudinal compression; see Fig. 33),

$$Y = \frac{F/a}{\Delta l/l} = \frac{\text{change in longitudinal stress}}{\text{fractional change in length}} = \frac{Fl}{a\Delta l}.$$

Bulk Modulus (B): For hydrostatic compression:

$$B = \frac{F/a}{\Delta v/v} = \frac{\text{compressional change in stress (pressure)}}{\text{fractional change in volume}} = \frac{p}{\Delta v/v}.$$

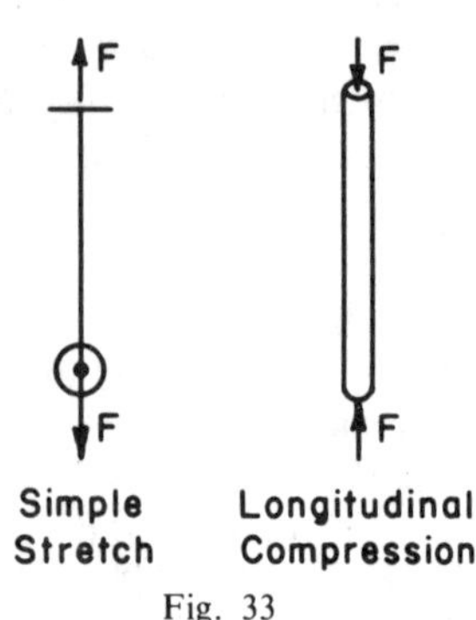

Fig. 33

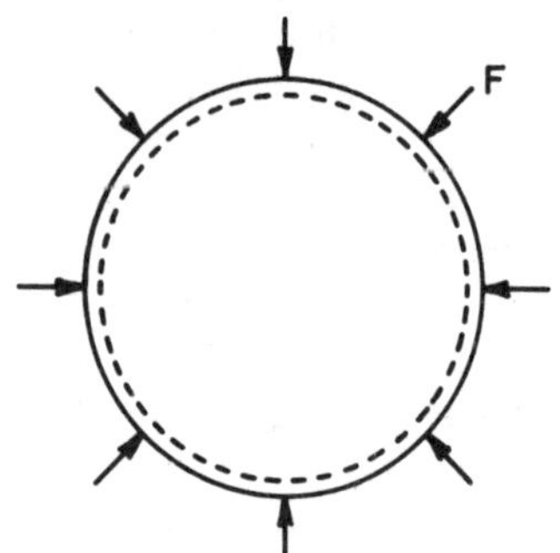

Fig. 34—Hydrostatic compression

In this case the force is always perpendicular to the surface upon which it acts. See Fig. 34. Such a force per unit area is called a *hydrostatic pressure.* The reciprocal of the bulk modulus is called the *compressibility coefficient.* The bulk modulus for most liquids is very large.

Shear Modulus (η): For a force applied tangentially to a surface, resulting in a *shear* or twist (see Fig. 35),

$$\eta = \frac{F/a}{\tan\theta} = \frac{\text{shearing stress}}{\text{fractional shear}}.$$

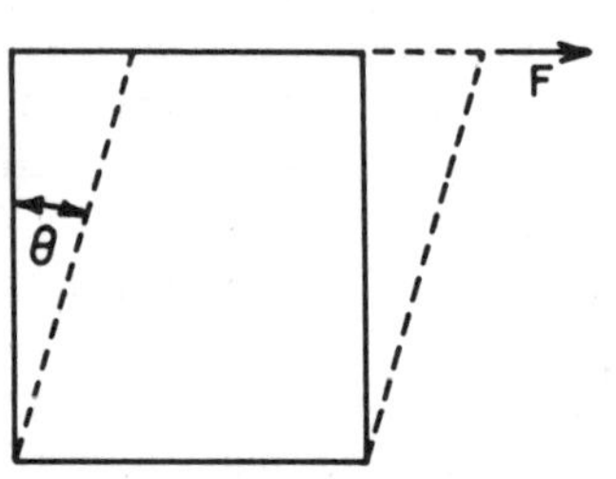

Fig. 35—Shear

The fractional shear is measured by the tangent of the angle of shear, and for small strains this is the angle itself measured in radians. The shear modulus is often called the *coefficient of rigidity.* Since a shearing strain involves a change of shape only, it is the lack of ability to withstand a shear that characterizes a fluid.

STUDY OF FLUIDS AT REST (HYDROSTATICS)

Fundamental Concepts. Density (d) is mass per unit volume $\left(d = \frac{M}{V}\right)$. The practical question of proper units in which to express density often arises. In British Engineering (B.E.) units, density should be expressed in slugs per cubic foot, but in engineering practice it is more common to use pounds per cubic foot. This procedure results from a failure to distinguish between true density and another concept, the weight per unit volume, sometimes called "weight density," which is often used. (Recall w = mg = dvg.) In C.G.S. (centimeter, gram, second) units, density is quite properly expressed in grams per cubic centimeter. In scientific work the above-mentioned concept of weight per unit volume (expressible in dynes per cubic centimeter) is never encountered. Thus the density of water is 1 gram per cm.^{3}, or 10^3 kg. per m.^{3}, or 1.94 slugs per ft.^{3} This is not inconsistent with the fact that 1 cubic foot of water *weighs* 62.4 lbs.

The *specific gravity* of a substance is the ratio of its density to the density of water considered as a standard substance. Specific gravity is dimensionless like all "specific" quantities. When metric units are used the numeric for density (number of grams per cm.^{3}) is the same as the numeric expressing specific gravity, because one cubic centimeter of water has a mass of one gram (practically). This identity does not hold when English units are used.

Due to the lack of shearing stresses in fluids, forces can act only normally to a fluid surface when it is at rest. The magnitude of such a normal force per unit area upon which it acts is called *fluid pressure* or *hydrostatic pressure.* $p = \frac{F}{A}$ (where $F \perp A$); more exactly $p = \frac{\Delta F}{\Delta A}$ as $\Delta A \rightarrow 0$.

Facts Concerning Fluid Pressure. At a given point within a fluid there is a force acting upon unit area (i.e., a pressure exists) and this *force* has the *same value in all directions* (i.e., the pressure exists regardless of the direction toward which the unit area faces). It would not be correct to state that the pressure is the same in all directions because pressure is not a vector quantity and, therefore, does not have a direction.

For a fluid of uniform density at rest acted upon by gravity alone, the pressure increases with depth (h).

$$p = hdg + p_0,$$

where p_0 is the pressure at the surface of the fluid. Consequently, the pressure is the same at all points on the same level.

Pascal's Law of the Transmissibility of Pressure: Increases in pressure are transmitted equally throughout a fluid. Thus if a force F_1 is applied to a surface area A_1 (Fig. 36) a pressure $p = \frac{F_1}{A_1}$ is established, which is transmitted through the fluid in such a manner that at some other surface A_2 (at the same level as A_1) a force $F_2 = pA_2$ is developed.

$$\frac{F_1}{A_1} = p = \frac{F_2}{A_2} \cdot \therefore \frac{F_1}{F_2} = \frac{A_1}{A_2}.$$

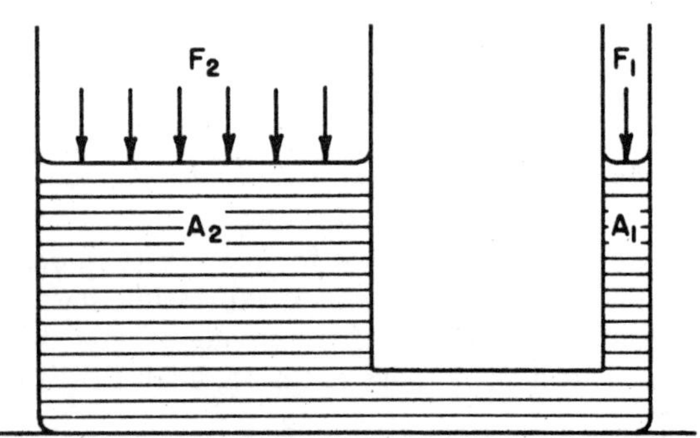

Fig. 36—Pascal's law of the transmissibility of pressure.

This multiplication of force is utilized in the hydraulic press, the hydraulic elevator, etc.

Atmospheric Pressure: The atmosphere is a fluid (although not of constant density because of its compressibility), and its weight is sufficient to exert a pressure of approximately 14.7 lbs. per sq. inch at the earth's surface. This pressure will support, in an air-free closed tube, a vertical column of mercury (specific gravity 13.6) approximately 76 cm. (30 inches approximately) high, known as a *barometric column.* (Fig. 37.) This fact was discovered by Torricelli. Thus the mercury barometer is used to determine accurately the pressure of the atmosphere and its variations, which are related to weather conditions. Other types of barometers are also commonly used, notably the aneroid barometer in which variations in atmospheric pressure actuate a delicately mounted indicating pointer. A sensitive barometer can be used to measure changes in altitude.

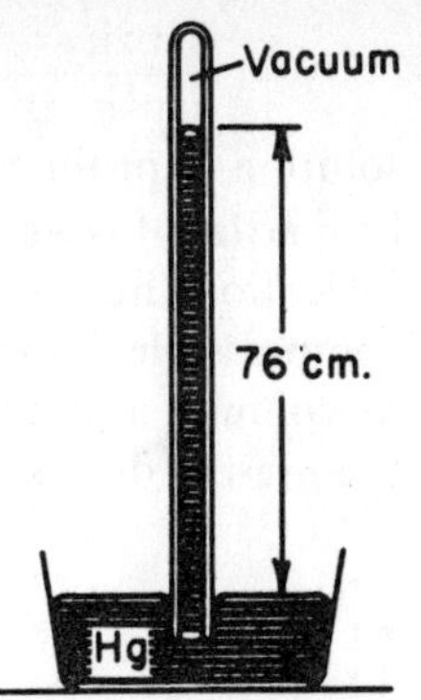

Fig. 37—Barometric column

Atmospheric pressure is utilized in the action of the lift pump, the common siphon, and other fluid devices.

Buoyancy and Archimedes' Principle. Due to the fact that below the surface of a fluid, pressure forces exist which point upward as well as in all other directions, a body immersed in a fluid is buoyed up in such a manner that it appears to undergo a decrease in weight. This is because the pressure forces at the bottom of an immersed object exceed those at the top. (Fig. 38.) *Archimedes' principle* states that a body wholly or partially immersed in a fluid is buoyed up by a force equal to the weight of the fluid displaced by it. It follows that bodies with specific gravities greater than unity sink in water, and conversely those with specific gravities less than unity float.

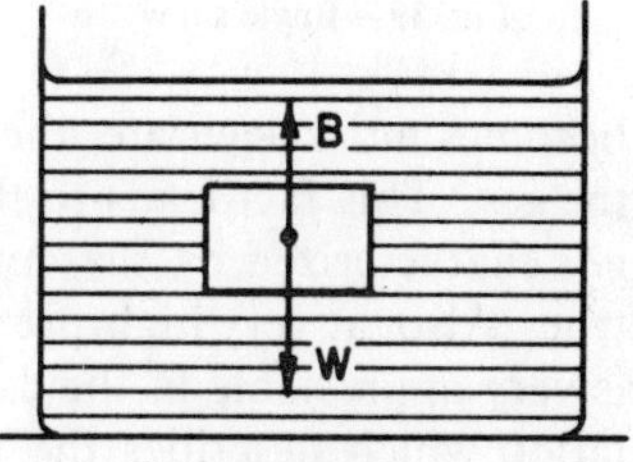

Fig. 38—Buoyancy

The fractional part of a *homogeneous* floating body (i.e., one with uniform density) that would be submerged in *water* can be shown to correspond to the ratio represented by its specific gravity. *Hydrometers* to determine specific gravities of liquids are constructed on this principle.

Analysis of Buoyancy Problems: Set up a force diagram indicating all upward and downward forces acting upon the "free body." Include the buoyant force (B) acting upward. Set the algebraic sum of these forces equal to zero (if equilibrium conditions exist) and solve for the unknown quantity, noting that $B = m_l g = v_l d_l g$ (where the subscript l refers to the liquid or fluid). Note also that if the body in question is completely submerged, $v_l = v_b$ (subscript b referring to the body). Moreover the facts that $W_b = m_b g = v_b d_b g$, and specific gravity of the body $= \frac{\text{density of body}}{\text{density of water}} = \frac{m_b v_b}{m_w v_b}$ are often useful aids in the solution of problems of this kind.

Properties of Gases. Since a gas is a fluid, all the preceding considerations hold true for gases. Gases, however, are much more compressible than liquids (i.e., they offer little resistance to change of volume) and display special properties, one of which fits into the present discussion.

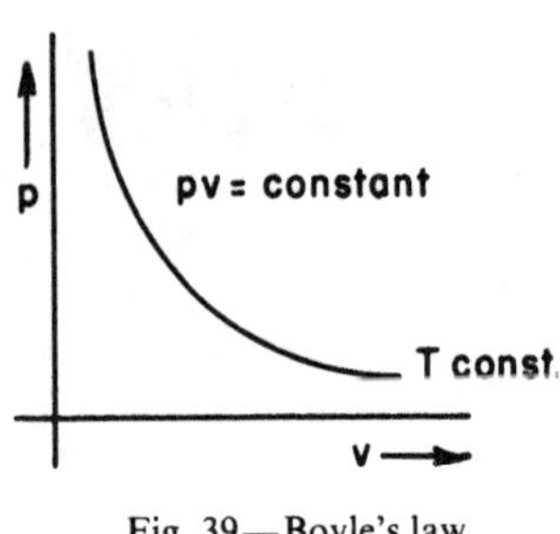

Fig. 39—Boyle's law

Boyle's Law: It is an experimental fact that if the temperature of a given mass of gas is maintained constant, an increase in pressure produces a decrease in volume such that the product of pressure times volume is approximately constant. (Fig. 39.) $p_1v_1 = p_2v_2$ or $\frac{p_1}{p_2} = \frac{v_2}{v_1}$ (at constant temperature). This relation becomes more accurate, the simpler the chemical constitution of the gas. This fact leads to the postulation of a hypothetical *ideal gas* characterized by the condition that Boyle's law be precisely true. Also, at very high pressures the departure from Boyle's law is very appreciable in the case of all real gases. An empirical relation which describes the situation somewhat more accurately than Boyle's law in the case of real gases is given by the *Van der Waals law:*

$$\left(p + \frac{a}{v^2}\right)(v - b) = \text{constant},$$

where a and b are constants differing for different gases. For the ideal gas, a and b are each zero, whence this relation coincides with Boyle's law (pv) = constant.

Surface Effects of Liquids (Surface Tension). Matter is held together by molecular forces. At surfaces of discontinuity these forces produce conspicuous effects. At the surface of a liquid the absence of liquid molecules above the surface causes these forces to behave in a manner suggesting the existence of a membrane stretched over the liquid surface to account for its observed tendency to shrink.

The *magnitude of a surface force* across (perpendicular to) a *unit of length* is known as the *coefficient of surface tension.* For pure water this tension (T), which varies markedly with purity and temperature, is about 70 dynes per cm. at room temperature.

Molecular forces between like molecules are called forces of *cohesion.* Molecular forces between unlike molecules are called forces of *adhesion.* When the adhesive forces between two different substances exceed the cohesive forces of one of them, the one substance is said to wet the other. Example: Water wets or clings to clean glass. Conversely, mercury does not wet clean glass but shrinks away from it. (Fig. 40.)

Adhesive forces cause liquids like water to rise up in glass capillary tubes to such height that for a tube of circular section $h = \frac{2T}{Rdg} \cos \alpha$ wherc R is the radius of the tube and α is the angle of contact between water and glass. (Fig. 41.)

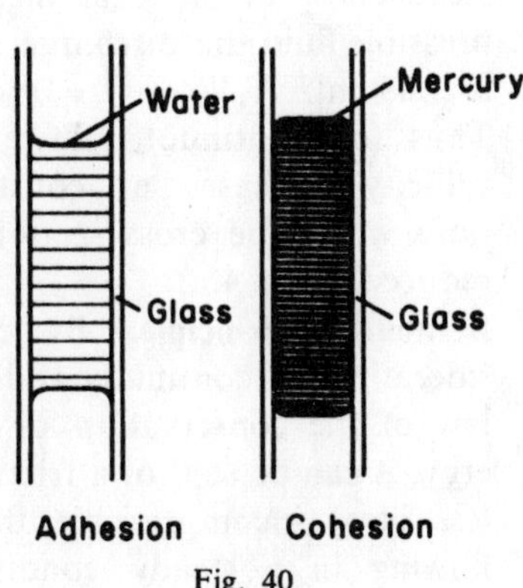

Fig. 40

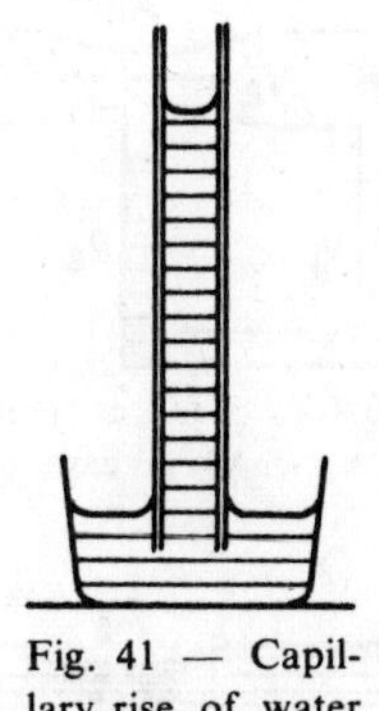
Fig. 41 — Capillary rise of water in glass tube

Surface tension, tending as it does to cause a surface to contract, requires that the pressure in soap bubbles, etc., be greater than the pressure outside. For a spherical bubble this excess pressure $p = \frac{4T}{R}$ (Fig. 42).

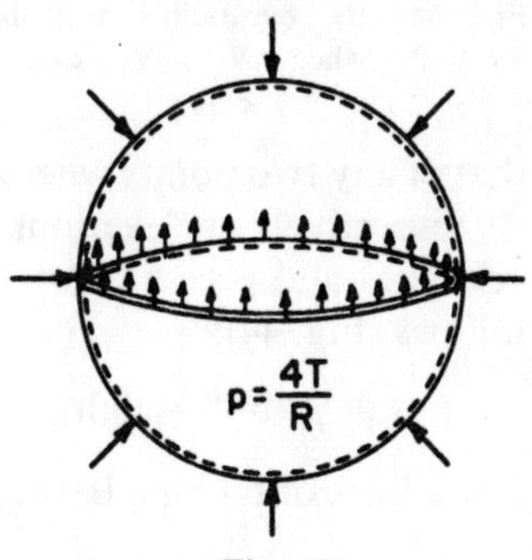

Fig. 42

HYDRAULICS (FLUIDS IN MOTION)

The case of fluids in comparatively slow, smooth, so-called streamline motion comes within the scope of an elementary presentation. Turbulent flow, however, cannot be considered here. Also only average over-all effects rather than instantaneous individual effects are considered.

Concepts and Definitions. *Steady flow* (sometimes called *stationary flow*) is such that the velocity of the fluid concerned has a fixed magnitude and direction at every point. The velocity does not change at a given point as time elapses but it may be different at different places. When the flow is *steady*, the paths actually followed by the moving particles of fluid are called *streamlines.*

Discharge rate (Q) refers to the volume passing a given point per unit time and is expressible in terms of the linear velocity (v) of the stream and the cross-sectional area; thus $Q = AV$.

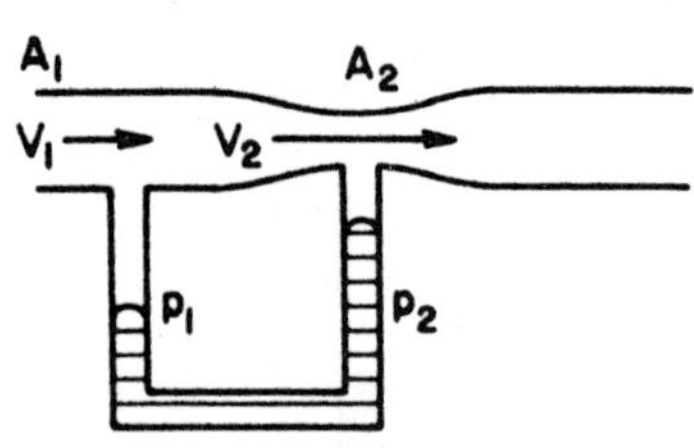

Fig. 43—$V_2 > V_1$ at constriction where $A_2 < A_1$ in case of steady flow

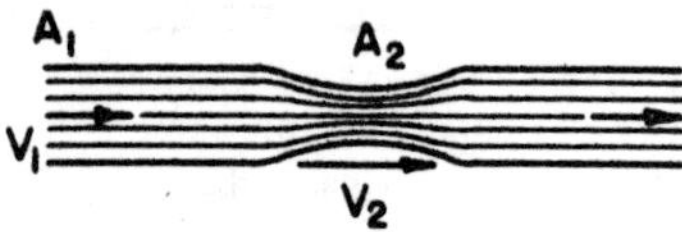

Fig. 44—By Bernoulli's principle: $P_2 < P_1$ when $V_2 > V_1$ due to $A_2 < A_1$

Law of Continuity. For the steady flow of an ideal incompressible fluid the discharge rate is constant. $A_1V_1 = Q = A_2V_2$. Thus for continuous flow the velocity increases at constrictions where the cross section is reduced. (Fig. 43.)

Bernoulli's Principle. By considerations of continuity and the law of the conservation of energy, it can be said of a frictionless ideal incompressible fluid, flowing in a steady condition through a pipe, that the total energy of a unit volume of the fluid is constant. This means that at any two points where the areas of cross section are A_1 and A_2 respectively at elevations h_1 and h_2 above some base level, the velocities and pressures of a liquid with density d are related as follows (Fig. 44):

$$\tfrac{1}{2}dv_1^2 + dgh_1 + p_1 = \tfrac{1}{2}dv_2^2 + dgh_2 + p_2.$$

For a horizontal pipe Bernoulli's principle simplifies to

$$\tfrac{1}{2}dv_1^2 + p_1 = \tfrac{1}{2}dv_2^2 + p_2 = \text{constant}.$$

This principle requires that at a constriction in a pipe the pressure is reduced, since at such a point the velocity must necessarily increase. The ideal conditions under which the preceding is quantitatively precisely true must be emphasized; but qualitatively, it is very readily demonstrated. Applications of this principle lead to or explain efflux from a tank. By Torricelli's principle, if a tank has an orifice a distance h below the level of the fluid in it, the velocity of stream-line efflux is given by $v^2 = 2\,gh$, as if a given mass of liquid were to fall freely from the liquid level to the orifice level and thereby acquire velocity.

Further examples are: the disk paradox, a ball supported by a jet of air or water, a curved spinning baseball (Fig. 45), the Ven-

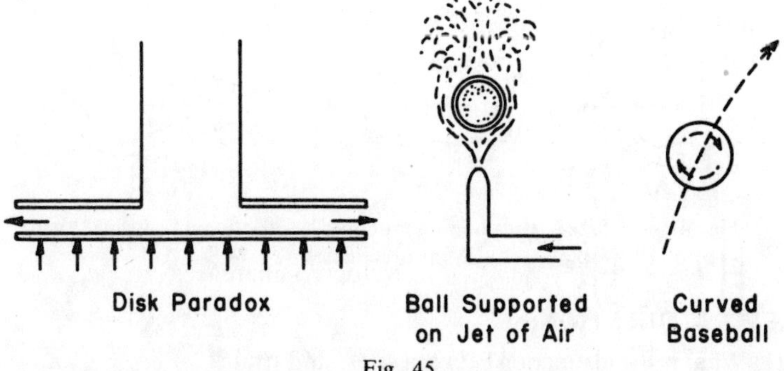

Fig. 45

turi water meter (Fig. 44), ship suction, the Flettner rotor-propelled ship, etc.

Fluid Friction. Below a certain critical velocity the effects of fluid friction are different from the effects at higher velocities.

For relatively slow motion (case of smooth-flow friction) most liquids flow as if they were divided into sheets flowing one over another with velocities proportional to the distance (d) away from that part of the liquid in contact with the walls of the liquid container and hence at rest. (Fig. 46.) The resistance offered to this type of flow, thought of as friction between the liquid layers, is called *viscosity*. The coefficient of viscosity (η) is the ratio of the tangential stress to the *velocity gradient* $\left(\eta = \frac{F/a}{v/d}\right)$ and is a

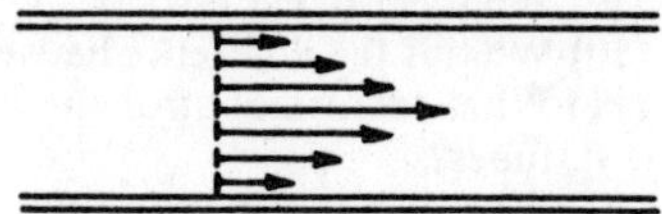

Fig. 46—Fluid friction (viscosity)

characteristic constant of a liquid for a particular value of temperature. This coefficient varies very greatly with temperature for most liquids.

When fluids are set into rapid motion, turbulent effects known as *eddy currents* or *whirls* are established which constitute a type of fluid resistance that varies greatly with the velocity of flow. This type of resistance is markedly reduced by "streamlining" the liquid container or any obstructions in the path of the moving fluid. For projectiles or other bodies moving very rapidly through fluids (liquids or gases), streamlining is very effective in reducing energy losses due to eddy currents. The best results are obtained by making the nose end of the projectile quite blunt and tapering the tail end. (Fig. 47.)

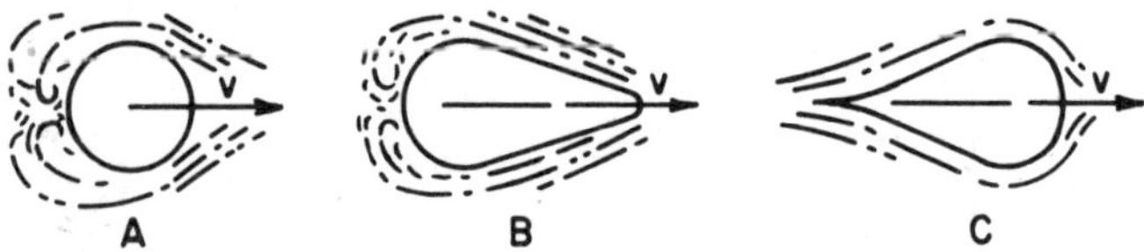

Fig. 47—In Case C streamlining produces less frictional resistance than in the other cases.

REVIEW QUESTIONS

(1) What is the distinction between stress and strain?
(2) What is Hooke's law? Under what restriction is it true?
(3) Define Young's, bulk, and shear moduli.
(4) If a mass of 1000 grams were suspended from a copper wire 10 meters long, of Young's modulus 10×10^{11} dynes per cm.^{2}, and of diameter .025 cm., with what period would it oscillate up and down? *Ans.* T = .28 sec. per vibration.
(5) What is meant by hydrostatic pressure?
(6) State Archimedes' principle.
(7) What fractional volume of a cake of ice floating in water is submerged if the specific gravity of ice is 0.90?
(8) What is the use of a hydrometer?
(9) What is Boyle's law?
(10) What is the difference between cohesion and adhesion?
(11) What factors control the height to which liquids rise in capillary tubes?
(12) What is meant by continuity in connection with fluid flow?
(13) State Bernoulli's principle.
(14) What is meant by viscosity?

8: Wave Motion and Sound

WAVE MOTION

Wave motion is the propagation of deformations through a deformable medium. As such, the study of wave motion is often properly referred to as the study of *dynamics of elasticity*. The deformation may be a single pulse or it may consist of a succession of periodic disturbances. The former is referred to as a *wave pulse*; the latter as a *wave train*. (Fig. 48.)

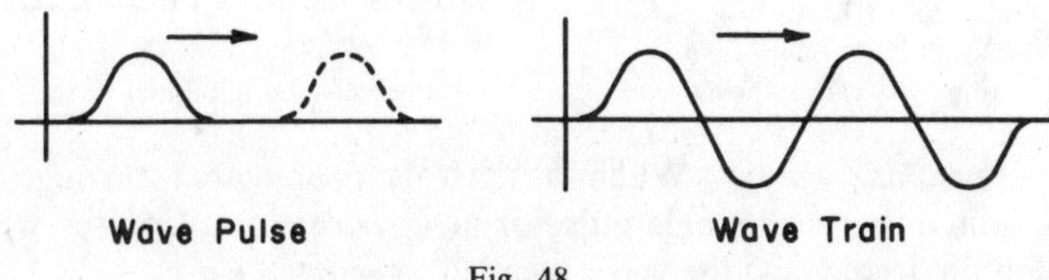

Fig. 48

In advanced treatments of wave motion, emphasis is placed on the mathematical equation of a traveling wave (see p. 57 for reference to the velocity of a wave). This has led to the acceptance of the definition of wave motion as that which can be described by the wave equation. Hence the original concept of the *elastic* wave in matter has been broadened to include the notion of wavelike radiation in free space, e.g., light waves and radio waves. For purposes of this outline, however, the original concept of the elastic wave suffices to explain elementary wave phenomena.

Characteristics of All Wave Motions. The motion of the medium is vibratory. Different parts of the medium vibrate successively, each back and forth about its own equilibrium position. The disturbance (not the medium) travels. In other words only energy is propagated.

Types of Waves. There are many well-known types of waves, of which the following are worth considering.

Transverse waves: When the direction of propagation of a wave is perpendicular to the direction of vibration of the particles of the medium in which the wave travels, the wave is said to be a *transverse wave.* (Fig. 49.) Such waves are due to shearing deformations; and since deformations cannot be produced in fluids, fluids cannot support transverse waves.

Longitudinal waves: These are waves such that the vibrations of the medium are in the same or opposite direction as the propagation. (Fig. 50.) They result from deformation due to tensions and compressions. Only this type of wave can be propagated through a fluid. Such waves can be propagated through air, and when capable of exciting the auditory nerve, they are called *sound waves.*

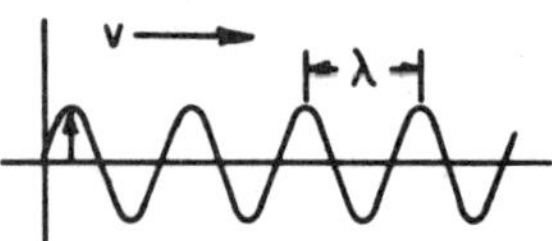

Fig. 49—Transverse wave

Fig. 50—Longitudinal wave

Torsional waves: When a twist is propagated through a medium either as a single pulse or as a succession of pulses with a definite frequency, the wave is called a *torsional wave.*

Plane waves, circular waves, spherical waves, ellipsoidal waves, etc. are also terms commonly encountered in wave considerations.

Representation of Waves. It is customary to limit elementary considerations of waves to the first two types mentioned, i.e., transverse and longitudinal. It is also customary to restrict the consideration to waves being propagated in a single direction, i.e., one-dimensional waves.

A transverse unidimensional plane wave (illustrated by a horizontal cord fixed at one end and acted upon by a periodic vertical force at its other end) is readily represented by a plane diagram which might be an actual picture indicating the transverse displacements of the medium at successive instants of time. (Fig. 49.)

A longitudinal wave is usually represented by a *graph* in which particle displacement is *plotted* at right angles to the time axis. Such a graph representing a longitudinal wave resembles the actual picture of a transverse wave, whence such a graphical representation is suitable for both types of waves. It must be clearly understood, however, that for the longitudinal wave, the graph is not a pictorial representation as it is in the case of the transverse wave.

Fundamental Wave Concepts. In the consideration of wave trains certain concepts and relations are fundamentally important.

For any wave train, the distance (along the direction of propagation) between two successive corresponding points on the wave is called the *wave length* (λ). This may be thought of as the distance from crest to crest or from trough to trough, for a transverse wave; from compression to compression, or from rarefaction to rarefaction, for a compressional longitudinal wave. (Fig. 49.)

The frequency (n) of a wave motion is the number of complete waves which pass a given point per second. The medium makes one vibration for each wave that passes; hence the frequency of a wave motion has precisely the same significance as the frequency of a periodic motion, discussed earlier.

The period (T) of a wave motion is the time required for a complete wave to pass a given point, or the time required for one complete vibration of the medium. It is the reciprocal of frequency. $T = \frac{1}{n}$.

From these definitions it is clear that the velocity of the wave motion, which is the velocity with which the disturbance spreads, is simply related to the frequency and wave length in a very fundamental manner thus: $v = n\lambda = \frac{\lambda}{T}$.

When waves are propagated from a source vibrating with harmonic motion the waves emitted are called *harmonic waves.* When simple harmonic displacements are plotted against time on a graph, the resulting curve is a sine (or cosine) curve; whence harmonic waves are *sine waves.* Such waves being so common (all elastic matter being capable of vibrating harmonically in accordance with Hooke's law), wave motion in general is naively represented by sine waves in the minds of all students.

The maximum displacement of particles of the medium is called the *amplitude* (A) of the wave.

The mathematical expression for a sinusoidal wave traveling in the positive x-direction is (recalling that $x = A \cos 2\pi nt$, p. 37):

$$y = A \cos 2\pi\left(\frac{t}{T} - \frac{x}{\lambda}\right)$$

where y is the displacement of a particle of the medium at a given time t at a position specified by the coordinate x. A represents the amplitude of the wave, and λ is the wave length. In terms of the velocity v of the wave, this reduces to

$$y = A \cos \frac{2\pi}{\lambda}(x - vt).$$

Superposition and Interference of Waves. Whenever two wave trains travel through the same point, the resulting displacement of that point is the sum of the displacements produced by each wave (vector sum, since displacement is a vector quantity). Harmonic waves have the significant property that the sum of two or more harmonic waves is also a harmonic wave. Consequently, any harmonic wave can be considered to be resolved into a number of component harmonic waves. This is *Fourier's theorem.*

Two waves are said to be *in phase* with each other if their corresponding parts are undergoing similar displacements at the same time, i.e., if they commence or end together. If one wave is one-half a wave length behind the other, there is said to be a phase difference of one-half a wave length. The phase difference between two harmonic wave trains is usually measured in angular units, as that fractional part of 360 degrees or 2π radians represented by the fractional part of a wave length of one wave behind the other.

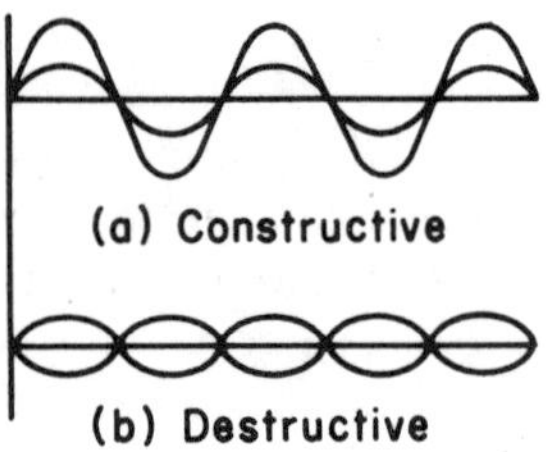

Fig. 51—Examples of wave interference

When two harmonic waves of the same period and in the same phase are superposed one on the other, the result is reenforcement or *constructive interference.* (Fig. 51-a.) When two harmonic waves of the same period but 180° out of phase with each other are superposed, the result is *destructive interference.* The destruction is complete only if the amplitudes of the two waves are the same. (Fig. 51-b.)

If two trains of similar waves of almost, but not quite, the same frequency are superposed, they will be completely in phase and later completely out of phase just as many times per second as the difference between their frequencies. This results in the formation of *beats.*

Reflection and Refraction of Waves. When a travelling wave meets an obstruction or comes to a surface of discontinuity between media of different elastic properties, part of the wave is reflected back into the original medium, and part is transmitted with a different velocity.

The velocity of a wave is governed by the elasticity and the density of the medium, increasing with the former and decreasing with the latter.

(a) For a compressional wave in a solid $v = \sqrt{\frac{E}{\rho}}$ (E is Young's modulus; ρ is density).

(b) For a compressional wave in a fluid $v = \sqrt{\frac{B}{\rho}}$ (B is the bulk modulus).

(c) For a transverse wave on a cord $v = \sqrt{\frac{T}{m}}$ (T is the tension; m is the mass per unit length).

A wave is said to be refracted when its velocity is changed as a result of the wave's passing from one medium to another. The ratio of the velocity of a wave in a first medium to that in a second medium is the *refractive index* of the second medium with respect to the first, for that particular type of wave. This change in velocity results in a bending of the wave, or a change in its direction, if the incident wave strikes the discontinuous surface in any but a perpendicular direction.

When a wave is reflected from a fixed surface, i.e., from a medium in which the restraining forces are greater, or one of greater density, the reflected wave undergoes a loss of half a wave length, or suffers a change of phase of 180° with respect to the original wave. Reflection from a free surface takes place without this change in phase. These facts are true for compressional as well as transverse waves provided the waves are displacement waves and not pressure waves.

When two waves having the same wave length and amplitude travel with the same speed but in opposite directions through a medium, *stationary waves* are formed. Parts of the medium separated by one-half a wave length are confronted by opposing tendencies which nullify each other's effects, whereas at points halfway between these regions the tendencies toward displacement are re-enforced. The former regions are called *nodal regions* and the latter, *antinodal regions,* or merely designated as *nodes* and *loops* respectively. When waves are reflected, the reflected wave may interfere in this manner with the incident wave to produce stationary or *standing waves.* Standing waves are further characterized by the fact that every part of the vibrating medium passes through its equilibrium position at the same time. Since stationary waves do not progress, there is no net transfer of energy involved. The increase of amplitude of vibration associated with constructive interference, such as displayed at antinodes, is often referred to as *resonance.*

Standing waves on cords are readily demonstrated by Melde's experiment. The frequency (n), the number of segments N (a segment being the part of the waves between two successive nodes), the length (L) of the cord, the tension (T) in the cord, and the mass of it per unit length (m) are related as follows:

$$n = \frac{1}{2L}\sqrt{\frac{N^2T}{m}}.$$

Since there can be only an integral number of segments, (i.e., N = 1, 2, 3, etc.) the corresponding frequencies of vibration are n, 2n, 3n, etc. The frequency n is called the *fundamental* frequency and the others are called *harmonic overtones.* The fundamental is referred to as the *first* harmonic, the first overtone as the *second* harmonic, the second overtone as the *third* harmonic, etc., where each represents a term in the so-called harmonic series, 1, 2, 3, 4, etc.

Chladni figures in sand sprinkled on vibrating plates demonstrate that standing wave patterns of loops and nodes are readily produced in plates, membranes, etc.

Doppler's Principle. When the vibrating source of a train of waves is caused to move in the direction of the wave propagation, the effect to an observer is as follows: If there is a relative approach of source and observer, the waves undergo an *increase in frequency*, or a decrease in wave length due to the waves being crowded into smaller space, necessitating a shortening of the length of each one. (Fig. 52.) If there is a relative separation of source and observer, the waves undergo a *decrease in frequency,* or an increase in wave length. In general, if n is the original frequency, v is the velocity of the wave, v_s is the velocity of source, and v_o is the velocity of the observer. $n' = n\,\frac{v \pm v_o}{v \mp v_s}$, where the upper signs refer to relative approach, and the lower signs, to relative recession. Doppler's principle enables an observer to measure the relative rate of travel, of source and observer, when the motion is along the line joining them. It is applicable to sound waves, light waves, etc.

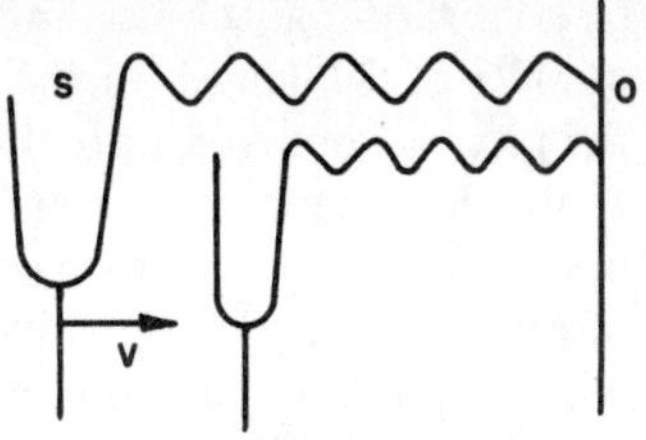

Fig. 52— Doppler's principle

SOUND

Sound has been defined as a wave disturbance capable of exciting the auditory nerve. More generally, it is any compressional disturbance propagated through a deformable medium. In so far as it is a wave phenomenon, the preceding wave considerations apply to sound. A formal study includes a consideration of sound sources, velocity, methods of analyzing sounds, and musical sounds.

All vibrating bodies produce audible sounds if the vibrations can be detected by the ear. The frequency range of such vibrations is limited to from approximately 16 to 20,000 vibrations per second, varying considerably with the individual observer. The amount of propagated energy in a sound wave is usually extremely small. Tuning forks in general emit very pure sounds, i.e., sounds lacking in harmonics.

Velocity of Sound. Sound waves travel with velocities dependent upon the elasticity and the density of the medium in which they travel. In general the velocity increases as the temperature of the medium is increased. For air: $v = v_o \sqrt{1 + \frac{1}{273} t}$ where v_o is the velocity under standard conditions (0°C. and 76 cm. Hg). The velocity of a sound wave in a given gas is readily determined by setting up standing waves of known frequency in a column of the gas in question, whereupon the length of the wave is twice the distance between two successive nodes or two successive loops, and then $v = n\lambda$.

Standing Sound Waves in Pipes. When standing waves are formed in air columns, as in organ pipes, for a pipe closed at one end and open at the other, a so-called *closed* pipe, the wave length of the fundamental tone is four times the length of the pipe, since the closed end must correspond to a vibration node, the open end to a vibration antinode, and the distance between must be one-quarter of the length of the longest standing wave producible in the pipe. Moreover, only the odd harmonics are possible because of the asymmetry of a closed pipe (one end closed and one end open). Hence the *first overtone* is the *third harmonic* for this type of pipe. For a pipe open at both ends, a so-called *open* pipe, the wave length of the fundamental tone is twice the length of the pipe, since each end must correspond to a vibration antinode, and the distance between two successive antinodes must be one-half wave length. In this case all harmonics are possible. Specifically, the *first overtone* is the *second harmonic*, etc.

Characteristics of Sound. Sounds are recognized by three characteristics: loudness, pitch, and quality.

The *loudness* of a sound depends upon the intensity level (β) of the disturbance, where the latter is defined by the logarithmic expression

$$\beta = 10 \log \frac{I}{I_o}.$$

The *intensity* I is the time rate at which energy is transferred across a unit area, and is proportional to the square of the amplitude of the pressure wave. I_o is arbitrarily taken as 10^{-16} watts/cm.^{2} for the faintest audible sound. β is expressed in decibels, a unit one-tenth as large as an earlier unit, the bel, thus accounting for the factor 10 in the expression. Two intensities differ by one decibel when the logarithm of their ratio is 1/10. Loudness levels range from the threshold of hearing (zero decibels) to the threshold of painful sound (125 or so decibels). Ordinary conversation would be 50–60 decibels.

The *pitch* of a sound is defined as the audible effect of the frequency of the disturbance producing it, and as such is a subjective attribute. For a sound of essentially one frequency, or one for which the fundamental frequency predominates, pitch is determined by that frequency. Pitch is measured in vibrations per second. Waves having frequencies greater than approximately 20,000 vibrations per second can be produced and are called supersonic waves. The limits of audition depend upon intensity as well as frequency. At the upper limit of intensity, i.e., around 120 decibels, the normal range of frequencies is from 20 to 20,000 cycles. Yet near the threshold of audibility the range may be reduced to frequency values between 500 and 5000. At 50 decibels, it is from about 50 to 20,000.

The *quality* of a sound depends upon the number of overtones present in it. Different sources of sound produce sounds of vastly different quality. It is in the number and relative loudness of overtones that different musical instruments can be distinguished even when they are emitting sounds of the same pitch. Complex sounds can be readily analyzed at the present time by analyzing devices such as the Phonodeik, the Helmholtz resonators, etc., but best of all by oscillating electrical currents. Open pipes are richer in quality than closed pipes because the former can have twice as many harmonic overtones as the latter.

Review Questions

(1) What is wave motion?
(2) Distinguish between transverse and longitudinal waves. Which type is illustrated by sound waves?
(3) State the fundamental wave relation.
(4) What is the phenomenon of beats?
(5) Define refractive index of a wave.
(6) Upon what factors does the velocity of a wave depend?
(7) What is meant by the loss of half a wave length at reflection from a dense surface?
(8) Distinguish between loudness, pitch, and quality of sound waves.
(9) Discuss Doppler's principle.
(10) What is meant by the term "standing waves"?

Part III: Heat

9: Nature of Heat and Temperature

INTRODUCTION

It was formerly thought that heat was a material substance, the calorific fluid, which when added to a body made it hot and when subtracted from a body made it cold. This view was weakened by the fact that the calorific fluid appeared to be weightless and, therefore, an abstraction rather than a material substance. The work of Rumford (1798), Joule (1842), and Rowland (1878) established the view that heat is definitely a form of energy and that a definite equivalence exists between a unit of heat and a unit of mechanical energy.

It is very significant that heat can be transferred from one body to another. That property which determines the direction of heat flow from one body to another in contact with it is qualitatively referred to as *temperature.* Heat flows of its own accord from regions of high temperature to regions of low temperature. Although temperatures can be estimated quantitatively by the sense of touch, more accurate measurements require a knowledge of certain thermal properties of matter. Attempts to refine such measurements disclose the necessity for a more detailed knowledge of the structure of matter than has hitherto been required in this study. Such information is also necessary to establish a quantitative definition of temperature.

KINETIC THEORY OF THE STRUCTURE OF MATTER

All matter is considered to be made up of *molecules,* which are the smallest known units of any given substance. These molecules themselves are made up of combinations of atoms, the atom being the smallest known unit of an elementary substance. Some one hundred or so such elementary substances are recognized, of which all known substances are composed. The atoms also have structures. They consist of combinations of positive and negative charges of electricity. The exact nature of the combinations is not completely understood. The negative charges are referred to as *electrons*, although positively charged electrons called *positrons* are now recognized, but they have no independent existence. The positive charges are referred to as *protons* and they differ from the electrons, both negative and positive, in that they have associated with them some eighteen hundred forty (1840) times as much mass. A subatomic unit called the *neutron* has been discovered. It has associated with it a mass approximately that of a proton, but it carries no net charge of electricity. Thus it appears that atoms have component parts, including the more recently discovered unstable and short-lived particles that are known as mesons, pions, strange particles, etc., but the electron, the proton, and the neutron are the most important.

The kinetic theory postulates that all these fundamental units of matter are in a state of motion, even the largest of these, the molecules. Moreover, it is supposed that this motion is pronounced, even for groups or aggregates of molecules. It is postulated that, to a first approximation at least, the molecules of a given substance are very small spherical particles, are all of the same size, and are in a state of random motion, continually colliding with one another and with the walls of the container in which they are held. The distinction between the three states of matter, solid, liquid, and gaseous, is assumed to be based upon the relative separation of the molecules, being by far the greatest for the gaseous state. In this state the molecules are supposed to be so far apart as to very seldom collide with one another, or even to get close enough together to have any appreciable potential energy due to the forces of attraction between them. Their energy is assumed to be all kinetic energy. They behave as if they were ideally elastic in that, at collision with the walls of their container, they rebound with undiminished speed. They do not all have the same velocity even for a given gas, but display a statistical distribution of velocities at a given temperature. Hence all conclusions regarding their effects are statistical conclusions. The total kinetic energy of these molecules may be divided into two classes, depending upon whether or not the motion of the molecules is regular and ordered (as in the case of a bodily translation or rotation of a whole mass of gas) or purely random and disordered (as the motion of the individual bees in a whole swarm). It is this latter kind of molecular kinetic energy which constitutes heat energy, such as results from the action of dissipative forces like friction, between which and mechanical energy there is the equivalence mentioned before. *Heat* is, therefore, *defined* as the total energy associated with the *random* molecular motion of a body. The addition of heat to a body increases this thermal agitation of its molecules. It can also be shown that the tendency for heat to be transferred from one body to another depends upon the average translational random velocity of its molecules. In view of this, the *temperature* of a body is *defined* in an absolute way as the average kinetic energy of translation of the random motion of its molecules. The absolute zero of temperature is that temperature at which all this random motion ceases. On this picture also, the pressure of a gas is accounted for in terms of the molecular bombardment of the walls of the container. Also the pressure of a gas becomes zero at the absolute zero of temperature. It can be shown that the pressure $p = \frac{1}{3} nmv^2$ for an ideal gas, when n is the number of particles per unit volume, m is the mass per particle, and v is the average molecular translatory velocity.

This theory predicts that at a given temperature the product of the pressure and the volume should be constant for a perfect gas, a result quite in accord with the empirical law of Boyle. It also predicts that all gases contain the same number of molecules per unit volume at a given temperature, a result quite in accord with the empirical law of chemistry known as Avogadro's principle, which states that all gases contain 2.71×10^{19} molecules per cc. at 0°C. and 760 mm. Hg pressure. It also predicts the constancy of the product of mass times velocity squared for different kinds of molecules at constant temperature (Maxwell's law). This has also been verified by experiment. Furthermore, this theory is very much supported by direct observation of the so-called *Brownian movement,* which is that random agitation of particles observed when a drop of highly diluted India ink, or some other colloidal solution, is viewed under the microscope.

Note: It must be carefully pointed out that this is a theory and as such is subject to many limitations, and is very ideal in its scope. Like all theories it does not necessarily portray the actual state of affairs, but it is a very fruitful picture. In many details it is already out of date, having been modified very considerably by concepts of a highly mathematical nature, but it is still worthy of consideration on many grounds.

THERMAL EXPANSION AND THERMOMETRY

Direct measurements of relative temperature are based upon observable thermal properties of matter, of which the expansion of solids and liquids, the pressure-volume-temperature (p-v-t) properties of gases, and certain electrical and optical effects are examples. Of these the first two will be considered in detail.

Expansion of Solids and Liquids. Most bodies expand when heated. If the expansion is restricted to one dimension, it is found to vary linearly with temperature. This phenomenon finds an application in the mercury-glass thermometer by which temperatures are measured with reference to the freezing and the boiling temperatures of water taken as arbitrary standards. There are two common temperature scales, centigrade and Fahrenheit. (Fig. 53.) The *centigrade scale* divides the range between the

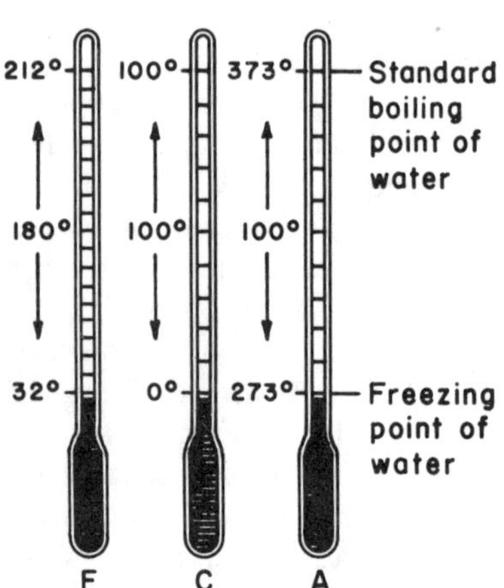

Fig. 53—Temperature scales

freezing point of water, arbitrarily called 0°, and the boiling point at standard atmospheric pressure, arbitrarily called 100°, into 100 equal divisions called centigrade degrees. The *Fahrenheit scale* is so chosen that the freezing point of water is called 32°, and the boiling point is 212°; thus the same range as before is divided into 180 equal parts called Fahrenheit degrees. Obviously, to change from one scale to the other

$$t_F = \frac{9}{5} t_C + 32.$$

The phenomenon of *linear expansion* is, of course, not limited in application to thermometry. Its many practical applications warrant its further consideration.

Experimentally, $L_t = L_0 (1 + \alpha t)$ within reasonable limits of temperature. Hence $\frac{L_t - L_0}{L_0 t} = \alpha$, or the *coefficient of linear expansion* referred to the specific temperature at which the length is taken as L_0, usually 0° C. Tables give values for α per degree C. or per degree F. for various substances.

When the expansion is not restricted to one dimension but is allowed to take place in three dimensions, the phenomenon is called *volume expansion.* Experimentally $v_t = v_0 (1 + \beta t)$, whence $\frac{v_t - v_0}{v_0 t} = \beta$, or *the coefficient of volume expansion* referred to the specific temperature at which the initial volume is designated v_0, usually 0°C. It can be shown that to a very close approximation $\beta = 3\,\alpha$ for all substances.

Expansion of Gases. It is found in the case of gases that changes in temperature not only affect the volume of a gas but produce simultaneous pressure changes, such that the three quantities, volume, pressure, and temperature, have to be considered together. If the pressure is kept constant by confining the gas in an expansible chamber, it is found that $v_t = v_0 (1 + \beta t)$ where β (the volume-temperature coefficient, as above, for solids and liquids) is found to be very nearly equal to .003667 or $\frac{1}{273}$. Here $\beta = \frac{\Delta v}{v_o \Delta t}$. If, however, the volume of the gas is kept constant by confining it in a rigid constant-volume container, it is found that the pressure changes such that $p_t = p_o (1 + bt)$ where b (the *pressure-temperature* coefficient) is found to be very nearly .003667 or $\frac{1}{273}$, or the same numerically as β. Here $b = \frac{\Delta p}{p_o \Delta t}$. These two effects are so uniform over such a wide range of temperature that gas thermometers are used in all standardization work in thermometry. The constant-volume hydrogen thermometer is universally recognized as a standard thermometer, against which mercury-glass thermometers are calibrated.

The facts that b is approximately equal to β for all gases, and that each is very nearly $\frac{1}{273}$, are very significant. It follows that if a gas at 0°C. should undergo a decrease in temperature of 1°C., its volume would shrink $\frac{1}{273}$ of its original value, whence the suggestion is made that if its temperature were to decrease to −273°C. its volume at constant pressure would shrink to zero. It also follows that the pressure of a gas at constant volume would be reduced to zero if the temperature of the gas could be lowered to −273°C. It is, therefore, concluded that −273°C. represents an absolute zero of temperature—in fact, the same absolute zero of temperature suggested by the kinetic theory. These facts added to other evidence to be discussed later serve to establish an *absolute scale of temperature,* the zero of which is −273°C. or −459°F. Temperatures are expressed on the *absolute centigrade* scale by adding 273° to the centigrade readings. (Fig. 53.) The absolute *Fahrenheit* scale is seldom used. It must be pointed out that the existence of absolute zero is not determinable by direct observation of the volume of a gas diminishing to zero at −273°C. because all gases liquefy at temperatures above this.

GENERAL GAS LAWS

The preceding facts about gases are simply expressed in terms of the ideal gas (previously discussed) in the following manner.

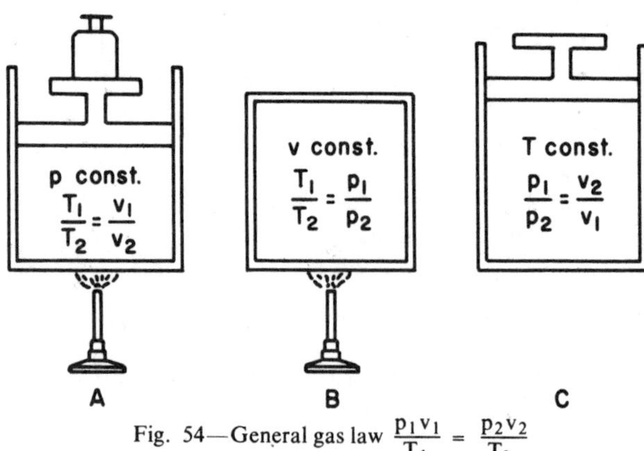

Fig. 54—General gas law $\frac{p_1 v_1}{T_1} = \frac{p_2 v_2}{T_2}$

If the absolute temperature of a given mass of gas is increased while the pressure is maintained constant, the volume increases proportionately. Thus in Fig. 54-A, where a gas is confined in a chamber whose volume is variable to maintain a constant pressure as heat is applied, $\frac{T_1}{T_2} = \frac{v_1}{v_2}$ (T expressed on the absolute scale).

If the absolute temperature of a given mass of gas is increased while the volume is maintained constant, the pressure increases proportionately. Thus in Fig. 54-B, where heat is applied to a gas confined in a sealed rigid container, $\frac{T_1}{T_2} = \frac{p_1}{p_2}$ (T absolute). These two relations taken together are known as Charles's or Gay-Lussac's law.

If these relations are combined with Boyle's law $\left(\frac{p_1}{p_2} = \frac{v_2}{v_1}\right)$ for a given mass of gas at constant temperature, suggested by Fig. 54-C., where the gas is confined in a container of variable volume so constructed that heat enters or leaves freely to maintain a constant temperature, we get $\frac{p_1v_1}{T_1} = \frac{p_2v_2}{T_2} = R$ (a constant) for a given mass of a given kind of gas. This is known as the general gas law, which, of course, is to be considered absolutely true only for the "ideal" gas, and approximately true for real gases. It is significant that this law is justified by the kinetic theory applied to gases. R is called the gas-constant per gram-mol. Its numerical value is, of course, dependent upon the units used for measuring pressure, volume, mass, and temperature. $R = 8.29 \times 10^7$ in ergs per gram per absolute centigrade degree.

Review Questions

(1) Give a qualitative and a quantitative definition of temperature.
(2) What are the basic assumptions upon which the kinetic theory of gases is built?
(3) What are molecules? atoms? electrons? protons? neutrons?
(4) What is Brownian motion?
(5) Review different methods by which temperature is measured.
(6) What temperature is the same on centigrade and Fahrenheit scales?
(7) What significance is attached to absolute zero?
(8) How much expansion must be allowed for in a steel bridge 3000 ft. long for a range of temperature from 100°F. in summer to −40°F. in winter? Consult tables for values of the coefficient of expansion.
(9) What is the general gas law?
(10) How deep must a pond be for a bubble of gas to triple its volume rising from the bottom to the top if the temperature at the top is 30°C. and that at the bottom is 15°C.?

10: Calorimetry and Thermal Properties of Substances

THE MEASUREMENT OF HEAT

Even though it has been shown that heat is a form of energy and that, consequently, it can be measured in energy units, it is nevertheless still convenient to think of quantities of heat, and units of heat quantity, as if heat were an independent substance.

Units of Heat Quantity. The amount of heat required to raise the temperature of one gram of water one degree centigrade is called the *calorie*. (Sometimes called gram-calorie.) Since this amount varies with the temperature, it becomes necessary to specify the temperature at which the measurement is made. The average value over the range 0°–100°C. coincides with the value at 15°C. whence 15°C. is specified as a standard temperature. The calorie is equivalent to 4.18 joules of mechanical energy, as will be pointed out later. One thousand calories are sometimes referred to as a *large calorie*.

The amount of heat required to raise the temperature of one pound of water one degree Fahrenheit is called the *British thermal unit*. One B.T.U. corresponds to 252 calories. The B.T.U. is usually standardized at 60°F.

Thermal Capacity and Specific Heat. The amount of heat required to raise by one unit the temperature of unit mass of a substance is called the thermal or *heat capacity* (c) of the substance. In scientific work it is usually expressed in calories per gram per degree centigrade. In engineering work it is usually expressed in British thermal units per pound per degree Fahrenheit. By definition, the numerical value of the heat capacity of water is unity in either system. The amount of heat necessary to raise the temperature of a body one degree is called the *heat capacity* (C) of the body. ($C = cm$.) This quantity is sometimes called the *water equivalent* of a body.

The ratio of the heat capacity of a substance to the heat capacity of water is defined as the *specific heat* (s) of the substance.

It is a dimensionless quantity, being just a ratio. Of course, numerically it is the same as thermal capacity of the substance in either system by virtue of the fact that the heat capacity of water is unity in either system. *(Ordinarily when the term specific heat is used, thermal capacity is intended, but because of the numerical identity, this distinction is often overlooked.)*

The specific heat of a body can be measured by the *method of mixtures.* If a body is heated to a relatively high temperature and then dropped into a quantity of water in a container of known specific heat, the specific heat of the body is readily determined since the total heat lost by the hot body is equal to the total heat gained by the water and its container. $m_1c_1(t_h - t_f) = m(t_f - t_i) + m_2c_2(t_f - t_i)$; i.e., (heat lost by hot body) = (heat gained by water + heat gained by container). m_1 is the mass of the body, c_1 is its heat capacity, equal numerically to its specific heat, m is the mass of water, m_2 and c_2 refer to the container, and t_h t_f t_i refer to the high, final, and initial temperatures respectively.

Since a gas can be heated with a change in volume, or a change in pressure, or both, a gas must have more than one heat capacity. As is more commonly stated, it has more than one specific heat. If the gas is heated at constant pressure, the volume must increase at the expense of the added energy. Hence more heat energy is required to raise, by unit amount, the temperature of unit mass of a gas at constant pressure than at constant volume. I.e., $c_p > c_v$. It can be shown that $c_p - c_v = R$, the gas constant, where R is expressed in cals. per degree per mol.

The *heat of combustion* is the amount of heat liberated when unit mass of a substance is completely burned.

CHANGE OF STATE AND ALLIED PHENOMENA

It has been previously pointed out that matter exists in solid, liquid, or gaseous form. Also it is significant that the particular form assumed depends upon the heat energy content and that changes from one form to another require the addition or subtraction of heat.

Vaporization. If heat is applied to a mass of water, a rise of temperature of one degree C. results from every calorie of heat added per gram of water, up to a certain temperature (100°C. under the normal atmospheric pressure of 760 mm. of mercury). At this temperature and pressure the addition of heat produces a change of state without change in temperature until the entire amount of water has been changed into steam (water-vapor). The amount of heat required to change unit mass of a liquid at a given temperature to a vapor without changing the temperature is called the *heat of vaporization.* For water at 100°C. it is approximately 536 calories per gram. Also, whenever a vapor condenses its *heat of vaporization* is liberated.

On the kinetic theory the molecules of a liquid, in their constant vibration, occasionally escape from the surface of the liquid and dart off with increased freedom as gas molecules. Such escaping of molecules at the surface of a liquid is called *evaporation.* If the vapor over a liquid is confined, it develops a pressure called *vapor pressure* which increases up to a value referred to as the *saturated vapor pressure,* at which an equilibrium condition is established. Under these circumstances the number of gas molecules entering the liquid becomes equal to the number of molecules escaping from the liquid in the same interval of time. The saturated vapor pressure of a substance increases with temperature. For water at 100°C. this pressure is 760 cm. of Hg (standard atmospheric pressure), whence the boiling point of water at standard atmospheric pressure is said to be 100°C.

The *boiling point* of a substance is defined as that temperature at which its saturated vapor pressure equals the atmospheric pressure upon its free surface. Hence the boiling point of a substance varies with the external pressure.

In a confined mixture of liquids and their vapors, each vapor develops its own vapor pressure independently of the others, such that the total pressure is equal to the sum of the pressures which each vapor would develop if it were alone. This is known as *Dalton's law of partial pressures.*

A gas cannot be liquefied by cooling alone. Yet there is a *critical temperature* above which pressure alone will not liquefy a gas. The pressure corresponding to the critical temperature is called the *critical pressure.*

Fusion. If heat is withdrawn from a quantity of water, the temperature is lowered by one degree C. for every calorie per gram subtracted, down to 0°C. At this temperature (at atmospheric pressure) the withdrawal of heat produces a change in state from liquid to solid (ice). The amount of heat required to make this change without changing the temperature is 80 calories per gram for water at 0°C. and is known as its *heat of fusion.* This quantity of heat must be added to a solid substance (ice) to change it to a liquid (water) without changing its temperature.

The freezing point of a substance is affected by pressure, but only by the application of very large pressures is it lowered appreciably for most substances. This phenomenon of the melting of ice under pressure followed by refreezing upon the removal of this pressure is called *regelation* and explains the process of skating on ice.

Upon freezing, most substances undergo a change in volume. Water and a very few other substances expand when they freeze.

Crystalline substances have definite melting points: *amorphous* substances do not.

Sublimation. *Sublimation* is the name applied to the direct change from the solid to the gaseous state, such as is often observed in the direct evaporation of snow. It is also observed in the evaporation of "dry ice" (solid carbon dioxide).

Pressure and Temperature. Water, like many other substances, can exist in equilibrium in each of its three states simultaneously if the pressure and the temperature are properly adjusted. If these two quantities (pressure and temperature) are plotted on a diagram, the states are indicated by the solid-liquid, liquid-vapor, and solid-vapor curves. (Fig. 55.) For water, these curves intersect at a point (p = 0.46 cm. Hg; t = .0075°); hence, this combination is often referred to as the *triple point* of water.

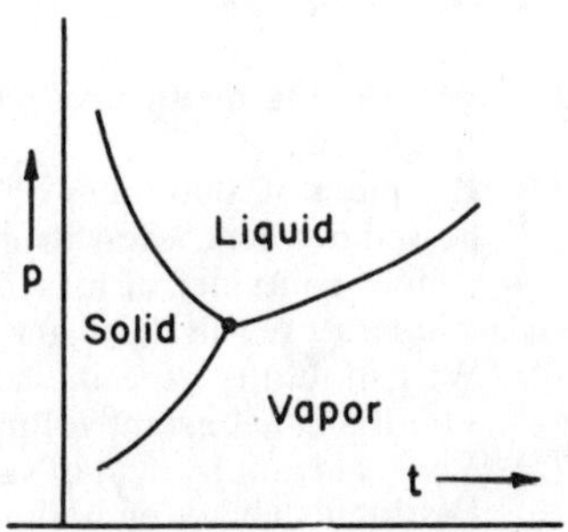

Fig. 55—Triple-point diagram

It is to be noted that the triple-point temperature for water is only slightly above zero on the centigrade scale. This, added to the fact that the triple point of water is readily reproducible, has led to the establishment of a new temperature scale called the *Celsius scale.* Its degree has the same size as the centigrade (or Kelvin) degree, and its zero point is such that the triple-point temperature of water is 0.01° (rounded to the nearest hundredth of a degree).

Water, like some other substances, can be *undercooled* and *superheated* beyond its normal freezing and boiling points respectively by very careful treatment, but such conditions are very unstable.

ATMOSPHERIC MOISTURE

When water evaporates into the atmosphere, the degree of saturation is an important *meteorological* factor. *Absolute humidity* is the mass of water vapor contained in a unit volume of air (in grams per cubic centimeter). *Relative humidity* is the ratio of the actual mass of water vapor present to the mass which would produce saturation at the given temperature. The *dew point* is the temperature at which the relative humidity would correspond to 100%, or saturation. When the atmosphere is cooled below the dew point, fogs and clouds are produced. Precipitation in the form of rain, hail, and snow results under the proper conditions of temperature in the upper atmosphere.

Review Questions

(1) How much energy is represented by a calorie? a British thermal unit?
(2) What is the distinction between heat capacity of a substance and specific heat?
(3) If a piece of aluminum of mass 200 grams and specific heat 0.2 is heated to 100°C. and dropped into 500 cc. of water at 20°C. in a copper container of mass 200 grams and specific heat .095, to what temperature will the water be raised?
(4) Why should the specific heat of a gas be greater at constant pressure than at constant volume?
(5) What is meant by heat of vaporization? of fusion?
(6) Distinguish between boiling and evaporation.

11: Heat Transfer and Thermodynamics

THE TRANSFER OF HEAT FROM ONE PLACE TO ANOTHER

Conduction. *Conduction* is the flow of heat along or through a substance. The details of the phenomenon are not completely understood, but in a general way the energy is passed along from molecule to molecule. The rate of flow is proportional to the area of cross section of the conductor and its *temperature gradient* (the difference in temperature between its two ends per unit of length), and varies with the substance of which it is made. $h = k\,a\,\frac{t_2 - t_1}{x}$ where h is the rate of flow (cal. per sec.) and k is called the *coefficient of thermal conductivity.* Gases in general are poor conductors whereas metals are very good conductors. Thermal conduction appears to be related to electrical conduction in that good conductors of electricity are also good conductors of heat. Poor conductors are good insulators.

Convection. *Convection* is the transfer of heat by a moving agent. By the addition of heat to a substance certain physical properties of the substance are often changed (as for example its density), with the result that a circulatory motion is established whereby heat is carried from one place to another. Hence this mode of transfer depends upon the establishment of *convection currents* of matter. Neither conduction nor convection can take place in a vacuum. Good ventilation is accomplished by the setting up of convection currents.

Radiation. *Radiation* is the transfer of heat such as is possible through empty space (vacuum), in a manner which appears to be wavelike. Radiant energy travels in straight lines in all directions with a velocity equal to the velocity of light. In fact, light is a form of radiant energy. Except in a very few instances, all known phenomena associated with radiation can be explained in terms of an electromagnetic wave motion in a hypothetical medium called *ether.* On this basis, radiation consists of waves ranging in wave length from hundreds of thousands of meters (radio waves) down to extremely small fractions of centimeters (light waves) and beyond to millionths of centimeters (X rays), thus comprising a whole spectral distribution of energy known as the *electromagnetic spectrum.* That part of the spectrum in which the radiant energy is predominantly heat is between the radio and the light waves. It is usually referred to as the infrared region.

Ideal Black Body: In the study of heat radiation it has been found desirable to postulate an ideal radiator known as the *ideal black body.* The ideal black body is a perfect absorber as well as a perfect radiator. The term "black" is not restricted to its visible color.

Stefan's Law of Radiation: It is a matter of observation that the rate at which energy is radiated from a hot body is proportional to the fourth power of the body's absolute temperature. This means that all bodies (cold as well as hot) radiate so long as their temperatures are above absolute zero. If W is expressed in watts (joules per second), Stefan's law states that $W = SAT^4$ for an ideal black body, where S is a constant (called the black body constant) equal to 5.32×10^{-12} in C.G.S. units, and A is the surface area of the body. Since all bodies radiate, one is usually interested in the *net* rate of radiation of a body with respect to its surroundings. This is given by $W = SA(T_1^4 - T_2^4)$ for a black body again.

Wien's Displacement Law: It has been pointed out by Wien that if the energy in the radiation spectrum is plotted as a function of wave length, and this plot repeated for different temperatures, the product of the absolute temperature of the radiator by the wave length corresponding to maximum energy is always constant. (Fig. 56.) In other words, $T\lambda_m$ = constant. From this it appears that the color of a radiator is an indication of its temperature.

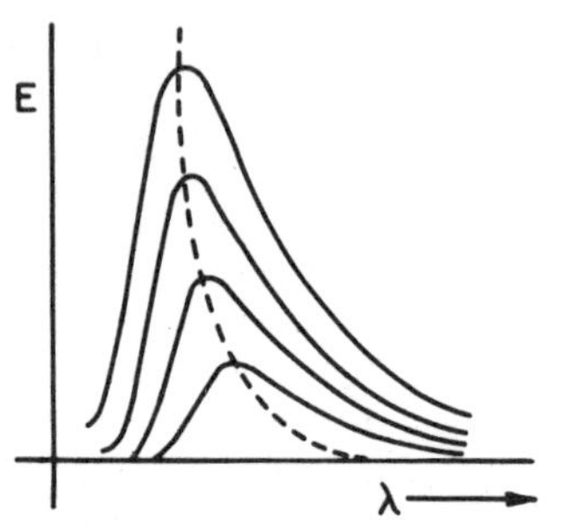

Fig. 56—Wien's displacement law

Planck's Quantum Theory: To describe analytically the curve of energy vs. wave length just referred to, Planck found it necessary to assume that radiation is not a continuous process, but that energy is emitted in small packets of various sizes always containing an integral multiple of units called *quanta*. On this basis he described the results in an equation $E = \frac{C}{\lambda^5(e^{c/\lambda T} - 1)}$ where C is a constant, λ the wave length, e the base of the natural logarithms, c another constant, and T the absolute temperature. The quantum theory has been very far-reaching in scope and has resulted in many changes in fundamental thought concerning the nature of things. In spite of the fact that its postulates seem at first artificial, it appears to be in complete accord with observable facts. Its chief disadvantage is the complexity of the mathematical language required for its complete understanding.

THE FIRST AND SECOND LAWS OF THERMODYNAMICS

The study of the problems of converting heat into other forms of energy, and vice versa, consists essentially in the deductions of consequences from two very general laws known as the *first* and the *second laws of thermodynamics*. A distinction has to be drawn between the thermodynamic and the atomic viewpoint. Atomics is concerned with specific processes, whereas thermodynamics is concerned with original and final conditions of a substance undergoing changes in energy content.

First Law of Thermodynamics. This is essentially the *law of the conservation of energy*, which states formally that energy may be changed in form but cannot be destroyed or created. Mechanical energy is convertible completely into heat energy to the extent that 4.18 joules are equivalent to 1 calorie (Joule-Rowland experiments). In other words, W = JH (J is the mechanical equivalent of heat = 4.18 joules per cal., or 778 ft.-lbs. per B.T.U.). If heat is added to a body, it shows up as external work done by the body plus an increase in its internal energy.

Thermodynamic Processes. Any process in which the temperature is kept constant is called an *isothermal process*. For an ideal gas, pv = constant, at constant temperature, whence this represents an isothermal process. *Note:* Heat must be added or subtracted in this process to keep the temperature constant. (Fig. 54-c.)

When no heat is allowed to enter or leave a substance during a process, the process is called *adiabatic*. (Fig. 57.) In the case of an ideal gas, adiabatic pressure-volume-temperature changes give

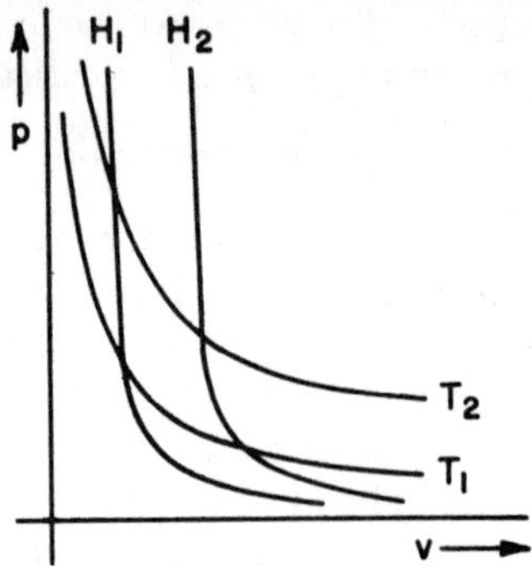

Fig. 57—Isotherms and adiabatics

(*a*) $pv^k = \text{constant} \left(\text{where } k = \frac{Cp}{Cv}\right)$; or (*b*) $T\,v^{k-1} = \text{constant}$; or (*c*) $p^{\frac{1-k}{k}}\,T = \text{constant}$.

A *reversible process* is one which can be made to take place in the opposite sense by an infinitesimal change (reversal) in the conditions. It is an ideal process which is never completely realizable in practice. Under *very slowly* changing influences a substance passes through a continuous series of states of thermal equilibrium in a manner suggesting an approximately reversible process.

An *irreversible process* is one characterized by some property which is *always* greater at the end than at the beginning. All natural processes are irreversible in actuality. Under *rapidly* changing influences a system tends to settle to a state of thermal equilibrium via irreversible processes.

If, by a process, a system is eventually brought back to its initial condition, the process is said to be *cyclic*. The *Carnot cycle* is one consisting of two reversible isothermal and two reversible adiabatic processes. It represents, of course, an ideal set of situations which might be realized by an ideal engine (Carnot engine) and is worth considering because it can be shown that the efficiency of such an engine is independent of the working substance and yet is limited (not unlimited), meaning that not all heat can be transformed into mechanical energy. In Fig. 57 any parallelogram such as the one indicated by the intersections of T_1, H_2, T_3, H_3, represents a Carnot cycle.

Second Law of Thermodynamics. Heat cannot pass directly from a cold body to a hot body of its own accord. This law restricts the direction in which the natural processes take place.

As a consequence of the second law, no irreversible engine can be as efficient as a reversible engine such as a Carnot engine working between the same temperature limits. The efficiency of a Carnot engine is equal to

$$\text{Eff.} = \frac{w}{JH_1} = \frac{J(H_1 - H_2)}{JH_1} = \frac{T_1 - T_2}{T_1},$$

where w is the work done and JH_1 is the energy supplied, J being the mechanical equivalent of heat. H_1 and T_1 refer to the heat taken in at the boiler and the absolute temperature of the boiler, and H_2 and T_2 refer to the heat given out at the condenser and the absolute temperature of the condenser.

Since the efficiency of a reversible engine is independent of the working substance, a general basis for the definition of temperature is established. Thermodynamic temperature (θ) is so defined that $\frac{\theta_1}{\theta_2} = \frac{H_1}{H_2}$ for an ideal engine, whence it follows that $\theta_2 = 0$ for 100% efficiency. Experimentally, temperatures on this basis coincide with absolute temperatures, whence added significance is given to absolute zero, namely that it is that temperature required of the exhaust of an ideal (reversible) engine working at 100% efficiency.

Since $\frac{H_1}{H_2} = \frac{T_1}{T_2}$, $\therefore H_2 = \frac{H_1}{T_1} T_2$. The quantity $\frac{H_1}{T_1}$ is called *entropy*, a quantity which measures thermodynamic degeneration. For all real processes there is an increase in entropy, whereas in an ideal (reversible) process the increase in entropy is zero. This means that although there is no gain or loss of energy in the universe, energy is nevertheless always becoming less available.

Review Questions

(1) Distinguish between conduction, convection, and radiation.
(2) What is an ideal black body?
(3) Why does a vacuum bottle keep liquids cold longer than it keeps them hot?
(4) What unique assumption is made by the quantum theory?
(5) State the first and second laws of thermodynamics.

Part IV: Electricity and Magnetism

12: Nature of Electricity and Electrostatics

INTRODUCTION AND EARLY THEORIES

Elementary Concepts. It is observed when certain substances such as hard rubber and fur are rubbed together and then separated from each other, that each of the substances is capable of exerting force upon the other and upon other bodies brought near it. Such forces, resembling the force of gravity in that they do not require a contact between the influencing body and the body being influenced, but differing from gravity in that repulsions as well as attractions are displayed, are called *electrical forces* and are said to be due to *electric charges* distributed upon the substances as a result of rubbing them together. Further consideration shows that the charge thus established on the fur behaves in the opposite way from the charge on the rubber rod, the former being designated as *positive*, and the latter as *negative*, merely by convention. It is also found that this distinction is relative and that similar effects of varying intensity are produced when almost any two substances are rubbed together. Moreover, these charges are readily carried from place to place by certain substances designated as *conductors*. Substances which do not have this property are called *insulators* or nonconductors. Actually, insulators are merely poor conductors since conductivity is also a relative property. An insulator is frequently referred to as a *dielectric substance.* These charges are subject to two experimental laws: (1) Like charges always repel and unlike charges always attract one another. (2) The magnitude of the attractive or repulsive force between two point charges is given by the expression $F = \frac{qq'}{Kr^2}$ where q and q′ are the charges, and r is the distance between them. This force is very much influenced by the medium in which the charges are located, which fact is indicated by the constant K, called the *dielectric constant,* arbitrarily taken as unity for a vacuum. This law is known as *Coulomb's law of electrical force.*

It is not uncommon to write $F = k\frac{qq'}{r^2}$, where the proportionality constant k, rather than $\frac{1}{K}$, is used. When C.G.S. units are used, $\frac{1}{K}$ is the more convenient because K has the numerical value of the dielectric constant of the medium. In M.K.S. units, however, k has the numerical value of 9×10^9 newton meter^2 per coulomb^2. See p. 89 for a discussion of electrical units.

Later Views. The above facts about electrical charges and forces were known hundreds of years ago when it was assumed that electricity consisted of *two fluids,* one positive and the other negative, an excess of either one on a body accounting for its state of electrification. These ideas were supplanted by a view advocated by Benjamin Franklin according to which a *single fluid* (positive electricity) accounted for either type of electrification by its excess or deficiency.

The present view of the nature of electricity is dictated by the electron theory of matter, according to which, as has been already pointed out, atoms of substances have a structure consisting of nuclei, intimately associated with positive charges of electricity called *protons,* surrounded by some sort of distribution of negative charges of electricity called *electrons.* Normally the electrons and protons maintain an electrical balance. Furthermore, the electrons are more or less free to move about in, and are in some cases readily removed from, substances (as when a hard rubber rod is rubbed with fur, the fur gives up large numbers of electrons to the rubber rod). On the other hand, the protons are for the most part rather closely bound to that part of the atom which displays practically all of the atom's inertia (said differently, the proton is some 1840 times more massive than the electron) and hence the protons are much less mobile than the electrons. Consequently, it is felt that the free electrons alone account for all the common electrical effects. This means specifically that a body contains an excess of electrons when it is said to be negatively charged, and that when a body is commonly referred to as being positively charged, what is meant is that the electron content is deficient. Thus a *single fluid* theory is in a way suggested, but it must be pointed out that this is a *negative* fluid and not the positive fluid proposed by Franklin. This view is not in the least altered by the discoveries of two other fundamental components of atoms: namely, the *neutron*, a neutral particle having approximately the same mass as the proton, and the *positron*, or what appears to be an electron with a positive charge. The positron plays a minor role in ordinary electrical phenomena, but the neutron plays a very important role in modern nuclear physics. See the chapter on nuclear physics.

Thus, all matter appears to be electrical in nature and all electrical phenomena are merely manifestations of energy different from those hitherto discussed. It must be pointed out that charges of electricity are never generated by frictional processes and the like, but that they already exist as integral parts of matter itself and are merely separated by these frictional devices.

Electrical Units. Coulomb's law provides a logical means of standardizing a unit of electric charge. Such a unit is that amount of charge which will repel an exactly equal amount of charge of like sign with a unit of force when the two are placed unit distance apart in vacuum (both charges considered to be pointlike). In the C.G.S. electrostatic system this quantity of charge is called the *stat-coulomb*. The coulomb is 3×10^9 stat-coulombs. Moreover, the electronic charge is -4.80×10^{-10} stat-coulombs.

In M.K.S. units, it proves to be more convenient to standardize the unit of current (rate of flow of charge). See Chapter 13. Consequently the coulomb, which is the unit of charge in this system, is a derived unit, being derived from the unit of current, the ampere, whereupon the proportionality constant k in Coulomb's law is not unity for vacuum.

Thus in C.G.S. units, $\frac{1}{K}$ has dimensions of $\frac{\text{dyne cm.}^2}{\text{stat-coulomb}^2}$ and a numerical value of unity. But in M.K.S. units, k has dimensions of $\frac{\text{newton meter}^2}{\text{coulomb}^2}$ and a numerical value of 9×10^9. Moreover, $k = \frac{1}{4\pi\epsilon_0}$ where $\epsilon_0 = 8.85 \times 10^{-12} \frac{\text{coulomb}^2}{\text{newton meter}^2}$.

Therefore:

$$F = \frac{1}{K}\frac{qq'}{r^2} \qquad = k\frac{qq'}{r^2} \qquad = \frac{1}{4\pi\epsilon_0}\frac{qq'}{r^2}.$$

(C.G.S.) K = unity for vacuum.	(M.K.S.) k = 9×10^9 for vacuum.	(M.K.S.) ϵ_0 refers to vacuum but is not unity.

CONCEPTS OF ELECTROSTATICS CONCERNING CHARGES FOR THE MOST PART AT REST

Electric Field Intensity. The region about a charged body is referred to as the electric field of force, or simply the electric field of the charged body. More generally, an electric field is said to exist at a point if an electrical force is observed to act on a charged body placed there.

The *intensity* of the electric field, or more simply the *electric field,* indicated by the letter E, is defined as the force that would be exerted on a unit positive charge placed at the point in question.

$$E = \frac{F}{q'} \underset{\text{(C.G.S.)}}{\left(\frac{\text{dynes}}{\text{stat-coulomb}}\right)} \text{ or } \underset{\text{(M.K.S.)}}{\left(\frac{\text{newtons}}{\text{coulomb}}\right)}.$$

With respect to a charge q at a distance r from it:

$$E = \frac{q}{Kr^2} \text{ (C.G.S.)} \quad \text{or} \quad E = \frac{q}{4\pi\epsilon_0 r^2} \text{ (M.K.S.).}$$

In terms of a concept called *potential* (to be discussed presently) E is frequently referred to as the negative *potential gradient.*

Considerations of the field intensity (E) at different points in the field of a charged body suggest the concept of *lines of force* to represent this quantity. (Fig. 58.) A line of force is the path that

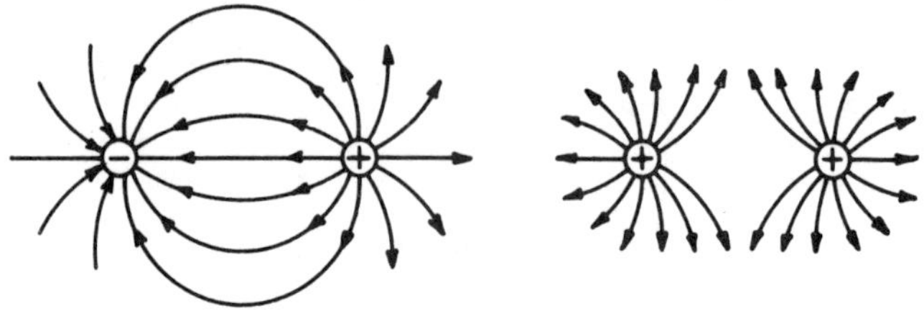

Fig. 58—Electric lines of force

would be taken by a free unit positive charge, and it is customary to imagine lines of force emanating from positive charges and entering negative charges (a unit positive charge being repelled from a positive charge and attracted toward a negative charge). The magnitude of E at a given point is represented by the concentration of lines of force at that place, measured in number of lines passing perpendicularly through unit area of surface. If we think of one line passing perpendicularly through one unit area of a spherical surface of unit radius completely enveloping a unit of charge, it follows that each unit of charge must emit 4π lines. No real significance is to be attached to these lines of force.

Distribution of Charges on Conductors. When electric charges are established on a conductor, they always are found on the surface of the conductor as a consequence of the mutual repulsions of like charges, and the freedom with which charges move in conductors. In the case of a spherical conductor the charges arrange themselves uniformly, but if the conductor displays an irregularly shaped surface the charges tend to crowd at pointed projections, due to the repulsive forces. (Fig. 59.) Moreover, if a charge is placed upon the inside surface of a hollow conductor it does not remain there but immediately travels through the conductor to the outer side. An interesting consequence of this is that the field intensity everywhere within a hollow conductor is always zero. (E = 0 everywhere within a hollow conductor.) Also for a sphere (hollow or solid) the field intensity (E) at any point outside the sphere is as if the entire charge on the sphere were concentrated at its center, behaving like a point charge, i.e., $E\,(\text{outside}) = \frac{kq}{r^2}$, where r is the distance from the point in question to the center of the sphere.

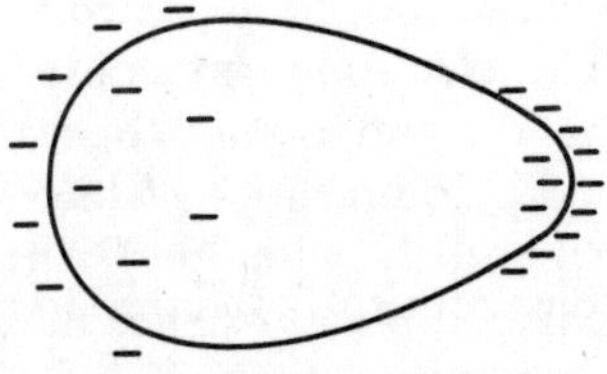

Fig. 59—Concentration of charges on points

The amount of charge on a unit of surface area is called the *surface density* of charge (σ).

Electric Induction (or Influence). Uncharged conductors (through which charges can move easily) develop "induced" charges when brought into electric fields. This is due to the fact that the free electrons, of which conductors have a generous supply, are readily attracted toward the near side of a conductor when it is brought into the field of a positive charge, and the positive charges (lack of negative charges) are repelled to the far side. This separation of the positive and negative charges in an *uncharged conductor* (one which has equal amounts of positive and negative charge, or just the right electron content to balance the total proton charge) is called *electric induction.*

If the body upon which charges are so separated (induced) by being brought into the field of a charged body, is grounded before it is removed from the field, it will, when removed, carry away a net charge of sign opposite to that of the body producing the field. The induction can be looked upon as a strained electrical condition which is relieved by grounding (charges enter or leave the ground, whichever the case may be to satisfy the situation), whereupon an excess of the charge of opposite sign remains upon the body when it and the body responsible for the strained condition are separated.

This phenomenon is displayed by the action of the *electrophorus*, a device of considerable practical importance, from which charges can be repeatedly taken as a result of a single rubbing. The electrophorus consists of a metal *plate* with an insulated handle and a *sole* consisting of ebonite, or hard rubber, or a rosin composition, which takes a negative charge when rubbed vigorously with fur. The plate is imperfectly touched to the charged plate, whence by induction its charges are separated so that positive charges line its lower surface and negative charges line its upper surface. (Fig. 60.) The plate is then grounded,

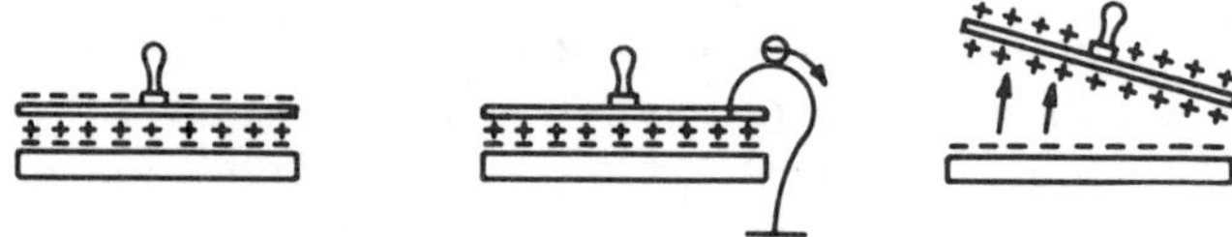

Fig. 60—The electrophorus

whence a path is provided for the excess electrons on the top of the plate to leave. Therefore, the plate upon being removed is found to have a net positive charge (having lost electrons when it was grounded). The process can be repeated many times, omitting the charging of the sole. It should be pointed out that removing the plate requires the expenditure of energy.

The various electrical machines such as the Wimshurst and Toepler-Holtz machines utilize the principle of induction.

Whereas the ordinary gold-leaf electroscope is readily

charged by transferring charges to it by direct contact with charged bodies, it is frequently charged by induction. This is the proper way to charge a very delicate electroscope. (Fig. 61.)

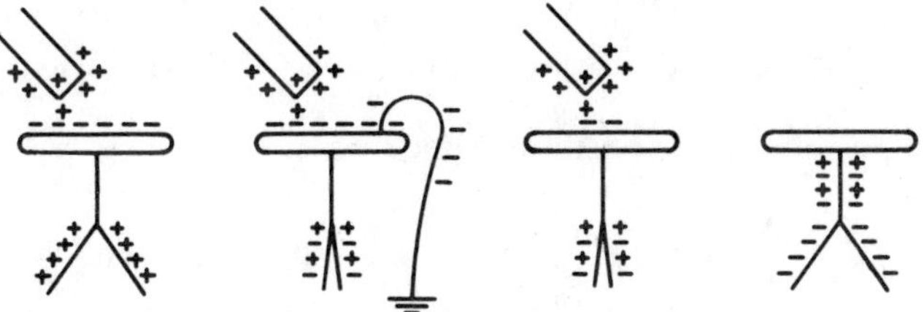

Fig. 61—Charging an electroscope by induction

Electrical Potential. It has been pointed out that electrical fields surround charges, meaning that at every point in the vicinity of a charge a force of definite magnitude and direction would act upon a unit positive charge if it were placed there ($E = \frac{kq}{r^2}$, where r is the distance from the charge q out to the point in question). Therefore, if a charge is moved toward or away from a charged body, a certain amount of work must be involved in the act since the product of a force multiplied by the distance through which its point of application is moved, in the direction of the force, represents work. It will be recalled from mechanics that whenever work is done against a conservative force (one dependent upon position alone), potential energy is acquired. The attractive or repulsive forces due to electric charges are conservative forces and hence electrical potential energy is acquired by a charge when it is moved through a distance against such forces. As in the case of gravitational potential energy where the difference in this quantity between two levels is more important than the absolute value of the quantity at a particular level, the difference in electrical potential between two points is more significant than its absolute value at any point. By definition, the difference in *electrical potential* between two points, A and B, is the amount of work which must be done on a *unit positive charge* in moving it from position A to position B. If in this process the work is positive work (i.e., work has to be done *on* the charge), B must be at a higher potential than A, and vice versa.

If A and B are at distances r_1 and r_2 respectively from a positive point charge q (Fig. 62, p. 94), the difference in potential be-

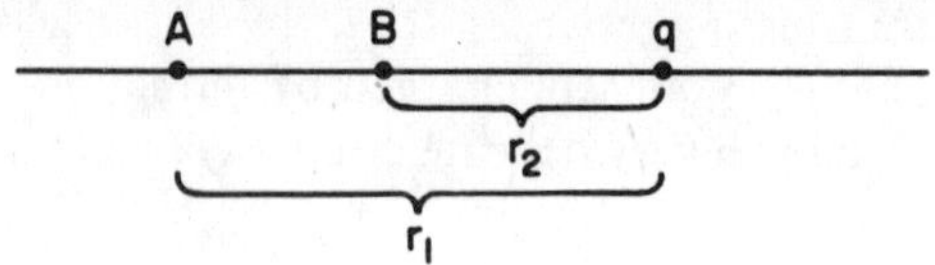

Fig. 62—Difference in potential between A and B due to q

tween position A and position B due to q is:

$$V_B - V_A = \frac{W}{q'} = E_{av}(r_1 - r_2) = \frac{kq}{r_1 r_2}(r_1 - r_2) = kq\left(\frac{1}{r_2} - \frac{1}{r_1}\right)$$

where this difference is expressed in ergs per stat-coulomb (*stat-volt*). In calculus language:

$$V_{AB} = \frac{W}{q'} = -\int_{r_1}^{r^2} E\cos\theta\, dr$$

$$= kq\left(\frac{1}{r_2} - \frac{1}{r_1}\right).$$

One stat-volt equals 300 *volts*. One volt is equivalent to one joule per coulomb and is the M.K.S. unit of potential. If A is infinitely far away from q, $\frac{1}{r_1} \rightarrow o$ whereupon V_A becomes zero, and it makes sense to speak of the absolute potential at point B as $V_B = \frac{kq}{r_2}$. Thus the *absolute potential* at a point in the field of a point charge q is defined as the amount of work that must be done upon a unit positive charge to bring it from an infinite distance away (i.e., from completely outside of the field) up to the point in question.

Potential is not a vector quantity but a scalar quantity, whence the potential due to a number of point charges is $V = \Sigma\frac{kq}{r}$. Potential difference can be readily measured by a calibrated electroscope or an electrometer.

The potential of a charged spherical conductor of radius a is:

$$V = \frac{kq}{r} \text{ where r is greater than a;}$$

$$V = \frac{kq}{a} \text{ for points on the surface, or for all points within the sphere, i.e., } r \leq a.$$

Note: V is constant inside a spherical conductor and is equal to the value at the surface, whereas E (field intensity) is zero inside a spherical conductor, whether it be solid or hollow.

$$dV = -E\,dr. \qquad E = -\frac{dV}{dr},$$

where $\frac{dV}{dr}$ is the potential gradient. See p. 90.

Electrical Capacity (Capacitance). When the charge on a conductor is increased, the potential is also altered in such a manner that the ratio of the new charge to the new potential is a constant called the *capacity* (or the *capacitance*) of the conductor. $\frac{q_1}{v_1} = \frac{q_2}{v_2} = \frac{q}{V} = C$. It must be pointed out that capacity has this technical significance and does *not* refer to the limiting amount of charge which the conductor can hold. The value of ratio q/v, or C, depends upon the proximity of other charged conductors, and also upon the dielectric substance of which the surroundings are composed.

When two conductors are separated by a dielectric, the combination is known as a *condenser* or *capacitor*. The capacity of a condenser depends upon the nature of the dielectric, the size of the plates, and the distance between them. The following relations indicate the capacities of different types of condensers:

(a) For a spherical condenser made of two concentric spheres of radii r_1 and r_2, $C = K\frac{r_1 r_2}{r_2 - r_1} = \frac{1}{k}\frac{r_1 r_2}{r_2 - r_1}$.

(b) For a single isolated sphere, $C = Kr = \frac{1}{k}r$.

(c) For a plane parallel plate condenser, $C = \frac{KA}{4\pi d} = \frac{A}{4\pi k d}$ where d is the thickness of the dielectric.

The unit of capacity (or capacitance) is the stat-coulomb per stat-volt, called the *stat-farad*. 9×10^{11} stat-farads = 1 farad.

The farad is the coulomb per volt. (Although the farad is the unit of capacity in the practical system, it is nevertheless so large a unit that the micro-farad [one-millionth of a farad], and the micro-micro-farad [one-millionth of a micro-farad] are commonly used.)

Condensers (or capacitors) can be combined in either one of two ways. When condensers are connected in *parallel,* the combined capacity of the combination is obtained by adding the capacities of the individual condensers.

$$C = C_1 + C_2 + C_3 + \cdots \text{ (parallel).} \qquad \text{(Fig. 63.)}$$

When condensers are connected in *series,* the capacity of the combination is found as follows:

$$\frac{1}{C} = \frac{1}{C_1} + \frac{1}{C_2} + \frac{1}{C_3} + \cdots \text{ (series).} \qquad \text{(Fig. 63.)}$$

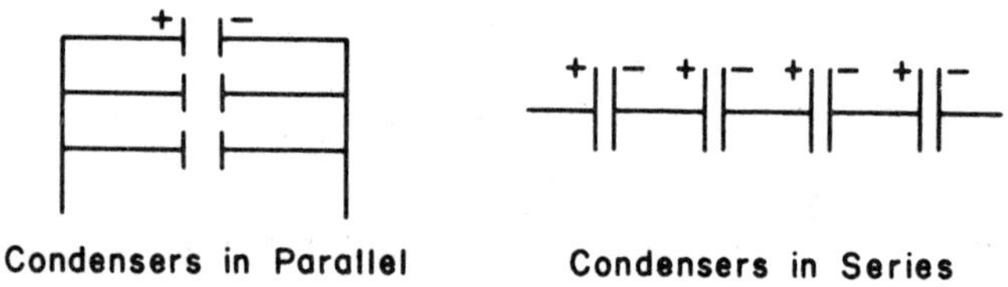

Condensers in Parallel

Condensers in Series

Fig. 63

Energy stored in a condenser is given by the relations $W = \frac{1}{2} q v = \frac{1}{2} C v^2 = \frac{1}{2} \frac{q^2}{C}$. It is this energy which shows up in the spark when a condenser is discharged. Since for a given condenser of capacity C, the energy stored up is proportional to the second power of the potential difference between the plates, it is desirable to store energy at high potential.

Review Questions

(1) What is the electrostatic unit of charge?
(2) Distinguish between positive and negative charges.
(3) What is Coulomb's law?
(4) What is meant by field intensity? potential?
(5) What is the "line of force" concept?
(6) Describe the manner of charging an electroscope by induction and indicate the sign of the resulting charge with respect to the sign of the charge on the charging body.

(7) What is the field intensity midway between a charge of +10 E.S.U. and a charge of −10 E.S.U., if they are separated by 10 cm.? What if the charges have the same sign? What is the potential at the same point in each case?

(8) Distinguish between electric capacity and dielectric strength of a conductor.

13: Electric Currents (Steady)

NATURE OF CURRENT

Intensity of Current. When two points, between which a difference in potential is maintained, are connected by an electrical conductor, a surge of electrical charges is established. This motion of charges is known as an *electric current* and its intensity (I) is defined as the rate of flow of charge.

$$I = \frac{q}{t} \text{ for steady flow.}$$

$$i = \frac{dq}{dt} \text{ at any instant.}$$

Also $i = A\,\Sigma nev$ in terms of charges moving through a conductor at various speeds, where A is the area of cross section of the conductor, n is the number of charged particles per unit volume, e is the charge on each particle, and v is the velocity of each particle along the conductor. This rate is expressed in *amperes* when q (coulombs) pass a given point in t seconds. By convention, the "flow" of electricity is from high to low potential in a conductor, the inference being that positive charges move due to a repulsion from regions of high potential and an attraction toward regions of low potential. The exact nature of electrical conduction is not any too well understood in detail, although it has been very definitely established that in reality, the "flow" in metallic conductors is chiefly a drift of electrons (negative charges) actually moving in an electrical field from low to high potential. This contradiction of the conventional direction of flow by actual facts is conceded by all; but, nevertheless, the convention persists due to a general feeling that nothing in particular would be gained by any widespread movement to change it.

Drift Speed of Electrons. Attention must be called to the not uncommon confusion between the drift speed of the electrons and the speed of propagation of electrical effects. The latter is exceedingly great, reaching a maximum of 3×10^{10} cm./sec. in vacuum, whereas the former is surprisingly small, usually of the order of magnitude of centimeters (or less) per second.

1 electron carries 4.80×10^{-10} stat-coulombs, or 1.60×10^{-19} coulombs.

1 ampere = 1 coulomb per second = 3×10^9 stat-coulombs per second.

$$\therefore 1 \text{ ampere} = \frac{3 \times 10^9}{4.80 \times 10^{-10}} = 6.25 \times 10^{18} \text{ electrons per second.}$$

Circulatory Nature of Current. At this time steady or unvarying currents will be considered. For such currents emphasis should be laid upon the *circulatory* nature of current. Electric charges behave like an incompressible fluid, and as such they cannot accumulate anywhere. If charges are set into motion at any point of a series circuit, they are nearly simultaneously set into motion everywhere in the circuit. This also means that at every branch point in a divided circuit, the currents which leave the branch point must total up to the sum of all currents entering that point.

Steady currents are best studied by certain effects which they produce. These are readily classified in three distinct groups as follows: *Chemical Effects; Heating Effects; Magnetic Effects.* In this outline these effects will be studied separately in this same order. Since, however, all steady currents require for their existence steadily maintained differences of potential, the sources of which are usually referred to as electromotive forces, the study of currents will be preceded by a study of electromotive force. The magnetic effect, requiring as it does a special discussion of magnetism, will be considered in a separate chapter.

ELECTROMOTIVE FORCE

The Voltaic Cell. If two electrodes of different metals such as copper and zinc are dipped into a solution such as sulphuric acid which attacks the zinc, chemical action sets up a difference in potential. The copper electrode acquires a positive charge and the zinc electrode acquires a negative charge, as can be shown with an electroscope. If the two electrodes are connected externally a current of electricity is established through the wire and also through the battery. (Fig. 64, p. 100.) The chemical action maintains a difference of potential between the metal electrodes until

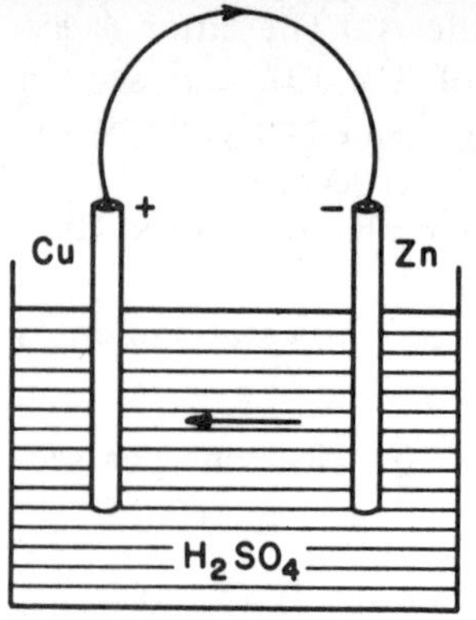

Fig. 64—Voltaic cell

the zinc electrode is completely disintegrated by the acid. Such an arrangement is called a *voltaic cell* or a *battery* and is referred to as a seat of electromotive force. The term *electromotive force* is used to refer to the setting up of potential difference, as this is accomplished by batteries, generators, etc. It is a quantity that is measured in the same units as potential difference, but differs from it in that the latter is not necessarily concerned with the manner in which it is established. The electromotive force of a circuit is that which is responsible for the flow of current in it and is defined as the work done in moving a unit charge completely around the circuit.

It is to be noted that whereas in the external circuit the *conventional flow* of current is from positive to negative, it is from negative to positive *within* the battery. This is analogous to the flow of water from low to high pressure within a pump whose function it is to establish the difference in pressure which makes possible a flow outside the pump from high to low pressure regions.

The electromotive force of a battery and the potential difference across its terminals are not to be confused. The latter, although measured in the same units, is always shown by measurement to be smaller than the former unless the measurement is made by an instrument which itself does not provide a closed path for the flow of current. The analytical relationship between these two quantities will be discussed at a later point.

Attention is called to the fact that a battery is in no sense a generator of electricity, because electrical charges are not capable of being generated, but merely of being separated. The processes involved represent transformations of energy only, by chemical, mechanical, or other means.

Electromotive forces can be established in a variety of ways other than by chemical processes as in the voltaic cell just discussed. A list of methods would include pyroelectricity (due to heating of crystals), piezoelectricity, and atmospheric effects, as well as the more common methods employed by so-called electromagnetic generators, and static (frictional) machines. Some of these will be considered at appropriate points as the subject is developed further.

CHEMICAL EFFECTS OF ELECTRIC CURRENTS

Electrolysis. When a steady current is passed through a solution capable of transferring charges, chemical effects are observed to take place at the place where the current enters the solution and also at the place where it leaves it. The phenomenon is referred to as *electrolysis.* Such a solution is called an *electrolyte.* The electrode at which the current (conventional current) enters the electrolyte is called the *anode*, and the one at which the current leaves the electrolyte is called the *cathode.* (Fig. 65.)

Electrolytic phenomena are accounted for by the Theory of Dissociation, according to which chemical decomposition is a process of matter breaking up into molecules or groups of molecules and atoms which carry free charges of electricity. These charged particles are called *ions* and they may be either positive (cations) or negative (anions). As the electrolyte becomes decomposed, the positively charged ions are attracted toward the cathode and the negatively charged ions are attracted toward the anode, if and when a difference in potential is established between them. It is supposed that in electrolytes the process of conduction is accounted for entirely by the motion of positive and negative ions. Whether an ion has a positive or negative charge is a matter of fundamental atomic structure closely related to the chemical valence of the substance from which the ions are produced. Hydrogen and metallic substances, having positive valence (i.e., being electropositive substances), form positive ions. Nonmetals and acid radicals, having negative valence (i.e., being electronegative substances), form negative ions.

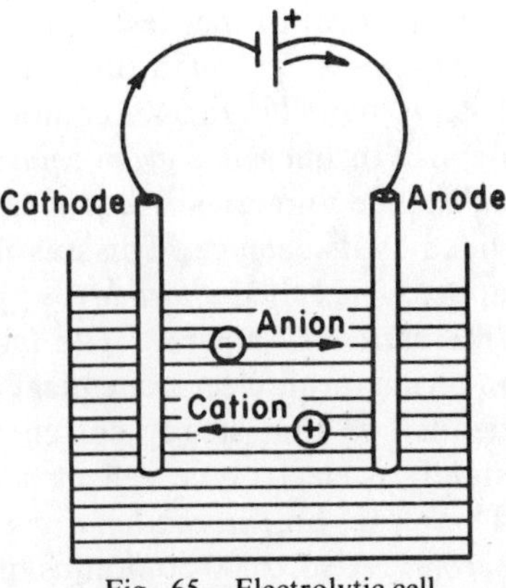

Fig. 65—Electrolytic cell

Electroplating. As the cations collect at the cathode where their charges are neutralized, it is obvious that the cathode becomes plated with the substance of these ions. In the case of copper ions in a copper sulphate solution, the cathode becomes plated with a coat of pure copper. This is the basis of electroplating. It is also the basis of a method of separating oxygen and hydrogen from water. Hydrogen accumulates at the cathode, and oxygen accumulates at the anode, the former collecting twice as rapidly as the latter.

Faraday's Laws of Electrolysis: (1) $M = ZIt = Zq$ for steady currents, where M is the mass of the substance deposited at the cathode (or also removed from the anode), I is the intensity of the current, t is the time, and Z is the *electrochemical* equivalent. (2) $Z\text{ (electrochem. equiv.)} = \dfrac{\text{atomic weight}}{\text{valence} \times 96540}$. From these laws it is evident that the rate of electrochemical deposit depends upon the chemical properties of the substance and the amount of electricity passed through the electrolyte. A certain amount of electricity, namely 96,540 coulombs (approximately), will always deposit or liberate a *gram equivalent* of a substance, i.e., a mass of substance numerically equal to the ratio of its atomic weight divided by its valence. This quantity of electricity (96,540 coulombs approx.) is called a *faraday*.

International Ampere. The *legal international ampere* is defined in terms of an electrochemical effect which it can produce. It is defined as that steady current which will deposit silver from a standard electrolytic cell at a rate of .001118 gram per second. Therefore, an *international coulomb* is an international *ampere-second.* Also, 3600 coulombs make one *ampere-hour.*

HEATING EFFECTS OF ELECTRIC CURRENTS AND GENERAL CIRCUIT CONSIDERATIONS

Joule's Law. It is the result of observation that when a current is established in a conductor heat is developed, and the rate at which it is developed is proportional to the second power of the intensity of the current. The proportionality factor is known as the *resistance* of the conductor. Thus for a steady current $\frac{W}{t} = \frac{JH}{t} = I^2R = P$ (the power dissipated). If P is expressed in watts (joules per second), and I is expressed in amperes, then R is expressed in *ohms.* J is the mechanical equivalent of heat equal to 4.18 joules per calorie.

Resistance. Although resistance is defined in the above manner, it is in reality a physical characteristic of a body. It is found to depend upon the length of the conductor, its area of cross section, and the material of which it is made, as follows: $R = \rho \frac{L}{A}$ where L is the length, A is the area, and ρ is the *resistivity* or *specific resistance* of the substance. The reciprocal of the resistivity is called the *conductivity* (c) or *specific conductance;* i.e., $c = \frac{1}{\rho}$.

When R is expressed in ohms, and L is given in cm., and A in cm.^{2}, ρ is then properly expressed in ohms-cm., which is the C.G.S. unit of resistivity. Engineers frequently express L in feet, and A in *circular mils,* whence ρ is properly expressed in ohms-mil-foot value. To calculate the area in circular mils, express the diameter in mils (thousandths of an inch) and square it. *Note:* The circular mil is not to be confused with a square mil to which it is proportional but not equal.

$$\left(1 \text{ circ. mil} = \frac{\pi}{4} \text{ sq. mil.}\right)$$

Resistance varies with temperature according to the approximate experimental law $R_t = R_o(1 + \alpha_o t)$ where R_t and R_o refer to the resistances at temperatures t and zero respectively. (Fig. 66.) Consequently $\alpha_o = \frac{R_t - R_o}{R_o t}$. α_o is the *temperature coefficient of resistance* referred to 0°C. It may be referred to any temperature, however. For metals α is a positive coefficient. Carbon displays a negative coefficient, i.e., its resistance decreases as the temperature rises. α is also negative for electrolytes and insulators in general.

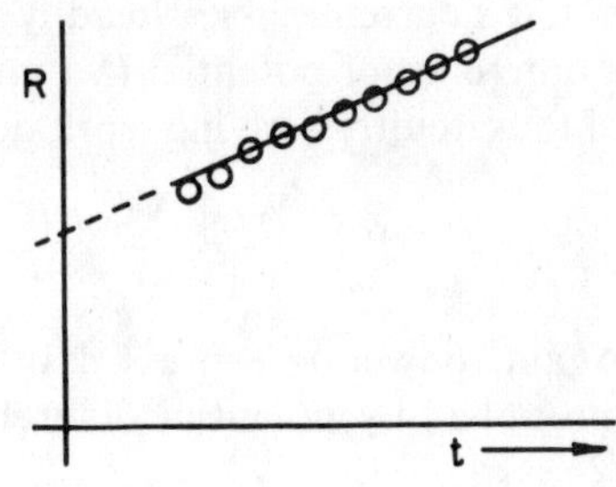

Fig. 66—Variation of resistance with temperature

For pure metals the value of α is approximately .0038 per degree C. It is interesting to note that numerically this is approximately the thermal expansion coefficient of a gas, suggesting a possible electrical effect associated with absolute zero. The facts are that some substances display extraordinarily high conductivities at very low temperatures within a few degrees of absolute zero. This phenomenon is called *superconductivity.* It is not a gradual effect, increasing with decreasing temperatures from 0°C., but occurs instead at very definite temperatures, different for different substances (yet always within a few degrees from absolute zero). The resistance starts to decrease very rapidly with temperature so that before absolute zero is reached all measurable resistance has vanished.

International Ohm. The *legal international ohm* is defined as the resistance offered to a steady current by a column of pure mercury 106.300 cm. long, of constant cross section, of mass 14.4521 grams, at the temperature of melting ice. These specifications require that the cross section be one square millimeter, corresponding to the density of mercury equal to 13.596 grams per $cm.^3$

Ohm's Law. It will be recalled that a seat of E.M.F. is a place where work (W) is done on an electric charge (q) in setting up a potential difference, and $E = \frac{W}{q}$ or $W = Eq$. The rate at which this work is done, i.e., the power $P = \frac{W}{t} = \frac{Eq}{t} = EI$ (for steady currents). The product of a current expressed in amperes multiplied by the electromotive force expressed in volts yields power in watts, or joules per second. If all this energy is dissipated in heat, then by Joule's law $EI = I^2R$ or $E = IR$. Furthermore, whether there is a seat of E.M.F. in a given part of a circuit or not, if a current passes steadily through such a part of the circuit, a difference of potential (V) must be maintained across that part of the circuit, involving work done at the rate of

$$P = \frac{W}{t} = \frac{Vq}{t} = VI = I^2R. \quad \therefore V = IR.$$

Again, power is expressed in watts if current (in amperes) is multiplied by potential difference (in volts). These two results $\left(I = \frac{E}{R} \text{ and } I = \frac{V}{R}\right)$, where the letter R does not have the same significance in each case, express *Ohm's law.* Stated in words, it says that the steady *current through* any portion of an electric circuit equals the *potential difference across* that portion of the circuit divided by the *resistance of* that portion of the circuit. If, instead of a portion of a circuit, a whole circuit, containing a battery or other seat of E.M.F., is considered, then the total electromotive force must be divided by the total resistance of the circuit (including the internal resistance of the battery itself) to get the current through the whole circuit. $I = \frac{E}{R_o + b}$ where b is the internal resistance of the seat of E.M.F. and R_o is the total *external* resistance of the circuit. (Fig. 67.) Consequently, $E = IR_o + Ib$.

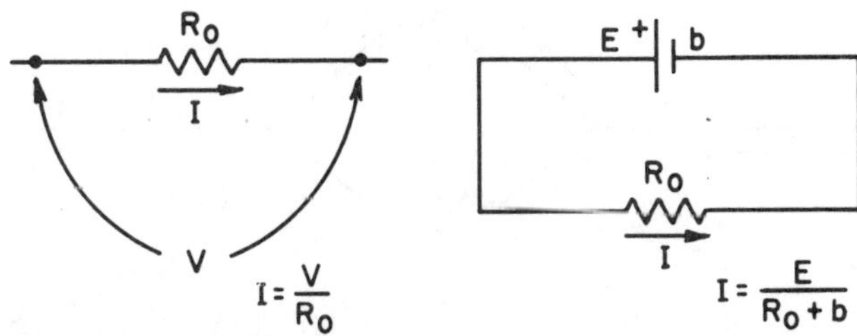

Fig. 67—Two cases of Ohm's law

According to the preceding discussion, IR_o represents the difference in potential across R_o. If the flow of current in R_o is from a to b, IR_o is called the *drop in potential* from a to b and is indicated by $V_{ab} = IR_o$. Obviously, if R_o represents the entire circuit external to the battery of E.M.F. (E), then V_{ba} also represents the potential drop across the battery itself, and the distinction between the electromotive force (E) of a battery and the potential difference (V) across its terminals is apparent ($E = V + Ib$). If no current were to flow, i.e., $I = 0$, then numerically E and V would be the same.

International Volt. The *legal international volt* is defined as that steady potential difference which will result in a flow of one international ampere through a resistance of one international ohm. This is *roughly* the E.M.F. of a standard Weston cell, but actually the E.M.F. of the latter equals 1.0182 volts.

Kirchhoff's Rules. A further consideration of potential drops, added to certain other very fundamental aspects of the nature of flow, suggests two important practical rules concerning steady currents in circuits. Obviously the net sum of all the potential drops across all the component parts of a closed circuit must be zero (considering the drops from a given point and passing around the whole circuit and arriving back at the starting point, and considering batteries as sources of negative potential drops, or potential rises). Also, by the incompressible nature of electric charges, previously referred to, no charges can accumulate at any point (if current is steady), especially at a branch point in a circuit. These facts lead to *Kirchhoff's rules:* (1) $\Sigma IR = \Sigma E$ in any closed loop of a circuit. (2) $\Sigma I = 0$ toward any branch point in a circuit; i.e., the sum of all currents toward a branch point is equal to the sum of all current leaving that branch point.

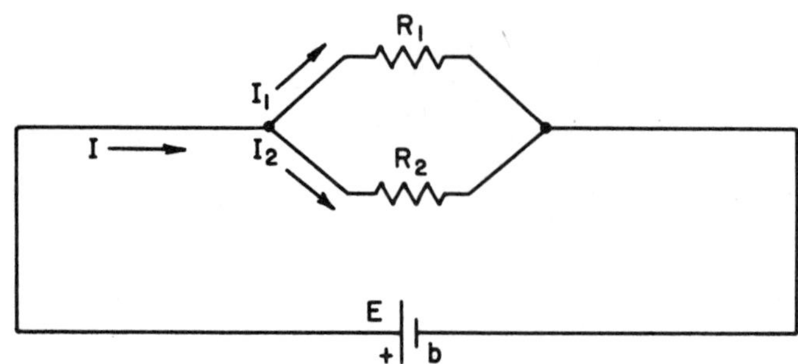

Fig. 68—By Kirchhoff's rules: $I = I_1 + I_2$; $E = I_2R_2 + Ib$

These rules are helpful in solving circuit problems, in that they yield a number of simultaneous equations to be solved for as many unknown quantities. (Fig. 68.)

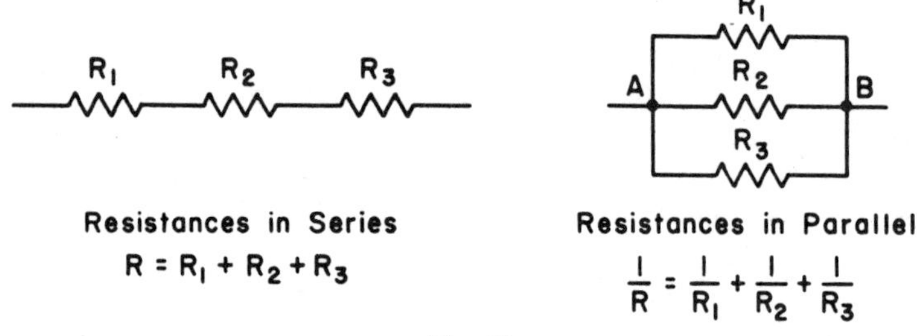

Fig. 69

Combinations of Resistance. It can be shown rather simply by a consideration of Ohm's law that for resistances in *series* (Fig. 69) $R = R_1 + R_2 + R_3 + \cdots$. For resistances in *parallel* (Fig. 69) (shunt) $\frac{1}{R} = \frac{1}{R_1} + \frac{1}{R_2} + \frac{1}{R_3} + \cdots$. In the latter case it is worth noting that the combined resistance of a number of resistances in parallel is less than the smallest of the combination. It may be worth pointing out that in the *parallel* case the currents are different through individual resistances (depending upon their individual resistance values) and the potential drop is the same across all; whereas in the *series* case, the current is the same through all, but potential drops across each differ according to the resistance value of each.

An interesting application of the laws of resistance combinations is the use of low resistance "shunts" for ammeters, and "multipliers" for voltmeters. Without considering the action of these meters except to note that ammeters are connected in series with a circuit to measure the current *through* the circuit, and that voltmeters are connected across parts of a circuit to measure potential drops, it can be shown that a given meter can be used for either purpose if it is sufficiently sensitive. In the use of an ammeter it is usually necessary that the resistance of the meter be low lest the drop in line potential be excessive and lest the meter burn up. This is accomplished by the use of low resistance shunts to divert a certain fraction of the entire current around the meter. In the use of voltmeters, it is necessary that the resistance of the meter be high lest the line current be affected appreciably by its presence. This is accomplished by inserting high resistances in series with the instrument. The proper values to use can be calculated by Ohm's law.

When cells are used in combinations, the internal resistances must be considered for efficient results. (Fig. 70.)

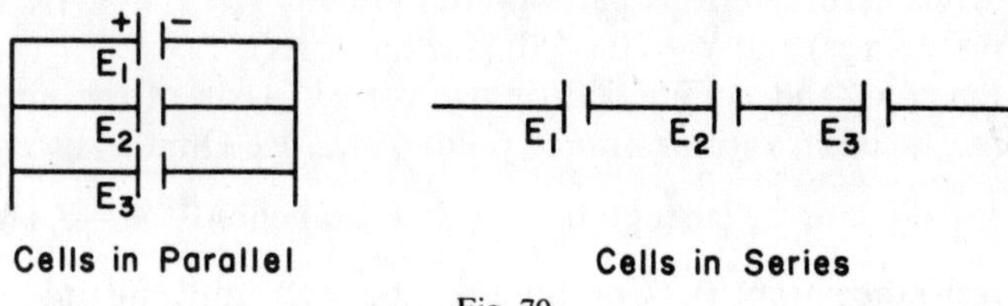

Fig. 70

For cells in series, Ohm's law gives $I = \dfrac{nE}{R_o + nb}$ where n is the number of cells each having an E.M.F. E, and an internal resistance b, and R_o is the external resistance. Therefore, a current advantage $\dfrac{I}{I_1}$ (where I_1 is the current drawn from one cell alone) equal to (n) is gained by this arrangement, if the internal resistance of one cell is very much smaller than the external resistance.

For cells in parallel, Ohm's law gives $I = \frac{nE}{nR_o + b}$. This arrangement yields a current advantage equal to n when the internal resistance of one cell is very much larger than the external resistance of the circuit.

It can be shown that the power output of a cell or a set of cells is a maximum when the combined internal resistance of the batteries is made equal to the external resistance of the circuit by properly combining the cells.

Problem Procedure for Electric Circuits.

(1) Draw a circuit diagram and label all batteries, resistances, branch points, etc., indicating the known quantities and specifying all the quantities to be determined.

(2) Replace all parallel resistance combinations by equivalent single resistances $\left(\frac{1}{R} = \frac{1}{R_1} + \frac{1}{R_2} + \cdots\right)$.

(3) Replace all parallel battery combinations by equivalent single batteries, expressing the equivalent E.M.F. and the equivalent internal resistance.

(4) Attempt to draw an equivalent simple series circuit.

(5) If (4) is possible, use Ohm's law to solve for current common to the series circuit $\left(I = \frac{\text{Net } E}{R_o + b}\right)$. *Note:* If I is known, this may yield the answer for E or R_o or b as the case may be.

(6) Once I is determined, use Ohm's law to determine potential drops across various parts of the circuit. I.e., $V = IR$ (for resistances) and $V = E - Ib$ (for batteries).

(7) Knowing the potential drops across all parts of the circuit, i.e., between various branch points, etc., use Ohm's law again to calculate the current in individual branches $I_1 = \frac{V}{R_1}$ (for a resistance branch). Continue this process until all unknown quantities are determined.

(8) If (4) is impossible, i.e., if an equivalent simple series circuit cannot be drawn—because, for example, of a branch line containing a battery and a resistance—this method will not work and an alternative method must be used. *See* Kirchhoff's rules, p. 106.

The Wheatstone Bridge and the Potentiometer Circuits. The *Wheatstone bridge* is a circuit used to compare resistances. (Fig. 71.) An unknown resistance is evaluated as a product of a known

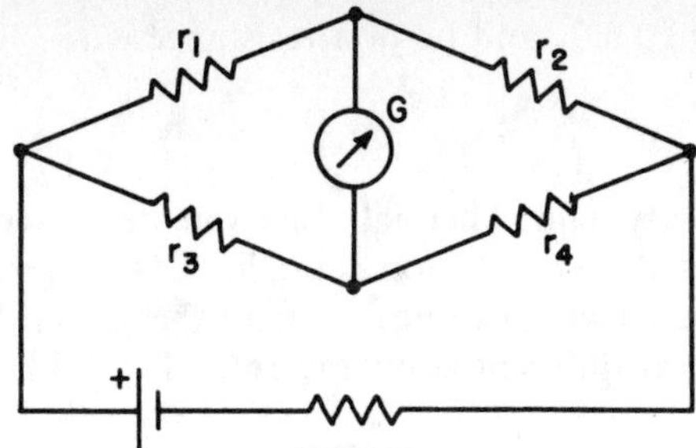

Fig. 71—The Wheatstone bridge circuit

resistance (standard) and the ratio of two other resistances. $r_1 = r_2 \frac{r_3}{r_4} = r_2 \frac{l_3}{l_4}$ where r_1 is the unknown, r_2 is a variable standard, and $\frac{r_3}{r_4}$ refers to two other resistances which need not be separately evaluated. Frequently r_3 and r_4 are two lengths, l_3 and l_4, of a resistance wire, the ratio of their resistances being determined as the ratio of their lengths, as in the slide wire type of Wheatstone bridge.

The *potentiometer* is a circuit by means of which electromotive forces may be compared. (Fig. 72.) An unknown E.M.F.

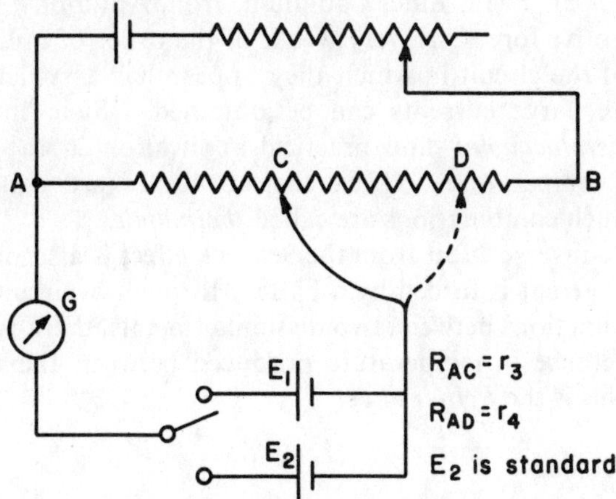

Fig. 72—The potentiometer circuit

is evaluated as the product of a known E.M.F. (standard) and the ratio of two resistances. As before, the ratio is often measured by comparing lengths, l_3 and l_4, of a resistance wire. $E_1 = E_2 \frac{r_3}{r_4} = E_2 \frac{l_3}{l_4}$.

Thermoelectricity and Thermal Electromotive Forces. In the *Seebeck effect,* if a closed loop is made of two dissimilar metals, current will be observed to flow around the loop if the two junctions are kept at different temperatures. (Fig. 73.) This current

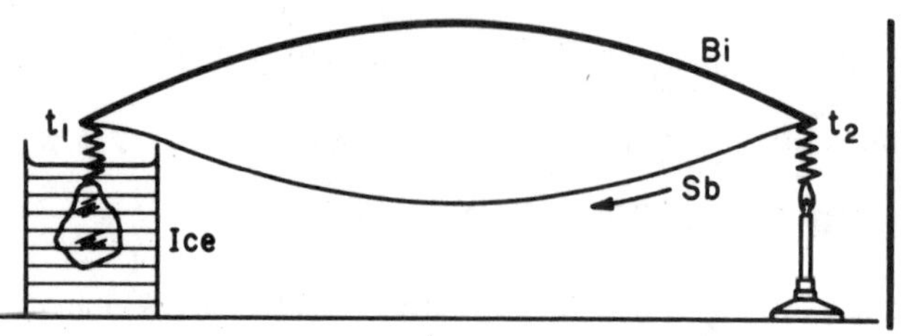

Fig. 73—Seebeck effect

is due to the development of a thermal electromotive force between the junctions which varies with the temperature difference between them. Current flows *across* the hot junction (e.g., from bismuth to antimony) as the junction consists of substances arranged in the following order: Bismuth, Nickel, Cobalt, Platinum, Copper, Lead, Zinc, Cadmium, Iron, Antimony. Thermal electromotive forces are very weak, of the order of millivolts per °C, but if the circuit in which they appear has a sufficiently low resistance, large currents can be obtained. Such metal-pairs, called *thermocouples,* find practical application in the measurement of temperature. Often thermocouples are connected in series. Such combinations are called *thermopiles.*

The converse effect from the Seebeck effect is also observable. When a current is forced by a battery through a circuit containing two junctions between two dissimilar metals, there is a noticeable difference in temperature produced between the two junctions. This is the *Peltier effect.*

Review Questions

(1) What is the nature of an electric current?
(2) Criticize the statement that "a current is started in a series circuit, and it flows around through the various devices in the circuit one after another."
(3) Outline three fundamental effects of an electric circuit.

(4) Does a current always travel from positive to negative (assume conventional flow)?

(5) What is electromotive force?

(6) Define the legal ampere.

(7) What are meant by anode? cathode? cation? anion? electrochemical equivalent?

(8) What is Joule's law? Ohm's law? Show that one is derivable from the other on the basis of fundamental definitions.

(9) What is the legal ohm?

(10) If two lamps of 200 ohms each are connected in parallel across a 100-volt line, how much current will be drawn? Compare the power dissipated by a series arrangement versus a parallel arrangement of the lamps.

(11) How is the legal volt defined?

(12) Describe the Wheatstone bridge method of comparing resistances.

(13) It is claimed that a certain thermoelectric device on the market passes a current of approximately 100 amperes resulting from a thermoelectromotive force. Realizing that thermal electromotive forces are of the order of millivolts or less, is the claim reasonable?

14: Magnetism and the Magnetic Effects of Currents

THE CONCEPT OF MAGNETISM

Magnetism. It was known at a very early date that a certain ore, now known as magnetite and earlier called lodestone, had the curious property of attracting to itself other bits of iron ore, and also that when a long thin sliver of this ore was suspended by a thread fastened around it as its center, it tended to orient itself in a north-south direction and so could be used as a compass. This property has been referred to as magnetism.

Early Ideas about Magnetism. It was realized that the magnetic effects of the bar magnet (sliver of lodestone or a long thin rod of iron previously rubbed with lodestone) were concentrated at the ends, which were called *poles,* one north and one south. It was also realized that magnetic effects are force effects which could be attributed to such poles, resembling the electrostatic forces which are observed between positive and negative electric charges. The view was further developed by Coulomb, whose experimental law of magnetic force between supposititious poles has the same form as his law of force between supposititious pointlike charges. $F \sim \frac{m\,m'}{r^2}$, where m and m′ refer to something called pole strength, and r is their separation. Moreover, like poles repel and unlike poles attract, resembling the repulsion and attraction of electric charges.

These views led to the development of magnetostatic concepts and terminology bearing considerable similarity to the concepts and terminology of electrostatics, but in no way suggesting any relation between the two.

The Earth as a Magnet. Because the lodestone compass tends to orient itself in a north and south direction it follows that the earth is a huge magnet having poles, one in each geographical hemisphere. Since the north pole of the compass points north, the earth's pole in the *northern hemisphere* is a *south pole,* and the earth's pole in the *southern hemisphere* is a *north pole.* The former is sometimes referred to as a *north-seeking* pole, and the latter, a *south-seeking* pole.

Due to the fact that the earth's magnetic poles, and consequently the earth's magnetic axis, do not coincide with the geographical poles and axis, in addition to other local magnetic factors, the magnetic meridian makes an angle, called the *angle of declination,* with the geographical meridian at most places on the earth's surface.

A compass needle pivoted at its center of gravity in such a manner as to allow vertical as well as horizontal motion does not assume a horizontal position in the magnetic meridian except at the magnetic equator. The angle made with the horizontal is called the *angle of dip* and in New England amounts to some 70° or so, the north end of the compass pointing downward.

Magnetic Lines of Force. If the region around a bar magnet is explored with a small compass it is found that the north end of the compass always points away from the north pole and towards the south pole of the magnet at every point. Imaginary lines are suggested that indicate the direction that a supposititious north magnetic pole would follow if free to move in the region. These are called *lines of force.* (Fig. 74.) They emanate from the north

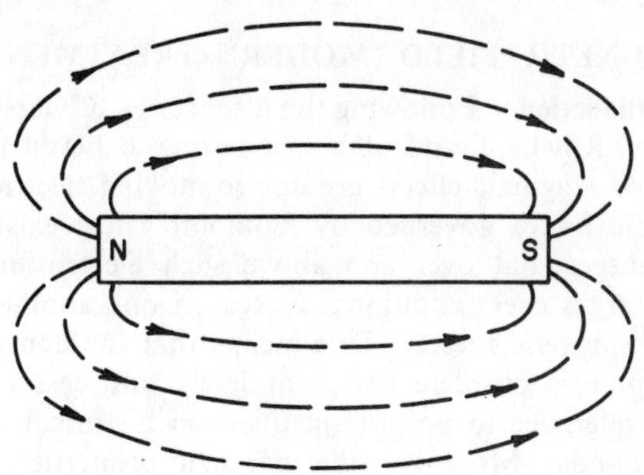

Fig. 74—Magnetic lines of force

end and enter the south end of the bar magnet, and provide a way of visualizing the direction of magnetic forces where such forces exist.

Oersted's Observation. About 1819 Hans Christian Oersted, a Danish scientist, observed that a pivoted compass needle was deflected when it was placed near a current-carrying wire. He thus discovered that *moving* electric charges produce effects which until that time were attributable only to supposititious magnetic poles. This is not to say that the current-carrying wire becomes magnetized and acts like a bar magnet with lines of force emanating from one end, but rather that magnetic effects are produced by the current and actually the lines of force encircle the current-carrying wire. The direction of the lines is given by the right-hand screw rule. If the current (conventional) points in the direction in which a right-hand screw advances, the direction of the lines is the direction of rotation required to produce the advance. It is also the direction that would be indicated by the fingers of the right hand if the right hand were imagined to grasp the conductor with the thumb pointing in the direction of the current. (Fig. 75.)

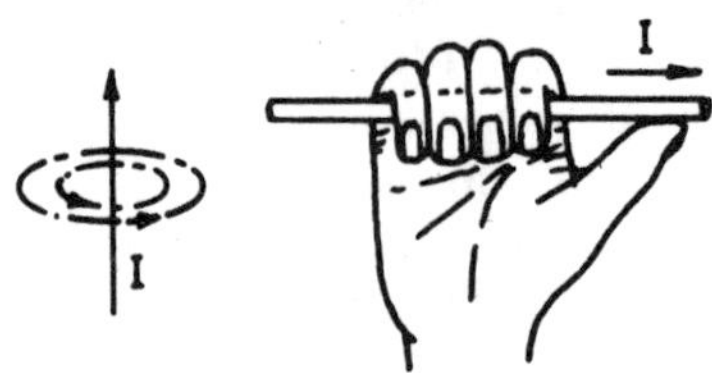

Fig. 75—Lines of magnetic force around a current

THE MAGNETIC FIELD (MODERN TREATMENT)

Magnetic Induction. Following the discoveries of Oersted, Faraday, Henry, Rowland, and others, it is now believed that *all* of the so-called magnetic effects are due to moving electric charges. Electrostatic forces governed by Coulomb's law exist between electric charges, but over and above such electrostatic forces, moving charges exert additional forces on one another. These are called *magnetic* forces. This means that the concept of the magnetic pole is obsolete and completely unnecessary, yet the foregoing reference to poles is justified on historical and pedagogical grounds. Moreover, the magnetic properties of permanent (bar) magnets are explained by the circulation of electrons within the magnets.

Any region where such magnetic forces are experienced is called a *magnetic field*. A magnetic field is characterized by a vector quantity called *magnetic induction,* represented by the symbol **B**. Had not the term "magnetic field intensity" been preempted for another concept involving the earlier pole concept (force per unit pole) it probably would have been used instead of "magnetic induction" to characterize the field.

To specify B quantitatively, one needs to consider the magnetic force acting on some test object such as a moving electron in a small cathode ray tube.

Direction of B. It is found by experience that in a magnetic field a stream of electrons in a cathode ray tube is deflected (i.e., a force acts on the moving charges) by an amount which varies with the direction of the motion of the charges. There is a direction for which it is zero and at right angles to which it is a maximum. The unique direction for which it is zero is defined as the *direction of the magnetic field* responsible for the force acting on the moving charge.

Magnitude of B. It is found, also by experience, that when the direction of the velocity of the moving charge is perpendicular to the direction of the field, the direction of the force is perpendicular to the directions of both the field and the velocity, and is proportional to both the magnitude of the moving charge and the magnitude of the velocity. (Fig. 76.) In general

$$B = \frac{F}{qv \sin \phi} \left(\frac{\text{newton}}{\text{coulomb meter/second}}\right).$$

Lines of Induction. Magnetic Flux. Whereas the concept of *lines of force* followed naturally from the earlier magnetic pole concept to represent the distribution of magnetic effects near magnetic poles, the concept of *lines of induction* is suggested to represent at each point in a magnetic field the direction of the magnetic induction vector. By conventionally numbering these lines per unit area perpendicular to the direction in question so as to be equal to the magnitude of the induction vector, not only the direction but the magnitude of the induction can be represented by lines, called *lines of flux*, such that the induction is the flux density.

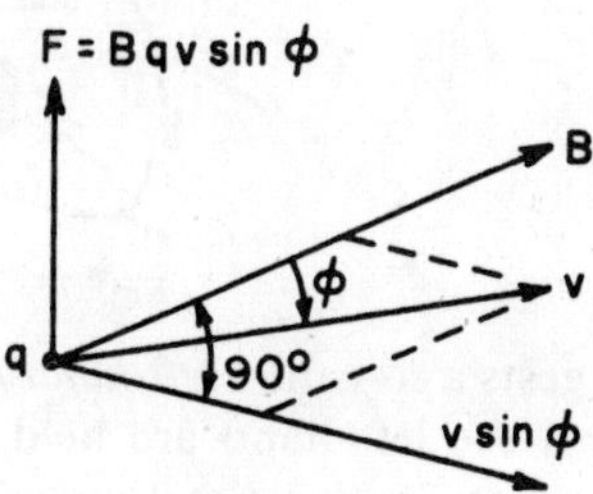

Fig. 76—Magnetic force acting on a moving charge

Denoting magnetic flux by ϕ, $B = \frac{\phi}{A} \frac{\text{weber}}{\text{meter}^2}$ where in M.K.S.

units, $1\ \frac{\text{weber}}{\text{meter}^2} = 1\ \frac{\text{newton}}{\text{coul.m./sec.}} = 1\ \frac{\text{newton}}{\text{amp. meter}}$.

In C.G.S. units, $1\ \text{gauss} = 1\ \frac{\text{maxwell}}{\text{cm.}^2}$,

$$\text{and } 1\ \frac{\text{weber}}{\text{m.}^2} = 10^4\ \text{gauss}.$$

The Sense of the Magnetic Induction Vector. The above reference to the direction of the induction vector does not consider the sense of it. This is a matter of convention. Although the negative electron is the natural unit of charge, the conventional direction of current is taken to be the direction of moving *positive* charge.

Whereas $B = \frac{F}{qv \sin \phi}$ or $F = Bqv \sin \phi$ involves three vector quantities, B, F, $v \sin \phi$, they are all mutually perpendicular. It is found by observation that, referring to moving *positive* charge, the directions of these quantities is given by Fig. 77, which sug-

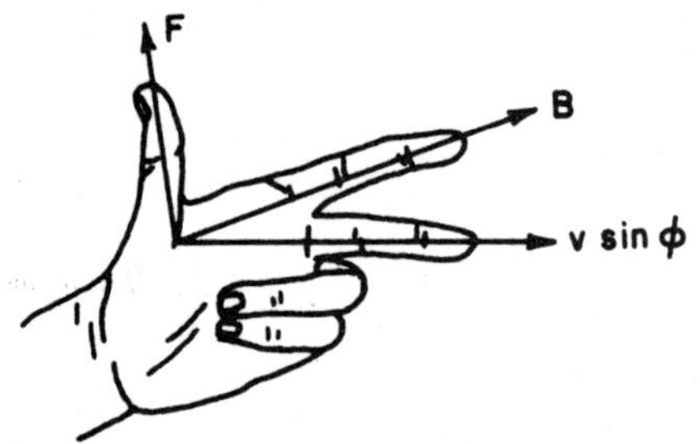

Fig. 77—Left-hand side thrust rule

gests a so-called *left-hand rule*. If the thumb and first two fingers of the left hand are held as indicated in Fig. 77, the forefinger points in the direction of the field (or induction B), the second finger in the direction of the velocity (or motion of the positive charge $v \sin \phi$), the thumb in the direction of the force (or thrust F).

Force on a Conductor Which Carries Current across a Magnetic Field. The side thrust forces on individual electrons in a current-carrying conductor are transmitted to the conductor as a whole. For the case in which B, v, and F are mutually perpendicular ($\phi = 90$ degrees in Fig. 76) and again referring to the direction of moving positive charge (opposite to the direction of electron motion),

$$F = Bqv \text{ per charged particle}$$
$$= BLI \text{ for a conductor of length L}$$
$$\text{carrying current } I = \frac{q}{t}.$$

In M.K.S. units: F in newtons, B in weber/meter^2, L in meters, I in amperes.

In C.G.S. units: F in dynes, B in gauss, L in centimeters, I in ab-amperes, where 1 ab-ampere = 10 amperes.

Directions are given by the *left-hand rule* because the conventional direction of current is the same as the motion of positive charge (forefinger-flux, center finger-current, thumb-thrust).

Torque on a Current Loop. It is obvious that if a wire carrying current across a magnetic field is urged sidewise, another wire of the same length L parallel to it, but carrying current in the opposite direction, will be urged to move in the opposite direction from the first. If these two are connected together at top and bottom so as to form a rectangular loop of length L and width d, then each length L carries the same current, but in opposite directions. Under these conditions, the side thrusts on each will develop a couple, or a torque, whose moment is Fd which will tend to twist the coil into a position across (perpendicular to) the field. (Fig. 78.)

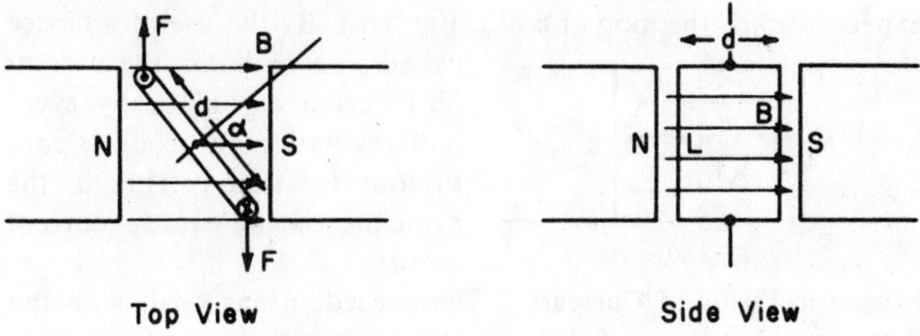

Fig. 78—Torque produced by side thrust

The magnitude of the torque τ is given by $\tau = BLId \sin \alpha$, where α is the angle between the direction of the field and the perpendicular (normal) to the plane of the loop. If instead of a single turn of wire there are N turns and if Ld is recognized as the area of the loop, then $\tau = NIAB \sin \alpha$. For a circular loop of N turns, the same relation holds if A is the area of the loop.

Applications of Side Thrust. The *D'Arsonval galvanometer* consists of a rectangular loop of many turns of wire suspended as an

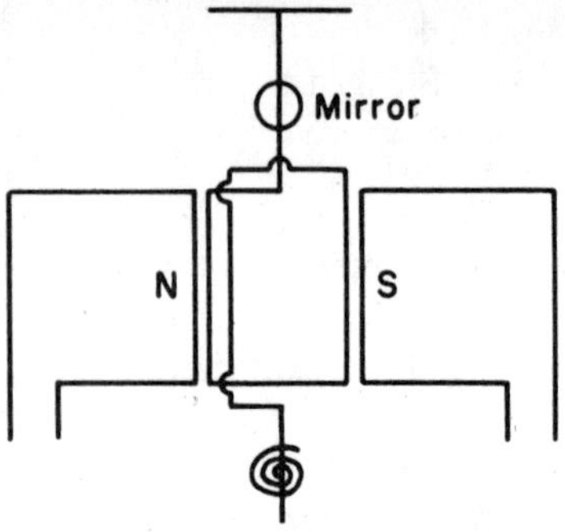

Fig. 79—D'Arsonval galvanometer

armature vertically between the poles of a permanent magnet (Fig. 79). This is essentially the same situation as that described in Fig. 78. When current is established in the coil, a torque is set up which tends to twist the whole suspension against the elastic restoring torque introduced through an external spring. The angle of twist, displayed by a beam of light reflected from a small mirror fastened to the suspension, is proportional to the current in the coil.

Voltmeters and *ammeters* are essentially D'Arsonval galvanometers whose armatures are usually mounted on pivots rather than suspended vertically.

In the *steady current motor,* if, just as the loop in Fig. 78 reaches a position directly across (perpendicular to) the magnetic field, the direction of the current in the loop is reversed, the direction of the side thrusts will be reversed and the loop will rotate a half revolution. If again, just as this half revolution is completed, the current is reversed, another half revolution will be experienced by the loop or coil. (Fig. 80.) By the use of a device called a *commutator,* the current be reversed automatically every half revolution to produce continuous rotation. This is the principle of the steady current motor.

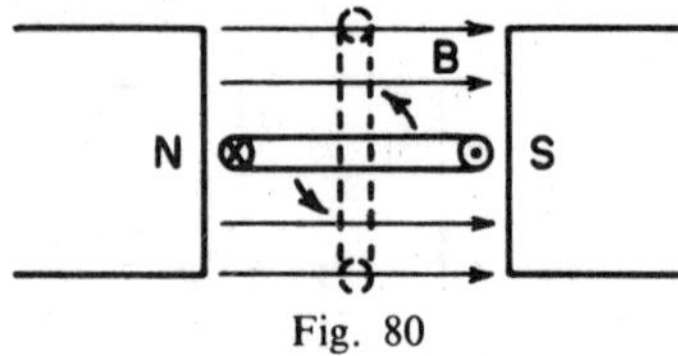

Fig. 80

Magnetic Fields of Currents. The preceding has dealt with the detection of magnetic fields and the quantitative specification of them by the forces which they exert on moving charges. The Oersted experiment indicates that a magnetic field is generated by a current, or a flow of charge, but as yet no mention has been made of any quantitative relationship between the intensity of the current and the magnitude of the induction. The direction of the induction vector **B** is always such as to encircle the conductor.

Ampere-La Place Rule, or the Law of Biot and Savart. The magnitude of the magnetic field at a given point in the vicinity of a current-carrying conductor is to be thought of as made up of contributions produced by every segment of the conductor's length. The increment of induction dB, at a given point P, resulting from a steady current I in a segment ds located at a distance r from the point (Fig. 81) is given by the relation

$$dB = k' \frac{I\,ds}{r^2} \sin\theta$$

where θ is the angle which ds makes with the radius vector from the point P. It is clear that the total amount of induction B

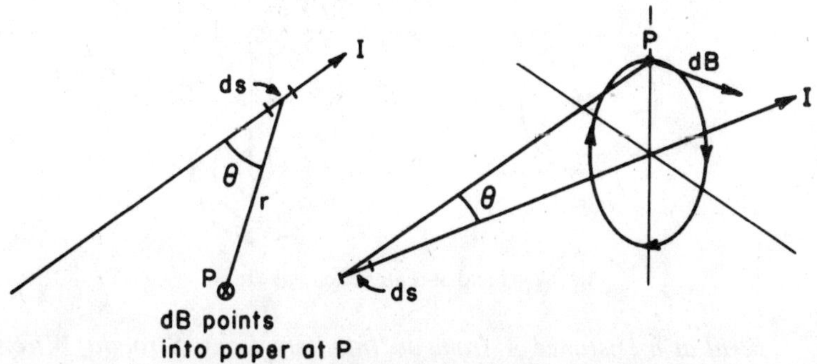

Fig. 81—Two representations of the Ampere-La Place rule

which results from the summation of all the increments dB is the integral of the above expression, the evaluation of which may be exceedingly difficult. Only three special cases are to be considered here.

$$B = k' \int I \frac{ds \sin\theta}{r^2} = \frac{\mu_0}{4\pi} \int \frac{I\,ds \sin\theta}{r^2}.$$

In C.G.S. units k' = unity, but I must be expressed in ab-amperes. In M.K.S. units, however, following the example of electrostatics where

$$k' = 9 \times 10^9 \frac{\text{n.m.}^2}{\text{coul.}^2} \quad \text{and} \quad E_0 = \frac{1}{4\pi k} = 8.85 \times 10^{-12} \frac{\text{coul.}^2}{\text{n.m.}^2},$$

$$k' = 10^{-7}\ \text{weber/ampere meter}$$

and a new quantity μ_0 is defined as $4\pi k' = 12.57 \times 10^{-7}$ weber/ampere m. Therefore $k' = \dfrac{\mu_0}{4\pi}$.

Field at Center of a Circular Turn of Radius R. The above differential equation, when solved for this case, yields

$$B = \frac{\mu_0}{4\pi} \frac{2\pi I}{R}$$

along the axis of the circle. (Fig. 82.) For N turns bunched into a cable $B = \frac{\mu_0}{4\pi} \frac{2\pi NI}{R}$.

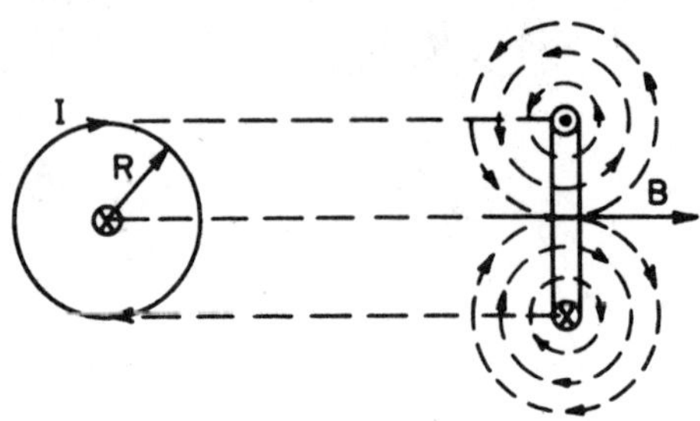

Fig. 82—Field at center of circular turn

Field at a Distance A from an Infinitely Long Straight Wire. (Fig. 83.) In this case the expression yields

$$B = \frac{\mu_0}{4\pi} \frac{2I}{A} \text{ weber/meter}^2$$

In C.G.S. units $B \text{ (gauss)} = \frac{2I}{A} \frac{\text{(ab-amperes)}}{\text{cm.}}$. This is the case which Biot and Savart discovered experimentally.

Field along the Axis of a Very Long Solenoid. It can be shown that in this case

$$B = \frac{\mu_0}{4\pi} \frac{4\pi NI}{L}$$

where N is the number of turns and L is the length of the solenoid. (Fig. 84.)

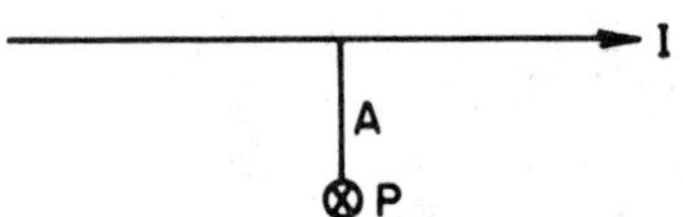

Fig. 83—Field near a long straight wire

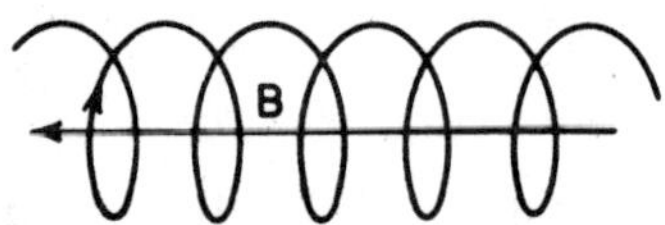

Fig. 84—Field along axis of a long solenoid

Force between Parallel Conductors. A long current-carrying conductor produces a certain magnetic field at a distance a from it. If a second current-carrying conductor is parallel to the first one and is separated from it by a distance a, it produces a magnetic field where the first one lies. Thus each wire will experience a thrust due to the current in the other one. If the two currents are in the *same* direction the mutual force is one of *attraction* and, vice versa, it is one of repulsion if the currents are in opposite directions. This force, per unit length of wire, turns out to be

$$\boxed{\frac{F}{L} = \frac{\mu_0}{4\pi}\frac{2II'}{a}}$$

where I is the current in one wire and I′ is the current in the other one.

Definition of the Ampere. The *ampere* is defined as that unvarying current which, if present in each of two parallel wires of infinite length and one meter apart in empty space, causes each conductor to experience a force of exactly 2×10^{-7} newtons per meter of length. Therefore 1 coulomb = 1 ampere second.

This means that the unit of charge in the M.K.S. system of units is defined in terms of force between *moving* charges rather than the electrostatic force between charges as in the C.G.S. system of units.

MAGNETIC PROPERTIES OF MATTER

Magnetic fields are set up by moving electric charges not only in air (or vacuum) but also in matter. In iron and certain other substances a magnetic field can be set up without any apparent motion of charge, but here it is assumed that electrons circulating within the substance are responsible for the magnetic field. Iron, cobalt, and nickel are the most conspicuously magnetic of the naturally occurring substances, with iron being by far the most magnetic. Alloys have been made, however, which are more magnetic than iron.

Magnetic Permeability. All substances can be classified as to their ability to become magnetized when brought into contact with a magnet, or when placed in a magnetic field. The situation is best described in terms of flux lines. Substances are called *paramagnetic* if they have the property of concentrating flux lines under these circumstances, and *diamagnetic* if they tend to disperse flux lines (Fig. 85, p. 122.)

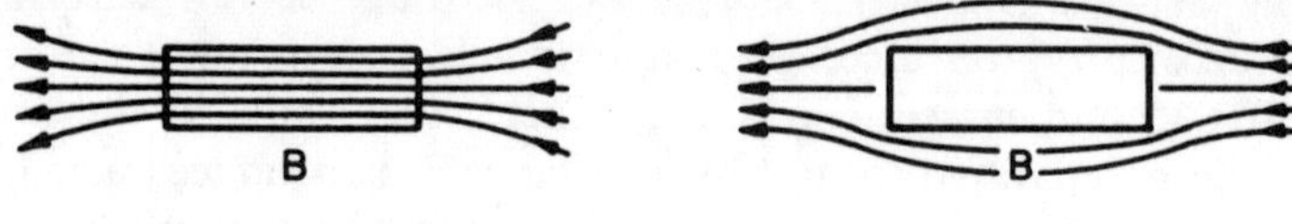

Fig. 85

It was shown on p. 120 that the field along the axis of a long solenoid coil is given by

$$B = \frac{\mu_0}{4\pi}\frac{4\pi NI}{L} = \mu_0 \frac{NI}{L}.$$

If such a solenoid is bent into a circular path (Rowland ring) it is found experimentally that such a ring with an iron core exhibits a different magnetic induction than does one with an air (or a vacuum) core. Denoting the former by B and the latter by B_0, the ratio

$$\frac{B}{B_0} = K_m \text{ (Relative permittivity).}$$

K_m = unity for vacuum.
$K_m >$ unity for a *paramagnetic* substance.
$K_m <$ unity for a *diamagnetic* substance.
If $K_m \gg$ unity, the material is said to be *ferromagnetic.*

Therefore
$$B = \frac{K_m \mu_0 NI}{L}$$

and
$$K_m \mu_0 = \mu \text{ (permeability)} \left(\frac{\text{weber}}{\text{ampere meter}}\right).$$

This may be compared to the electrical equation

$$K\epsilon_0 = \epsilon \text{ (permittivity)} \quad \text{where } K = \frac{C}{C_0}.$$

Magnetic Poles and Magnetic Intensity H. The flux lines in a Rowland ring are continuous, and the iron core of such a device, being a solid doughnutlike object, has a wholly contained magnetic field when it is magnetized by a current in the winding. If, however, a slit is cut in this ring to form a C-shaped object, lines of induction cross the surfaces of the object at places called poles (see earlier discussion of magnetic poles). So-called bar magnets

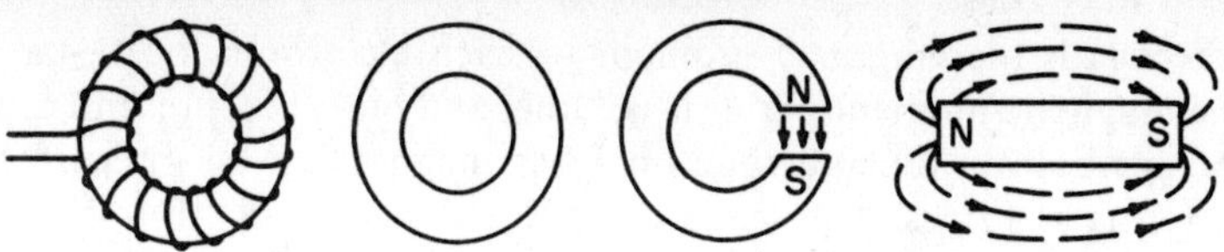

Fig. 86—Permanent magnets exhibit poles if they have free ends.

can be thought of as slotted rings which have been straightened out into bars. (Fig. 86.)

Moving electric charges are acted upon by a force when near *poles* as well as when near other *moving charges*. A vector quantity called *magnetic intensity* H is defined to account for both magnetic effects (see page 114); i.e., it has two aspects, the one to express the effects of current and the other to express the effects of the so-called poles. In the absence of pole effects (as in a Rowland ring) the effect of currents is independent of the material and is expressed by the Ampere-La Place-Biot law without the factor μ_0.

$$dH = \frac{1}{4\pi} \frac{I\,dl \sin\theta}{r^2}.$$

Along the Rowland ring (for example)

$$H = \frac{1}{4\pi} \frac{4\pi NI}{L} = \frac{NI}{L} \frac{(\text{amperes})}{\text{meter}}$$

whereas $\quad B = \mu \dfrac{NI}{L}.$

The ratio $\quad \dfrac{B}{H} = \mu\,(\text{permeability}) = K_m \mu_0.$

$$\left(\frac{\text{weber meter}}{\text{meter}^2\ \text{ampere}} = \frac{\text{weber}}{\text{ampere meter}}\right)$$

In empty space μ becomes μ_0, and $K_m = \mu/\mu_0$.

Note: μ is definable in terms of H as well as in terms of the permittivity K_m.

Torque in a Bar Magnet, and Pole Strength m. Treating a bar magnet as if it were made up of a series of n electronic loops per unit volume, all aligned the same way with each experiencing a torque τ = Bia, it follows that a bar magnet of length L and cross section A experiences a torque

$$\tau = B\,(\text{niaA})\,L = \text{Bm}\,L = FL,$$

where ia is the magnetic moment of each electronic loop, nia is the magnetic moment per unit volume, and niaA is represented by the symbol m. Since torque on a bar magnet can be interpreted in terms of forces at its ends (or poles) the quantity Bm can be considered a force, and m is referred to as the pole strength.

$$m = \text{niaA (ampere-meter)} = \frac{F}{B}.$$

It can also be shown that between two point "poles" of strengths m and m′ there is a force given by

$$\boxed{F = \frac{\mu_0}{4\pi}\frac{mm'}{r^2}}$$

This is one and the same as the experimentally discovered law of Coulomb referred to earlier expressed in terms of supposititious poles, suggesting that although the concept of the pole is physically obsolete and unnecessary, it is one which the student will do well to recognize if he is to read the physics literature.

Intensity of Magnetization. The ratio of the induced pole strength to the area of cross section of a magnet (this being the same as the magnetic moment per unit volume) is called the *intensity of magnetization* and is usually denoted by $I = \frac{m}{s}$ (s is cross-sectional area).

Magnetic Susceptibility. Whereas the ratio of B to H is permeability (μ), the ratio of I to H is called *susceptibility* (k) and obviously is a measure of the ease with which a substance is magnetized. The following relations hold: $B = H + 4\pi I$; $\mu = 1 + 4\pi k$. It will be noted that negative susceptibilities correspond to fractional permeabilities, and, therefore, to diamagnetic substances.

B-H Diagrams and Magnetic Hysteresis. Curves of B plotted against H display considerable information about magnetic substances. They show that μ is far from constant in general, usually diminishing with increasing H until a state of magnetic saturation is reached. A complete B-H curve including negative values of both quantities is in general a closed loop referred to as a *hysteresis loop,* which is characteristic of a given substance. Magnetic hysteresis is then a lagging of the magnetization behind the magnetizing influence. The B-intercepts on such a loop indicate the *residual magnetism* or *remanence,* and the H-intercepts indicate what is called the *coercive force* of the substance. (Fig. 87.) Although iron is in a class by itself among the magnetic elements, magnetic alloys of enormously high permeability have been made. These include "permalloy" and the *Heusler alloys,* the latter of which is interesting in that, of the three substances of which it is made, namely, copper, manganese, and aluminum, none are themselves magnetic to any appreciable extent.

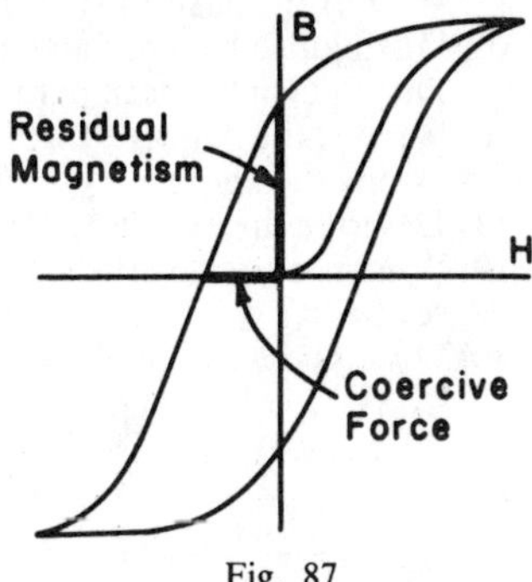

Fig. 87

The Magnetic Circuit. It is frequently desirable to know the total amount of magnetic flux associated with a given electric current I in a given winding of an electromagnet.

In the case of an endless solenoid (Rowland ring) with no air gap, $B = \mu \frac{NI}{L}$ where L is the length of the magnetic path (the mean circumference of the Rowland ring), whereupon

$$\phi = BA = \frac{\mu NIA}{L} = \frac{NI}{L/\mu A}.$$

Referring to the ring as a magnetic circuit, and recalling that for an electric circuit $\frac{L}{\rho A}$ is the resistance, and that the current is given by the ratio $\frac{\text{electromotive force}}{\text{resistance}}$, by analogy it is suggested that magnetic flux is the ratio $\frac{\text{magnetomotive force}}{\text{reluctance}}$. Thus M.M.F. = NI (ampere turns), and reluctance $= \frac{NI}{\phi}$ (the required number of ampere turns per weber flux produced).

Magnetic Proof that Current Is a Flow of Electric Charges. Rowland proved conclusively that electric charges in motion constitute an electric current. He did this by rotating a charged insulated disk at a very high speed about its axis and observing that a magnetic field was established.

Review Questions

(1) How is magnetic induction defined?
(2) What is meant by magnetic-field intensity? Magnetic moment? Line of force?
(3) What is the basis for the claim that the earth is a magnet?
(4) Distinguish between angle of dip and angle of declination.
(5) Distinguish between para- and dia-magnetic substances.
(6) What is the Ampere-La Place rule?
(7) Define the ampere.
(8) Describe the action of the D'Arsonval galvanometer.
(9) What is meant by the side thrust phenomenon? What hand rule describes it?
(10) Discuss the action of a steady current motor.

15: Electromagnetic Induction, Oscillations, and Waves

INDUCED ELECTROMOTIVE FORCE

Induction Viewed as the Inverse of Side Thrust. In view of the side thrust associated with a conductor carrying current across a magnetic field, the question naturally arises as to the possibility of inducing a current in a conductor by merely moving it across a magnetic field, i.e., the inverse of the former effect. This should be a reasonable expectation because the motion of a conductor means motion of the electric charges out of which it is made, and according to Rowland's experiment, charges in motion constitute an electric current, which in turn experiences a side thrust if it occurs in a magnetic field. Further analysis shows that this side thrust on the electric charges should be in such a direction as to urge the charges along the length of the conductor, thus establishing a difference of potential between the ends of the wire so that if these ends should be connected by a conductor, current would be observed to flow. Also, the direction of the current is predicted (for a given direction of motion) to be opposite to the direction of current which, by the side thrust, would produce motion in the same direction. Thus the *right-hand* rule is quite naturally suggested instead of the left-hand rule, which applied to the opposite effect. The magnitude of this predicted electromotive force is suggested since the force f on each individual electronic charge q is f = Bqv (due to side thrust), and if q is moved a distance L (the length of the conductor in the field), then

$$\frac{W}{q} = f\frac{L}{q} = E = BvL.$$

Experimentally, these predictions are found to be true. When a conductor of length L is moved perpendicularly across a magnetic field of flux density B with a velocity v, it is found upon closing the circuit of which this conductor is a part that current flows (Fig. 88, p. 128), and in a direction given by the right-hand rule.

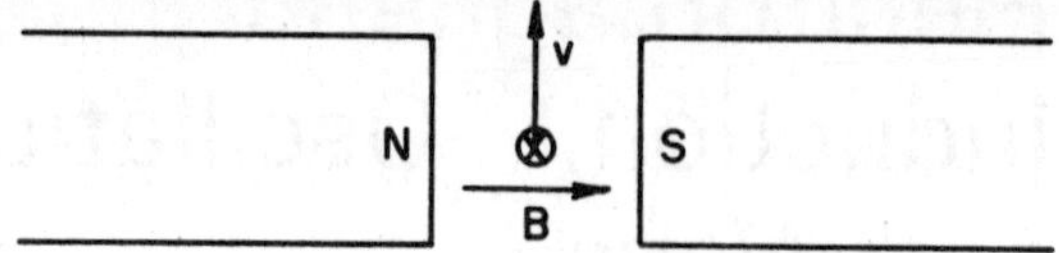

Fig. 88—Induced current

(Fig. 89.) The forefinger points in the direction of the field, the thumb points in the direction of the motion, and the second finger points in the direction of the induced current.

By the law of the conservation of energy, a consideration of power gives the magnitude of the induced electromotive force to be $P = Fv = BLIv = EI$, or $E = BLv$, as predicted.

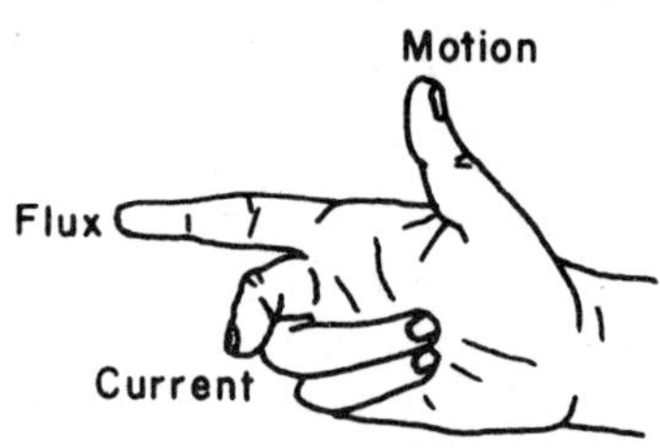

Fig. 89—Right-hand rule (generator)

In M.K.S. units, induced electromotive force is expressed in volts when B is in webers per square meter, length is in meters, and v is in meters per second. In C.G.S. units, the *absolute electromagnetic unit of electromotive force* is defined as that electromotive force induced when a conductor of unit length (1 cm.) is moved perpendicularly across a uniform magnetic field of unit flux density (1 gauss) with unit velocity (1 cm. per sec.). It is called the absolute volt or *ab-volt* (10^8 ab-volts = 1 volt).

Faraday and the Magnetic-Flux Viewpoint. It is often very convenient to picture the preceding discussion of a conductor moving across a magnetic field, as the conductor "cutting the lines of flux" which by convention represent the field. It can be shown that the induced electromotive force is proportional to the time-rate at which the lines are cut, or more specifically that the induced electromotive force depends upon the rate at which the number of flux lines enclosed by the circuit is decreased. See Fig. 90, in which the lines of flux **B** are represented by dots to indicate that they are perpendicular to the plane of the moving conductor.

$$E = -k\,\frac{\phi_2 - \phi_1}{t_2 - t_1} = -k\,\frac{\Delta\phi}{\Delta t}\ (k = \text{proportionality factor}).$$

k is made equal to unity in the C.G.S. system of units by defining a new unit of E (the ab-volt) equal to one line cut per second.

$$\therefore E\ (\text{ab-volts}) = -\frac{\Delta\phi}{\Delta t}\ (\text{lines/sec. or maxwells/sec.}).$$

In M.K.S. units, $E\ (\text{volts}) = -\dfrac{\Delta\phi}{\Delta t}\ (\text{webers/sec.})$.

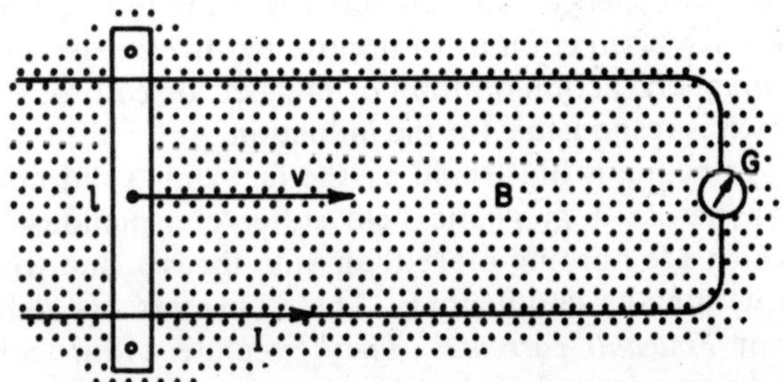

Fig. 90—Cutting lines of flux. $E = Blv = -\dfrac{\Delta\phi}{\Delta t}$

Faraday showed by experiments in 1831 that the idea of cutting lines of flux can be generalized to mean any manner of flux change with respect to time, as follows (Fig. 91):

An iron magnet thrust in or out of a coil connected with a galvanometer induces a current while the magnet is being moved, the direction of the current depending upon the direction of the motion. An electromagnet brought up to the same coil similarly induces a current during the motion of the electromagnet. The insertion of an iron core in the electromagnet does the same thing. Opening and closing the circuit of the electromagnet while

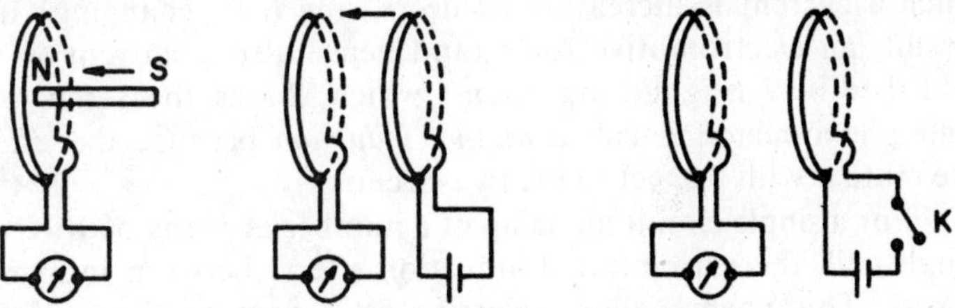

Fig. 91—Examples of electromagnetic induction

it is held steady near the same coil induces currents in the coil due to the changing flux associated with the changing current in the circuit. This latter effect is increased by winding the electromagnet on the same iron core as the coil in which the current is induced, so as to form an iron-core transformer. In all these cases

$$E = -\frac{\Delta\phi}{\Delta t} \text{ and } I = -\frac{1}{R}\frac{\Delta\phi}{\Delta t}.$$

Lenz's Law. All the above facts concerning induced electromotive forces resulting from changing magnetic fields is summarized in *Lenz's law,* which results from considerations of the conservation of energy. The law states that the induced current is always in such a direction as to oppose by its electromagnetic action the magnetic action (motion of magnet, or coil, or change of field) which is responsible for the induction.

This principle is illustrated by the fact that solid conductors in motion across a magnetic field suffer conspicuous damping forces which are nothing more than side thrusts due to currents induced within the conductors. These currents are called *eddy currents* or *Foucault currents.* They circulate within conductors and may be very intense if the resistance is very small. Considerable energy may be dissipated in heat by eddy currents, and so it is often desirable to minimize them. This is accomplished by *lamination.* The eddy current pendulum illustrates the damping effect. The effect is frequently utilized to damp the swings of a galvanometer by merely short-circuiting the armature.

When a motor is running, the motion of the armature across the field results in the development of an induced E.M.F. called a *back E.M.F.* Consequently, the potential drop across the armature is less than the potential difference impressed across the brushes by just the amount of this back E.M.F. It is the reaction to this back E.M.F. that accounts for the useful output of the motor.

Mutual Induction and Self-Induction. It has been shown that when a current is increasing or decreasing (i.e., changing) in a circuit, an electromotive force (and hence also a current) is established in a neighboring circuit which shares the same field. This phenomenon is called *mutual induction* because the effects are mutual with respect to the two circuits.

For a single circuit made up of a number of turns of wire in a single coil, there are mutual induction effects between individual turns. This phenomenon, referring as it does to the inductive action of a current upon itself, is called *self-induction.* (Fig. 92.)

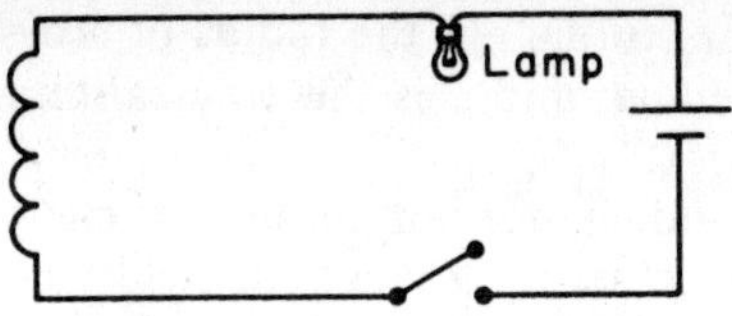

Fig. 92—Illustrating self-induction

The effect of self-induction is to oppose the growth of a current by an oppositely directed induced E.M.F. and to oppose the decay of a current by a forward induced E.M.F., or in a general way to oppose any change in the current. Self-induction is, therefore, commonly referred to as electrical inertia and is analogous to mechanical mass. The coefficient of self-induction (L), more commonly called *self-inductance* or just *inductance*, is the proportionality factor by which the induced E.M.F. is proportional to the time-rate of change of its current.

$$E = -L\frac{I_2 - I_1}{t_2 - t_1} = -L\frac{\Delta I}{\Delta t}\left(\text{as } F = M\frac{\Delta v}{\Delta t} \text{ in mechanics}\right).$$

It is that property of an electrical circuit by virtue of which a counter E.M.F. is induced in itself. It exerts a choking effect upon an increasing current (as when a circuit [Fig. 92] is closed, the lighting of the lamp is delayed) and it exerts a sustaining effect upon a decreasing current (as when a circuit is opened). This latter effect is often made visible by sparking at the switch.

The M.K.S. unit of inductance is the *henry*, defined by the equation $L = -\frac{E}{\Delta I/\Delta t}$, or it is the induced E.M.F. per unit rate of change of current when E is in volts and I is in amperes. In C.G.S. units, the absolute henry (ab-henry) is given in ab-volts per ab-ampere per second. (1 henry $= 10^9$ ab-henries.)

Another expression for self-inductance L is $L = \frac{N\phi}{I}$, where it is treated as flux linkage per unit current. Therefore $N\phi = LI$.

The direction of the induced E.M.F. in a circuit having self-inductance is opposite to that of the current if current is increasing, but is in the same direction as the current if current is decreasing. In other words, the change in current is opposed by the induced E.M.F. (Lenz's law).

The inductance of a long solenoid can also be calculated in ab-henries from the following formula $L = \frac{4\pi^2 N^2 r^2 \mu}{l}$ where N is the total number of turns, r is the radius of cross section, l is the length of the solenoid, and μ is the permeability, all expressed in C.G.S. units.

By virtue of inductance, an amount of energy equal to $W = \frac{1}{2} L I^2$ is required to set up a magnetic field when a current is established in a circuit. This energy is liberated, when the circuit is broken, in the form of heat, light, and radiation.

Applications of Induced Electromotive Forces. These effects are applied practically in the use of choke coils for theater light-dimmers, lightning arresters, induction coils, transformers, telephones, etc.

In the case of the transformer (Fig. 93) used to step up or step

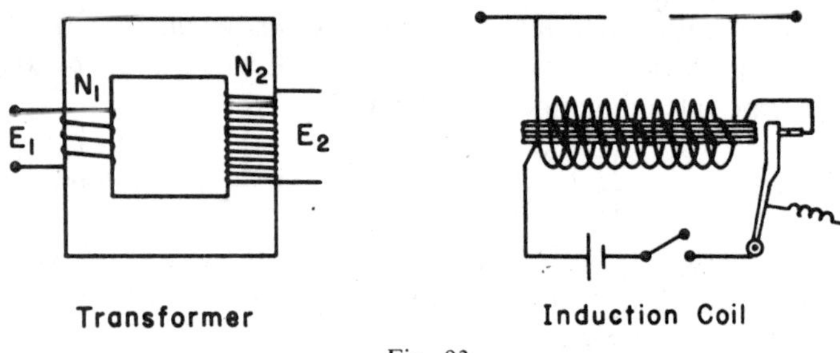

Fig. 93

down a fluctuating electromotive force, the following is approximately true: $E = -N_1 \dfrac{\Delta \phi}{\Delta t}$, whence

$$\frac{\Delta \phi}{\Delta t} = -\frac{E_1}{N_1} = -\frac{E_2}{N_2}. \quad \therefore \frac{E_1}{E_2} = \frac{N_1}{N_2} = \frac{I_2}{I_1}.$$

The induction coil (Fig. 93) is a modified transformer.

Alternating Electromotive Force. When a coil, consisting of a number of circular turns in a uniform magnetic field, is set into rotation with constant angular velocity about an axis through its diameter and perpendicular to the field, the induced electromotive force varies sinusoidally with time as follows: $e = E_{max} \sin \omega t$ where ω is the angular velocity (radians per sec.) and t is the time. (Fig. 94.) The small (e) is used to indicate instantaneous value. Such an E.M.F. is very important because of the prac-

Fig. 94—Graph of "alternating" E.M.F.

tical importance of rotating machinery, and it is always referred to by the technical name, "*alternating electromotive force.*"

For such an alternating E.M.F. and the alternating current which it produces in a simple resistance circuit, it becomes necessary to define a quantity called the *effective value.* Obviously the average value of a sinusoidally varying current is zero, but yet it is known that an alternating current will produce steady effects such as heating and lighting. It is found that such effects depend upon the second power of the current ($JH = I^2Rt$) whence the *effective current* is defined as the square root of the average value of the second power of the current, and is called *root-mean-square value* (R.M.S.). For sinusoidal variations, the R.M.S. value is .707 times the maximum value of the quantity considered. A.C. voltmeters and ammeters indicate R.M.S. values, which are usually designated as E_v and I_a respectively.

ALTERNATING CURRENTS

When an alternating E.M.F. is impressed across a circuit containing resistance alone, the current which flows is also alternating, and the alternations of the current faithfully correspond to the alternations of the E.M.F. (Fig. 95.)

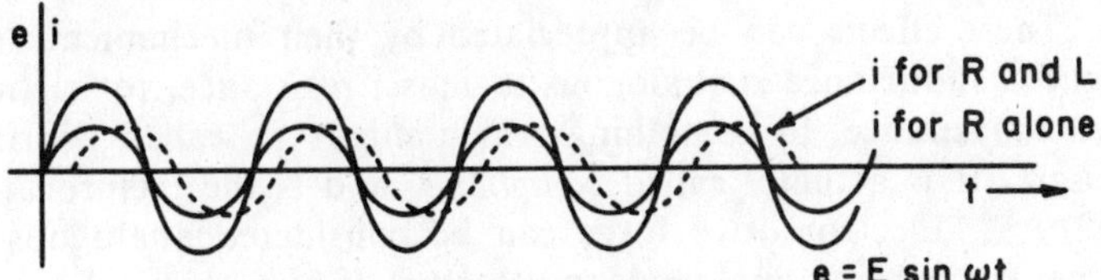

Fig. 95—Example of lagging current due to inductance

A circuit containing resistance alone is very rare. Almost every circuit has some inductance and some capacitance associated with it, so that all three factors must be considered for the general case. If an alternating E.M.F. $e = E \sin \omega t$ is impressed across a series circuit containing resistance R, inductance L, and capacitance C, a consideration of Ohm's law leads to an expression for the instantaneous value of the current in the circuit as follows: $i = \dfrac{E_M \sin(\omega t - \phi)}{\sqrt{R^2 + (\omega L - 1/\omega c)^2}} + Ae^{-R/Lt}$ where ϕ is an angle whose tangent is $\dfrac{\omega L - 1/\omega c}{R}$ and where the exponential term vanishes in a very short interval of time after the circuit is closed. In the steady state (after the exponential term has vanished) $i = I_M \sin(\omega t - \phi)$, where $I_M = \frac{E_M}{Z}$, and Z is called *impedance.* The impedance is a sort of generalized resistance, in that for A.C. considerations it plays the same role as resistance alone does for D.C. Also $Z = \sqrt{R^2 + X^2}$ where X (called *reactance*) is given by the following: $X = \omega L - \frac{1}{\omega C}$. ωL is called *inductive* reactance and $\frac{1}{\omega C}$ is called *capacitive* reactance. The current is thus seen to be also sinusoidal, having the same frequency $\omega = 2\pi n$ as the E.M.F., but differing in phase from the E.M.F. by the factor ϕ, called the phase lag, expressed as a fractional part of a complete oscillation which is designated by a 360° angle.

A preponderance of inductive reactance in the circuit makes the quantity $(\omega t - \phi)$ less than $\omega t \left(\phi = \tan^{-1} \frac{X}{R}\right)$, whence the current follows, or "lags" behind, the electromotive force. (Fig. 95.)

A preponderance of capacitive reactance in the circuit makes the quantity $(\omega t - \phi)$ greater than ωt, whence the current leads the electromotive force.

These effects can be appreciated by their mechanical analogues. Inductance is analogous to mass; resistance, to friction; and capacitance, to something which might be called "springiness." It is actually called *compliance* and is the reciprocal of stiffness. Electromotive force can be considered analogous to force; and current, analogous to velocity. If a mechanical system containing these factors were set into mechanical vibration by a sinusoidally varying force (the graph of which with respect to time would be a sine wave), then a graph of velocity plotted on the same diagram would display the same frequency of oscillation, but it would either lag behind or lead the force graph, depending upon the preponderance of the mass or the spring factor. If these two factors were to completely offset one another a condition referred to as *resonance* would be encountered, in which the oscillations might become very violent, and yet not require the expenditure of more energy than just enough to overcome friction. This is the familiar situation involved in "pumping" a swing, previously referred to in the discussions of vibratory motion. A particular frequency called the *resonant frequency* is involved. $\left(2\pi n L = \frac{1}{2\pi n C}. \therefore n = \frac{1}{2\pi} \sqrt{\frac{1}{LC}}\right)$.

The *power* or rate of dissipation of energy at any instant in an alternating current circuit is given by the product of the instantaneous value of the electromotive force multiplied by the instantaneous value of the current. When these quantities are sinusoidally varying quantities it is worth considering the average value of this product, which is *not* zero. Nor is it the product of an A.C. voltmeter reading multiplied by an A.C. ammeter reading, as might be suspected since these readings are R.M.S. values. Average power is actually given by the relation $\bar{p} = E_v I_a \cos\phi$, where E_v is voltmeter value E, I_a is ammeter value I, ϕ is the phase lag previously discussed, and $\bar{p}$ is the power expressed in watts. Cos ϕ is referred to as the *power factor.*

ELECTROMAGNETIC OSCILLATIONS

When a condenser (or capacitor) is discharged, it is found that under certain conditions of the circuit the discharge is oscillatory. If the circuit contains only a condenser and an inductance, the resistance being negligible, it is found that the frequency n of the oscillations is given by $n = \frac{1}{2\pi}\sqrt{\frac{1}{LC}}$, which happens to be the same frequency as the resonant frequency just discussed. A mechanically analogous situation is shown in Fig. 96.

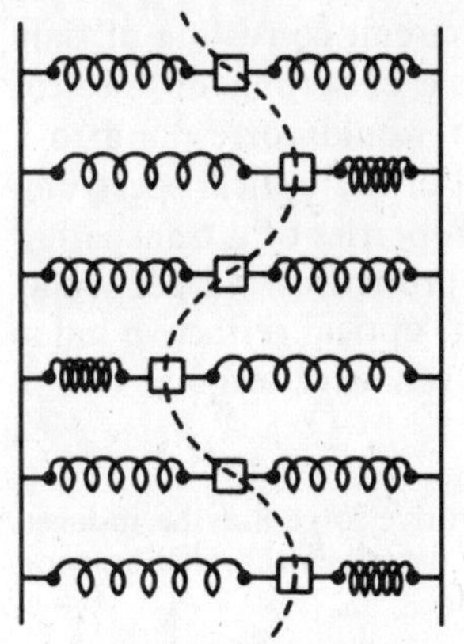

Fig. 96—Mechanical model of an oscillating circuit

If, however, the considerations are extended to include the case of resistance, it is found that the frequency is

$$n' = \frac{1}{2\pi}\sqrt{\frac{1}{LC} - \frac{R^2}{4L^2}}$$

such that if the factor $\frac{R^2}{4L^2}$ for the circuit should exceed the factor $\frac{1}{LC}$, there would be no oscillations.

When electromagnetic oscillations are thus established in a circuit, it is observed that in a similar circuit placed nearby, similar oscillations are produced, and these latter oscillations become particularly strong if the second circuit is "tuned" to resonance with the first, i.e., if the inductance and the capacitance of the second circuit are so adjusted as to give this circuit the same natural frequency as the first one. This means that energy must have been transferred from the first to the second circuit by radiation of some sort.

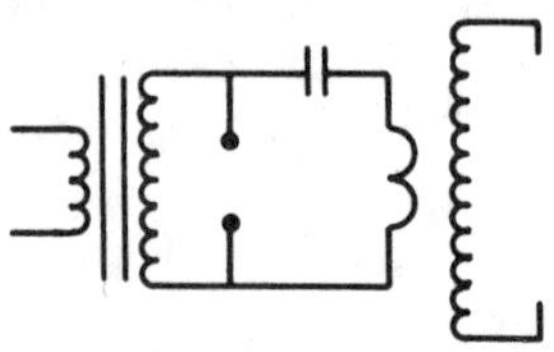

Fig. 97—Tesla coil circuit for producing high frequency and high potential oscillations

The Tesla coil (Fig. 97) is a high frequency transformer capable of radiating electromagnetic radiation at very high potential. Analysis shows that the electromagnetic radiation thus produced is essentially a transverse wave phenomenon consisting of electric and magnetic intensity being propagated through a hypothetical medium, called the ether, with a velocity of 3×10^{10} cm. per second. These waves are commonly known as *radio waves.*

Maxwell predicted, from purely mathematical considerations, the existence of such waves. He also set forth the view that light is a phenomenon of this sort, i.e., an electromagnetic disturbance propagated through the ether at a rate of 3×10^{10} cm./sec., which is the known velocity of light. In view of the more recent discovery of the electronic structure of matter this view has gained considerable ground, since an electrical circuit consisting of only two vibrating electrons would be capable of setting up electromagnetic oscillations of a frequency that would correspond to a wave length in the near ultraviolet region of the optical spectrum. It is also well known that the electrical properties of a transparent medium are closely related to its optical properties. In particular the dielectric constant (K) is related to the optical refractive index (n) by the simple relation $K = n^2$ for a given wave length.

Review Questions

(1) Describe methods by which an electromotive force may be induced in an electrical circuit. What hand rule describes the phenomenon of induction by the motion of a conductor?
(2) State Lenz's law.
(3) What are eddy currents?
(4) Define inductance, and suggest some of its consequences in a circuit.
(5) Diagram and discuss the action of the transformer; the induction coil.
(6) Describe the general result of impressing an "alternating" E.M.F. across a circuit containing inductance, capacitance, and resistance.

(7) What is meant by root-mean-square values of E.M.F. and current?
(8) What is impedance? How is it measured?
(9) Describe a mechanical situation that will present analogies to an electrical circuit containing inductance and capacity.
(10) What is the power factor?
(11) What factors determine the natural frequency of electromagnetic oscillations?
(12) Diagram and describe the action of the Tesla coil.
(13) What is the nature of a radio wave?

16: Gaseous Conduction, the Electron, and the Nuclear Atom

CONDUCTION OF ELECTRICITY THROUGH GASES

Atmospheric Ionization. Dry air under normal conditions, like most gases, is an insulator, but under a sufficiently intense electrical field (30,000 volts/cm.) it breaks down and becomes a conductor, due to the formation of positive and negative ions. A small number of residual ions are always present under normal conditions, but the effect of an intense field is to accelerate these ions to such a degree that collisions taking place liberate sufficient energy to knock electrons completely out of atoms and form other ions. The process is cumulative like an avalanche, and in a very short interval of time a disruptive discharge, called a spark, has taken place.

The average length of path between collisions of a given ion with neighbors is referred to as its *mean free path.* It is of the order of magnitude of 10^{-8} cm. at atmospheric pressure.

The velocity acquired by an ion between collisions depends upon its mean free path thus: $v = \sqrt{\frac{2Ee}{m}}\,\lambda$ in cm. per sec., where E is the field intensity, e is the charge on the ion, m is the mass of the ion, and λ is its mean free path. It will be noted that as the pressure of a gas is decreased, the mean free path is increased (there being fewer particles with which to collide) and, consequently, the field intensity necessary to produce a discharge is decreased.

Nature of a Gaseous Discharge under Decreasing Pressures. The behavior of the discharge between electrodes in the ends of a long glass tube slowly undergoing evacuation is worthy of consideration.

At a pressure of 30–40 mm. Hg, the discharge takes the form of an irregular, violet-colored, streaked spark. The potential difference necessary to produce the discharge decreases markedly as the pressure is decreased, down to something less than a millimeter of mercury, beyond which the necessary potential difference increases rapidly.

As the exhaustion proceeds, these streaks give way to a pink glow throughout the whole tube. Corresponding to a pressure of a few millimeters of mercury, the pink glow appears to become separated by a dark space from the cathode (negative electrode) which itself becomes surrounded by a violet glow. The pink glow which seems to be definitely associated with the anode (positive electrode) is called the *positive column.* The violet glow around the cathode is called the *negative glow,* and the dark space is known as the *Faraday dark space.*

Further exhaustion (approx. one mm. Hg or less) produces a second dark space called the *Crookes' dark space* between the cathode and the cathode glow, while at the same time the pink positive column, which still occupies most of the tube, breaks up into a transverse striated pattern. (Fig. 98.)

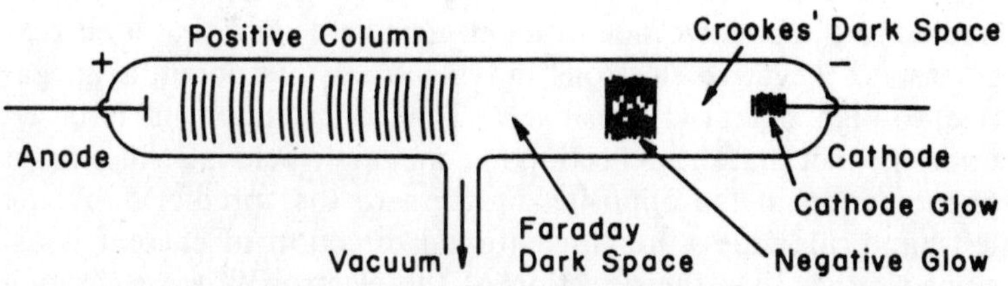

Fig. 98—Phenomenon of electrical discharge through a gas at reduced pressure

As the pressure is still further reduced, the pink positive column turns white, the striations get coarser, the Faraday dark space travels toward the anode (shortening the length of the positive column), and the Crookes' dark space increases in size, until at a pressure of about .001 mm. Hg it completely fills the entire tube. By this time the positive column, the Faraday dark space, and the cathode glow have completely disappeared at the positive end of the tube.

Coincident with the Crookes' dark space filling the entire tube, a greenish fluorescence appears upon the glass walls of the tube. It is now noticed that any object inside the tube casts a sharp shadow upon the positive end of the tube, indicating the emanation in straight lines of some kind of radiation from the cathode. These rays are known as *cathode rays,* and have been found to be streams of electrons. The greenish fluorescence of the glass walls of the tube is due to the bombardment of these walls by the cathode rays, which are found to cause many substances to fluoresce with a wide range of colors. Tubes made to fluoresce in this manner with different kinds of substances, liquid and solid, are called *Geissler tubes*.

When cathode rays impinge upon metallic substances within the exhausted tube, *X rays* are produced, which constitute a very penetrating radiation. They are sometimes called *Roentgen rays* after their discoverer. The degree of vacuum necessary for this is frequently referred to as an X-ray vacuum.

Nature of Cathode Rays. Cathode rays travel in straight lines. They leave surfaces normally (whence they can be focussed by a concave cathode). They can produce fluorescence and heating effects. They can pass through very thin metal foils and produce ionization.

Cathode rays are deflected by magnetic and electric fields. This proves that they consist of electrons in motion (an electric current) and that the electron carries a negative charge (being attracted to the positive side of an electric field) and that a current consists of negative electrons moving from low potential (negative) to high potential (positive). This latter statement is based upon the fact that the deflection in a magnetic field is a side thrust phenomenon in the opposite direction to that predicted by the left-hand rule unless the conventional direction of current is assumed rather than the direction of the electron flow originating in the cathode. According to the side thrust law $F = BIL = B\frac{q}{t}L = Bqv = Bev$, if e is the charge on the electron.

THE ELECTRON AND ITS PROPERTIES (Electronics)

The ratio of the charge to the mass of an electron was determined in a very ingenious manner by J. J. Thomson. A stream of electrons was first subjected to an electric field of measured intensity, which produced a certain deflection of the stream toward the positive side of the field. Then a magnetic field was applied perpendicularly to the electric field, of sufficient intensity to nullify the deflection. In terms of measurable quantities the ratio e/m was thus obtained. Its value is 1.77×10^7 ab-coulombs per gram or 1.77×10^{11} coulombs per kilogram.

The value of the charge (e) on the electron was measured very ingeniously by Millikan. The experiment is referred to as the *Millikan oil-drop experiment*. Fine droplets of oil are sprayed into a region between two metal plates which can be maintained at a controlled difference of potential. A particular droplet is watched through a microscope and its rate of fall under the influence of gravity alone is first determined. Then the electric field is established between the plates and it is observed that electric charges are picked up by individual droplets, making themselves evident by abrupt changes in the droplet's motion. In terms of measurable quantities such as the density of the oil, the velocity of the droplet, etc., it becomes possible to determine, in a relative manner, the amount of charge acquired by a given droplet. The interesting fact is that every charge observed is a multiple of a certain fundamental charge; and assuming that a droplet of oil cannot acquire less than a single electronic charge, it is concluded that this observed fundamental charge is the charge on an electron. It amounts to 4.80×10^{-10} E.S.U. (stat-coulombs) or 1.6×10^{-19} coulombs.

Using this value for e and J. J. Thomson's value for e/m (1.77×10^7 ab-coulombs per gram), it follows that m (the mass of an electron) is 9×10^{-28} grams.

ELECTRONIC PHENOMENA

Thermionic Emission. It is a fact that hot bodies, particularly metals, in a vacuum emit electrons. This effect was observed by Edison (1883) but was not understood by him. He observed that current flowed through a vacuum tube in which a heated filament and a metal plate were mounted, when the plate was connected to the positive side of a battery, but not when it was connected to the negative side. The effect is known as the *Edison effect* and is the basic principle upon which the modern vacuum (radio) tube functions. (Fig. 99.) Tubes having two, three, four, five and even more electrodes, utilizing all known variations of this principle, have been successfully employed as rectifiers, amplifiers, and modulators, etc., of electric currents to such an extent that the modern vacuum tube is one of the most important of all electrical devices. (See Fig. 100, p. 142.)

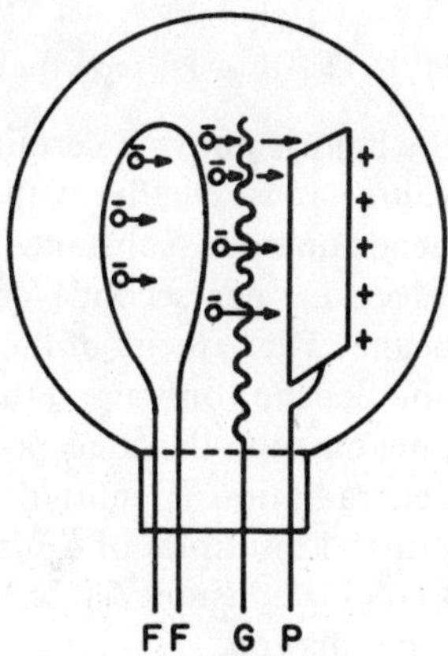

Fig. 99—Three-electrode vacuum tube

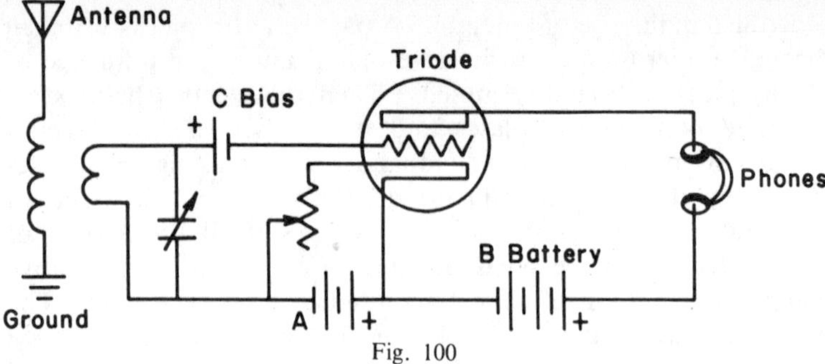

Fig. 100

Photoelectric Effect. It is observed that an electroscope charged negatively is readily discharged by ultraviolet light, but when positively charged is unaffected by such light. It appears that electrons are virtually drawn out of the surface of a body by the action of light. The effect is known as the *photoelectric effect.* (Fig. 101.) Under certain circumstances the action can be so intense as to produce an electric current which, although feeble in itself, is capable of enormous amplification with unlimited consequences. The phenomenon is subject to the following laws.

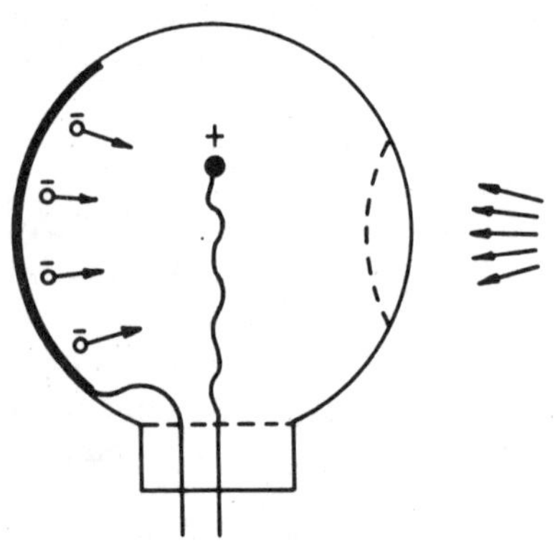

Fig. 101—Photoelectric cell

The emission takes place only when the frequency of the light is above a certain critical value known as the threshold value. It is usually in the ultraviolet, but its exact location depends upon the substance concerned. The amount of the emission (electrons per second) depends upon the intensity of the light beam. The velocity of the emission is independent of the intensity and depends only upon the frequency of the light. To explain this phenomenon the concepts of the *quantum theory* must be invoked, i.e., radiation is emitted intermittently in bundles consisting of integral multiples of a fundamental amount. $E = h\nu$ where h is Planck's constant 6.6×10^{-27} ergs sec. and ν is the frequency of the radiation.

Electronics. Practically all that is commonly referred to as "electronics" is the application of electrons to useful ends. These electrons are usually liberated by thermionic emission, photoelectric emission, or collision with other electrons or ions in tubes more or less evacuated. As they stream from one electrode to another —usually in high vacuum tubes—they constitute portions of electric circuits which are very easily controlled by electric fields, magnetic fields, beams of light, condensers, resistors, inductance coils, batteries, etc. Applications include:

(1) *Radio.* All radio tubes operate on these principles. Usually feeble oscillating currents are amplified by multi-element tubes (detectors, amplifiers, etc.).

(2) *Rectifiers.* Alternating currents are rectified by electron tubes (kenotrons).

(3) *Relays.* Feeble currents trigger off circuits involving considerable power (power tubes, thyratrons, etc.).

(4) *Electric Eye.* This is simply a photoelectric tube usually connected in a relay circuit to control electrical devices.

(5) *Television and Sound Motion Pictures.* These employ phototubes and amplifier tubes to convert beams of light of variable intensity into electric currents with corresponding variations of intensity, and vice versa.

(6) *Airplane Detectors.* These utilize the directional propagation qualities of very short radio waves (wave lengths of a few cm. or so). These waves are produced by special vacuum tube oscillators. They behave much like waves, but penetrate darkness and fog to detect objects which reflect them (radar).

(7) *X Rays.* These also come under this classification of electronic phenomena. In the Coolidge tube the electrons are liberated by thermionic emission.

ATOMIC AND NUCLEAR PHYSICS

Radioactivity. A certain class of substances, of which radium and actinium are particularly conspicuous, is known to emit spontaneously a radiation that has been designated as radioactive. It has been shown that this radiation consists in general of three distinct types. *Alpha particles* are ionized helium atoms, i.e., nuclei of helium atoms. *Beta rays* are ordinary electrons with their customary negative charges. *Gamma rays* are high frequency rays like X rays. These radiations involve the spontaneous liberation of large amounts of subatomic energy.

The Structure of the Atom. The isolation of the electron by

Thomson in 1897 and the discovery of radioactivity by Becquerel at about the same time indicated that the atom, instead of being the smallest indivisible particle of matter as previously supposed, had structure. Modern physics has been concerned largely with the nature of this structure and its component parts. As indicated earlier (see pp. 88–89) the present view of the atom is that of a positively charged nucleus enveloped or surrounded by some kind of distribution of negative electric charge.

The *Bohr atom* pictures the outer structure as consisting of electrons which revolve in elliptical orbits about the nucleus, a single electron in the case of hydrogen, and an increasing number as more complicated atoms are considered up to lawrencium, the most complicated one in the periodic table of the natural elements. In the Bohr model various orbits are possible for the electrons depending upon the excitation state of the atom, the larger ones being associated with more energy than the smaller ones. Discrete *energy levels* appear to be more important, however, than the concept of orbits. Optical and X-ray spectra are explained by the emission of radiation as electrons fall in from outer to inner orbits or from higher to lower energy levels. The spectrum of hydrogen (see Chapter 19) is practically completely so accounted for, but discrepancies are found in spectra of more complex substances.

The differences in energy levels between the Bohr orbits, and consequently the amounts of radiation emitted, are multiples of the basic *quantum* of action suggested by Planck's quantum theory (see p. 80). Thus it is supposed that atomic phenomena are governed by the laws of *quantum mechanics* rather than those of Newtonian or classical mechanics. According to the *uncertainty principle* of quantum mechanics, there is an ultimate limit to the precision with which events can be determined. There are basic uncertainties. For example, the position and the momentum of a particle cannot both be measured simultaneously with unlimited precision. As the precision of determination of the one increases, the limit of certainty of the other decreases. The product of the uncertainties of these two quantities is approximately equal to Planck's constant h. This principle becomes significant only for particles of atomic size or smaller. It is completely obscured in the case of phenomena in the macroscopic world.

Thomson not only isolated the negative electron but also showed the existence of rays of positive ions emitted by the anode in a discharge tube. Subjecting these to a transverse magnetic field, he discovered that atoms of a given chemical element may have different masses. The different forms of an element are called its *isotopes*. The mass spectrometer is used to separate isotopes by selective deflections of ions of different masses. The *deuteron* is an isotope of hydrogen with twice the mass of the proton. So-called heavy water is composed of this isotope.

Atom-smashing devices include various high voltage devices such as the Van de Graaff generator, the Lawrence cyclotron, the Kerst betatron, the cosmotron, the syncocosmotron, the bevatron, etc., all created for the original purpose of smashing atoms to learn as much as possible about their structure.

Cosmic rays constitute a source of nuclear particles. Originating in outer space, they have been discovered to penetrate the earth's atmosphere. Although primarily protons, they produce secondary cosmic radiation in shower bursts as they collide with matter.

The Nucleus of the Atom. The nucleus appears to be made up of components known as nucleons which are held together by forces not well understood. Consequently the details of its structure are not yet altogether clear. Two basically different theories are current; the liquid drop model and the shell model. Nuclear forces considerably greater in magnitude than coulomb forces of electrostatic attraction or repulsion are considered in the first model to behave in a manner analogous to surface tension forces to cause the components of the nucleus to coalesce into something analogous to a liquid drop. In the other model closed shells involving discrete energy levels are postulated after the manner of the shells or energy levels associated with atomic structure.

Nuclear components include the *proton,* the *neutron* (a particle having the mass of a proton but no net electric charge), the *positron* (essentially a positive electron), various *mesons* (particles considerably more massive than electrons and charged negatively or positively), and innumerable other nondescript particles called *pions, muons, strange particles,* and so-called *anti-particles* of various kinds.

Devices for detecting nuclear components include the following. The *Geiger-Mueller counter,* a device in which a wire mounted coaxially inside a metal cylinder, but insulated electrically from it and raised to a high potential difference with respect to it, discharges momentarily when a charged particle (alpha or beta) happens to pass through a very thin metal foil window into the tube. The *Wilson cloud chamber* is a device in which droplets of water vapor condensing upon minute particles when the vapor is adiabatically expanded form tracks which can be observed visually or photographically, and which indicate the recent presence of said particles. *Photographic emulsions* can be used to detect particles. *Bubble chambers* use supersaturated liquid hydrogen to make tracks of particles. *Scintillation counters* consist of multiple photo cells so oriented as to multiply minute photoelectric currents.

Nuclear Reactions and Transformations. Rutherford in 1919 showed that nitrogen bombarded by alpha particles (helium nuclei) was transformed into oxygen with the release of protons according to the reaction

$$_2He^4 + {}_7N^{14} \rightarrow {}_8O^{17} + {}_1H^1.$$

Also lithium, when bombarded with protons, is transformed as follows to form helium.

$$_1H^1 + {}_3Li^7 \rightarrow {}_2H_e{}^4 + {}_2H_e{}^4$$

Note. The subscript to the left in the above notation indicates the so-called *atomic number* Z, while the superscript to the right indicates the so-called *atomic mass* A. A is 16 for oxygen, i.e., it is the nearest whole number to the atomic weight. Z is the number of protons in the nucleus, i.e., it specifies the amount of positive charge which the nucleus exhibits. Neutrons were first produced in 1930 by Chadwick, who bombarded beryllium with alpha particles according to the following:

$$_2H_e{}^4 + {}_4Be^9 \rightarrow {}_6C^{12} + {}_0N^1$$

Radioactive Decay and Half Life. The spontaneous emission of alpha and beta particles from the naturally (in contrast to the artificially) radioactive substances is accompanied by changes in the position of a substance in the periodic table of the elements. The ejection of an alpha particle represents a loss of two protons and two neutrons, i.e., the mass number A *decreases* by four units whereas the atomic number Z *decreases* by two. The emission of a beta particle means a loss of negligible mass but an *increase* of the atomic number Z by one unit. Thus the radioactive materials decay, usually by well-defined steps, to some final stable substance, usually some isotope of lead for the heavier elements like radium, uranium, thorium, actinium, etc. The *half life* is that time required for a substance to lose one half its activity, which happens in an exponential manner. Half lives vary from fractions of a second to millions of years for different isotopes, but each has its own characteristic value.

Nuclear Binding Energy. When nuclear transformations take place and nucleons combine to form nuclei (as when neutrons and protons combine to form helium nuclei), or when nuclei disintegrate naturally (natural radioactivity) or artificially by bombardment with other nucleons (artificial radioactivity), the mass of the nucleus is usually not the same as the combined masses of the component nucleons. The difference is called the *binding energy* in view of Einstein's relationship between mass and energy $E = mc^2$, where c is the velocity of light. The binding energy per nucleon is a function of the mass number A, and is greatest for the elements near the center of the periodic table and least for elements at the extreme ends of the table.

Fission and the Atom Bomb. When neutrons are allowed to bombard certain substances, notably the 235 isotope of uranium, nuclei of the latter, under appropriate circumstances, are observed to split into components which have been identified to include atoms of barium and krypton, i.e., substances located near the middle of the periodic table rather than at either end. Along with the splitting (*fission*) is observed the liberation of high intensity gamma radiation (electromagnetic waves) and additional neutrons, which themselves can be made to collide with more nuclei of the uranium isotope to produce more components and more radiation and more neutrons, etc. This process can be controlled by the use of moderators like cadmium or water (preferably heavy water), or can be allowed to get out of control, resulting in a chain reaction which is the basic principle of the *atom bomb*. The radiation is the equivalent of the binding energy being released in accordance with the Einstein relation $E = mc^2$, which collectively for the billions and billions of atoms involved in a few pounds of uranium represents a fantastic amount of energy (comparable with the energy released by the explosion of tons of T.N.T.).

Fusion and the Hydrogen Bomb (Thermonuclear Device). Temperatures produced in the fission process are sufficiently great to produce the *fusion* of hydrogen nuclei (protons) and neutrons into helium nuclei (alpha particles) with the release, in the form of radiation, of the excess energy beyond that necessary to bind these nucleons together (hydrogen and helium are at the lower extreme of the periodic table where the binding energies are not the greatest). Thus the *hydrogen bomb,* theoretically unlimited in size, became available following the development of the atom bomb, before which the necessary temperatures were not only unavailable but inconceivable of attainment. Incidentally less radioactive debris is produced by the H bomb than the A bomb.

Molecular Binding. Molecules, being aggregates of atoms, are held together by various forces. For those molecules which are simple combinations of positive and negative ions, coulomb forces seem to suffice. For diatomic molecules like H_2 the atoms appear to share the two electrons by what are called *exchange forces.* The *Pauli exclusion principle* suggests that when one atom approaches another to form a molecule the electrons of the one penetrate the occupied energy shells of the other, but some are forced into higher states because crowding of shells is not allowed. This explains how attractive forces are developed to hold the molecule together in spite of the coulombic repulsion of two positive nuclei.

Solid State Physics. The atoms of a solid are held together by forces which result in a crystalline structure. In metals the valence electrons are free to migrate through the crystal from atom to atom because they do not appear to be permanently associated with any particular one.

Whereas classically the vibrational energy of molecules and atoms is assumed to be zero at absolute zero, quantum mechanics predicts a residue of atomic energy at 0°K. The quantizing of vibrational waves in crystal lattices gives rise to the concept of the *phonon,* an elastic counterpart of the electromagnetic *photon.*

In a solid the energy levels of the component atoms become broadened to form what are called *energy bands.* At 0°K. the electrons are in the lowest possible band or level, i.e., the lowest levels are filled, but as the temperature is raised electrons become excited and tend to occupy higher bands. In metals the so-called conduction bands are not completely filled. *Conductors, semiconductors,* and *insulators* are distinguished by the extent to which the conduction (upper) bands are filled. The so-called *Fermi level* in a substance is that level at a given temperature for which the probability that an electron occupies any available state at that energy is 50%.

Impurity semiconductors are formed when small amounts of a foreign substance are added (an example is arsenic added to a germanium crystal). This alters the distribution of electrons in the valence band and conduction band (separated by the Fermi level). An arsenic atom provides an extra conduction electron and is called a *donor* impurity and produces a so-called n-type semiconductor. *Acceptor* impurities result in so-called p-type semiconductors in which missing electrons produce so-called *holes* available for conduction.

The *transistor* is an n-p-n junction which has found important applications as an amplifier in a device which has replaced the electronic vacuum tube in many electronic circuits.

The *laser* is a solid-state device in which atoms are excited from lower to higher energy states by a novel process in which light of higher frequency than that emitted by the atoms when they return to their original states is so-to-speak pumped into them. This results in a greater than normal number of atoms in the higher states so that when radiation is stimulated, it is greatly amplified while the frequency remains the same as that of the stimulating source and therefore is said to be coherent.

Review Questions

(1) Describe the phenomena associated with the conduction of electricity by a gas in a tube undergoing exhaustion.
(2) What is meant by positive column? Faraday dark space? Crookes' dark space? Cathode rays? X rays?
(3) List the properties of electrons.
(4) What is the fundamental action of a three-electrode radio tube?
(5) Describe the photoelectric effect. What is the "electric cye?"
(6) What are alpha particles? Beta particles? Gamma rays?
(7) Describe the Bohr atom.
(8) Discuss the uncertainty principle of quantum mechanics.
(9) Give two devices for detecting nuclear components.

Part V: Light

17: The Nature of Light: Its Propagation and Measurement

HISTORICAL INTRODUCTION

The subject of optics has attracted the attention of philosophers and scientists since about 4000 B. C., around which time the magnifying glass was discovered. From that time up to and including the present, the nature of light has been questioned, and attempts have been made to explain it, without complete success. Two theories, the one a *corpuscular theory* and the other a *wave theory,* have persisted. The present view is compromising in that it suggests the probability that light is both corpuscular and wave-like, the one aspect predominating for a given set of conditions, and the other predominating for other conditions.

Newton's Influence. In the seventeeth century Huygens proposed a wave theory to account for the known facts, but this view was unacceptable to Newton, who felt that the available evidence favored a corpuscular view, on which luminous bodies were supposed to give off corpuscles capable of traveling rapidly in straight lines and of exciting the eye to vision. He had in mind particularly the phenomena of rectilinear propagation and shadow formation. Newton's influence upon scientific thought was so great that for a hundred years or more the corpuscular theory thrived.

Fresnel, Young, and Maxwell. About the middle of the eighteenth century the wave methods of explaining light were revived, especially by the work of Fresnel and Young on the subject of interference. These views were ultimately established when in 1864 Maxwell developed, by rigorous mathematical argument, the electromagnetic wave theory in so perfect a form that all doubt disappeared as to the correctness of the wave nature of light. Of course, the medium (the ether) in which these waves were postulated to travel, was quite ficitious and somewhat vague, but this objection was considered relatively unimportant. On this theory light waves form a part of the entire electromagnetic spectrum which ranges in length from long radio waves down to ultrashort

X rays. (Fig. 102.) The wave-length range of the visible waves is from about .00008000 cm. for red light to about .00004000 cm. for violet light. This range comprises just about one octave.

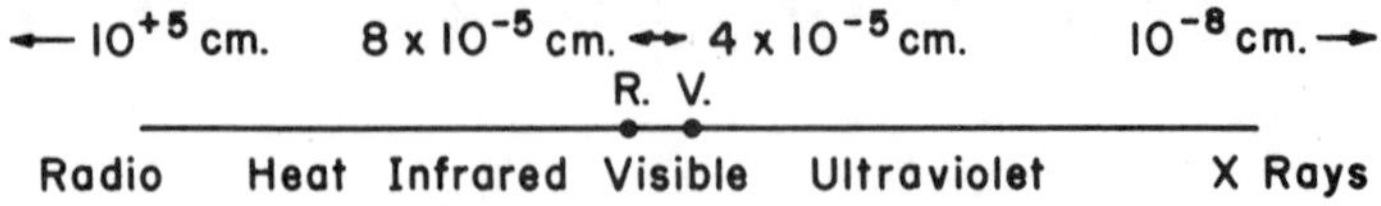

← 10^{+5} cm. 8 x 10^{-5} cm. ↔ 4 x 10^{-5} cm. 10^{-8} cm. →
R. V.

Radio Heat Infrared Visible Ultraviolet X Rays

Fig. 102—Electromagnetic spectrum

The Photon. Since the latter part of the last century, however, an increasing degree of uncertainty about the wave theory has been developing due to the discovery of the photoelectric effect, the quantum theory, and a number of allied phenomena, and due also to a detailed investigation into the nature and physical properties of the ether. Also, during this period a great deal has been learned about the structure of the atom which is not altogether limited to a wave picture of light. Hence the *photon,* or a light corpuscle, has been postulated. It must be pointed out, however, that the photon differs from Newton's "corpuscle" in that it is postulated that the photon is a bundle of waves and as such has wave properties. Thus the present view considers light both *corpuscularlike* and *wavelike.*

THE NATURE AND FUNCTION OF A PHYSICAL THEORY

The preceding consideration discloses the necessity for clarifying the *function of a theory* in physics, and particularly in optics. It must be concluded that there are any number of ways of explaining anything, and that the best way is the one which explains the most on the fewest assumptions, or in the simplest manner. If one theory best explains a given phenomenon, as the corpuscular theory best explains the rectilinear propagation of light and the photoelectric effect, then it is to be considered the correct theory for the purpose. But if another theory is better suited to explain other phenomena, as the wave theory better explains the interference effects of light, then it is to be considered the correct one for that purpose. In general then, whichever theory best explains a given phenomenon is to be considered the correct theory for the purpose, although a particular phenomenon may be explainable by more than one theory.

It is probably worth pointing out that there are a very large number of optical phenomena which a satisfactory theory has to explain. A *partial* list of these will now be made, and although it is not the purpose of this outline to completely exhaust the detailed knowledge associated with each of these phenomena, it is nevertheless a fact that optics is concerned with the study of these phenomena and hence the remainder of this outline will be devoted to a consideration of many of them.

The partial list includes: (1) rectilinear propagation; (2) photometry (the quantitative measurement of light); (3) geometric optics (regular reflection and refraction, and the fact that both take place simultaneously); (4) the fact that light involves a transfer of energy; (5) the scattering of light by diffuse reflections; (6) fluorescence (the change of wave length or color of light by matter); (7) dispersion (the spreading out of light into its component colors); (8) the Zeeman effect (the action of a magnetic field upon light); (9) the fact that light has a definite velocity in free space; (10) the fact that light is slowed up by matter; (11) interference (the superposition of multiple light beams to produce re-enforcement and annulment); (12) diffraction (the bending of light around edges); (13) polarization (the fact that light vibrations can be restricted to particular modes); (14) the radiation aspect of light; (15) the photoelectric effect; (16) the fact that light can be spread out into a variety of different kinds of spectra; (17) the Compton effect (pertaining to the collision of photons with matter).

Note: The preceding list has been arranged in a definite order. The first nine phenomena are explainable by either a corpuscular or a wave theory. In each instance, however, one theory is more satisfactory than the other. Topics from (10) to (13), inclusive, pertain to phenomena explainable best on the basis of the wave aspects of light. The remainder, (14) to (17) inclusive, can be explained best on the basis of corpuscular considerations.

RECTILINEAR PROPAGATION

Light travels in straight lines with a velocity measurable by a number of methods. The value of this velocity in vacuum according to the last measurement by Michelson is $2.99796 \pm .00004 \times 10^{10}$ cm./sec. (approx. 186,000 miles per second).

Nature of Propagation by Waves and Corpuscles. On the wave picture, the path taken by the light is called a ray. By *Huygens' principle,* a wave is propagated by virtue of the fact that every

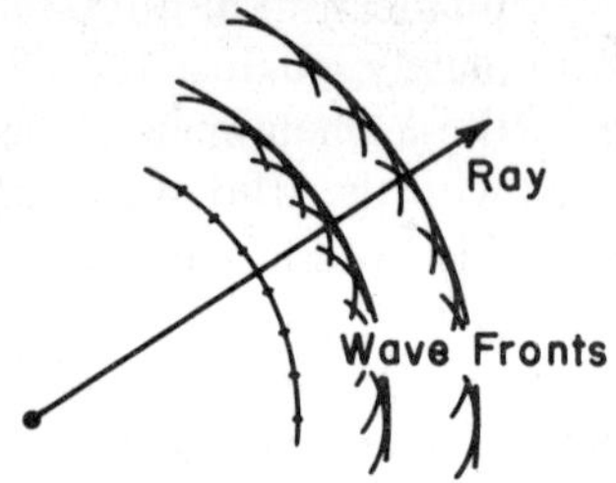

Fig. 103—Huygens' wave principle

point on a wave front acts as the source of new wavelets, the tangent to, or envelope of, which constitutes the new *wave front.* The wave front is always perpendicular to the ray. The propagation of light can equally well be described in terms of successive wave fronts, or in terms of rays. (Fig. 103.) On the corpuscular picture it is obvious that the path taken by the corpuscles streaming out from a luminous point must coincide with the ray of the wave picture.

PHOTOMETRY (Measurements of Light Quantities)

Fundamental Concepts and Definitions.

Light Flux. If light is emitted by a very small source it can be treated quantitatively as if it were emanating in straight lines in all directions from a geometrical point, i.e., as a flux. Flux is measured in *lumens.* One lumen corresponds to one *flux line.* It has been found by experiment that the amount of light emitted by a hot filament depends upon the color (wave length) of the light and the rate at which energy is dissipated in producing it. It has been established by convention that one lumen of green light is emitted by the dissipation-rate of 0.00161 watts, or that one watt corresponds to 685 lumens at wave length .0000555 cm. The lumen is a power unit and not an energy unit. Flux = $\frac{\text{Light Energy}}{\text{Time}}$.

Spherical Angle (solid angle). Corresponding to the radian of circular measure, so defined that every complete circle is measured by 2π radians (the radian being an angle bounded by an arc equal in length to the radius of curvature) and the number of radians in a whole circle being the circumference divided by the radius, i.e., $\frac{2\pi r}{r} = 2\pi$, a unit of solid angle called the *ster-radian* has been defined in such a manner that all space about a point is measured by 4π ster-radians (the number of radians in space being equal to the area of a spherical surface enveloping the point, divided by the square of the radius, i.e., $\frac{4\pi r^2}{r^2} = 4\pi$).

Intensity of a Point Source. The number of flux lines or lumens emitted in a ster-radian (unit solid angle) serves as a measure of the intensity (I) of the light source in *candle power* or *candles.* Obviously the total flux (F) emanating from a point source of candle power intensity (I) is $F = 4\pi I$.

Note: There has been considerable confusion among engineers and physicists concerning many of the photometric conventions and standards. It was formerly customary to measure the intensity of a point source in comparison with a standard candle constructed in a specified manner and then to define a lumen as the amount of light emitted by a standard candle in one ster-radian. This procedure has given way, however, to the one already mentioned.

Luminance of an Extended Source. If a source is not a point source but has an appreciable size (as all real sources do), it is not customary to refer to the intensity of such a source, but to its *intrinsic brightness* or *luminance* (B) expressed in lumens emitted per square centimeter of emitting surface (lamberts) or in candles per square centimeter of emitting surface (assuming the light to come from a point source behind the extended surface). One candle/cm.^{2} = π lamberts.

Illuminance of a Surface. The amount of light flux, or the number of lumens, incident upon unit area of surface (not necessarily normally) is referred to as the *illuminance* (E) of the surface. $\left(E = \frac{F}{A}\right)$. One lumen per square foot of illumination is called a *foot-candle.* One lumen per square centimeter is called a *phot.* (This last unit is not very comon.)

The illuminance of a spherical surface of radius r enveloping a point source of candle intensity (I) is given by

$$E = \frac{F}{A} = \frac{4\pi I}{4\pi r^2} = \frac{I}{r^2}.$$

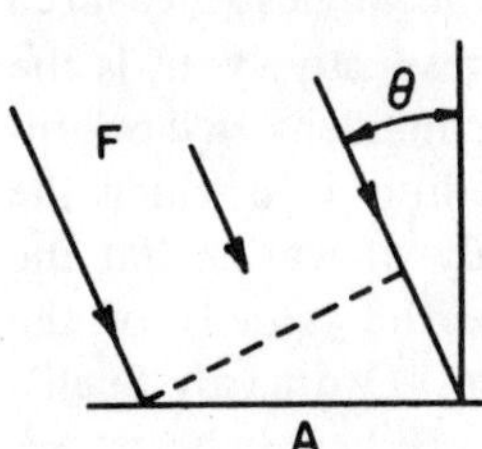

Fig. 104—Illumination

$E = \frac{F}{A} \operatorname{Cos} \theta$

For a plane surface at a distance r from a point source of candle intensity I, $E = \frac{I}{r^2} \cos \theta$, where θ is the angle between the ray and the normal to the surface. (Fig. 104.)

Photometric Measures. For equal amounts of illuminance (E) due to two sources of different intensity at different distances:

$$E = \frac{I_1}{r_1^2}. = \frac{I_2}{r_2^2}. \quad \frac{I_1}{I_2} = \frac{r_1^2}{r_2^2}.$$

For different values of illuminance (E_1) and (E_2) at different distances from the same source:

$$E_1 = \frac{I}{r_1^2}; \; E_2 = \frac{I}{r_2^2}. \quad \therefore \frac{E_1}{E_2} = \frac{r_2^2}{r_1^2}.$$

The order of magnitude of illuminance is suggested by the facts that full sunlight gives E = 10,000 ft.-candles (approx.); full moonlight gives E = .02 ft.-candles; and good reading illumination is of the order of 10 ft.-candles.

REGULAR REFLECTION AND REFRACTION

Whenever a light wave or a light ray strikes a surface of discontinuity, part of it is *refracted* and part of it is *reflected* just as any wave would be. If the surface is polished like a mirror the reflection is said to be *regular reflection* in contrast to *diffuse reflection,* which results when light is reflected in all directions from a surface that is more irregular in an optical sense.

The law of regular reflection states that the angle of incidence (angle made by the incident ray with the normal to the surface) equals the angle of reflection (angle made by the reflected ray with the normal), i.e., $i = r$, and that the incident ray, the normal, and the reflected ray all lie in the same plane. (Fig. 105.)

Snell's law of refraction states that when a light ray strikes a surface making an angle i with its normal, the refracted ray, which lies in the same plane with the incident ray and the normal, makes an angle with the normal in accordance with the relation, $n_1 \sin i = n_2 \sin r'$ where i and r′ refer to the angles (measured with the normal) of incidence and refraction respectively, n_1 is the refractive index of the medium in which the incident ray originates, and n_2 is the refractive index of the medium into which the ray passes. It will be recalled from the study of waves that the refractive index of a medium is the ratio of the velocity of the wave in vacuum to its velocity in the medium. Ordinarily Snell's law leads to the following conclusions: (1) When light passes from a rare to a denser medium (optically speaking) the ray is bent *toward* the normal. (Fig. 106.) (2) When light passes from a dense to a rarer medium, the ray is bent *away from* the normal.

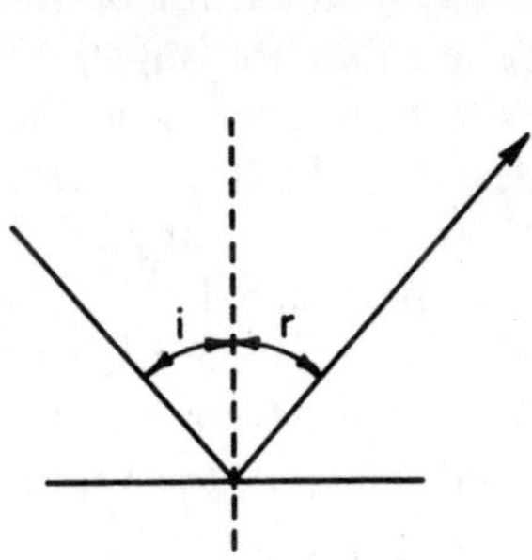

Fig. 105—Regular reflection

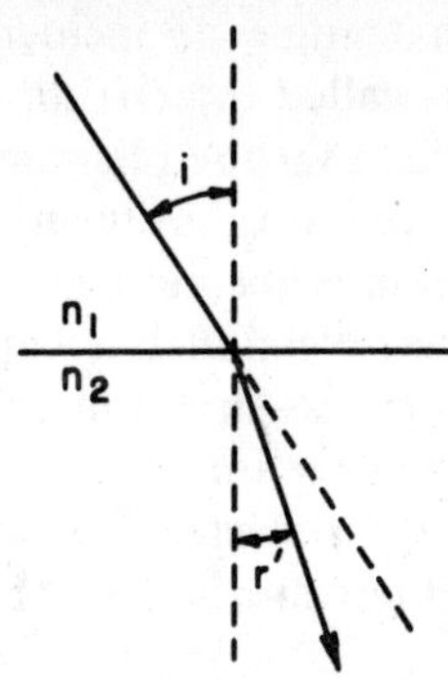

Fig. 106—Regular refraction. $n_2 > n_1$

It should be pointed out that the intensities of the reflected and refracted rays at a surface of a transparent medium depend upon the angle of incidence. For small angles of incidence (made with the normal) the fraction transmitted is large and the fraction reflected is small. As the angle increases, the amount reflected increases at the expense of the transmitted portion.

An interesting case of refraction and reflection arises when the ray of light originates in a medium whose refractive index is greater than that of the medium into which it passes. For such a case the angle of refraction must exceed the angle of incidence. It will be noted, however, that the angle of incidence corresponding to the refraction angle of 90° represents a critical incidence angle because for an incidence angle greater than this, the angle of refraction would be required to have a sine value greater than unity, an impossibility. The result is not refraction, but reflection back into the original medium, as if the surface were mirror-coated. (Fig. 107.) This phenomenon is called *total internal reflection,*

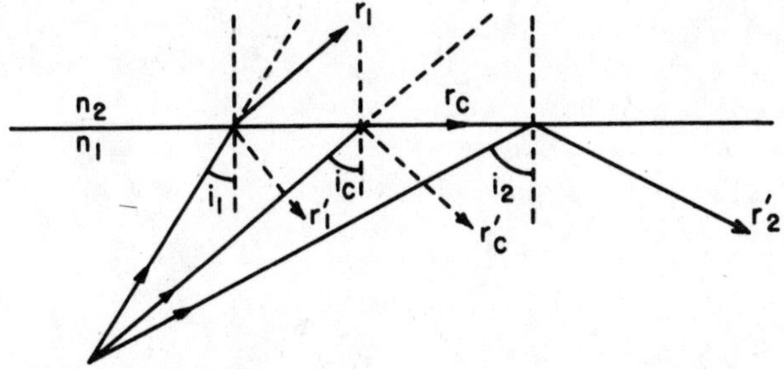

Fig. 107—Total internal reflection $n_1 > n_2$; i_c = critical angle

and that angle of incidence, greater than which the refraction fails, is called the *critical angle of incidence.* It must not be interpreted that the phenomenon is abrupt, i.e., that for angles of incidence less than the critical angle the reflection is zero and the refraction is absolute, and for greater angles, the refraction is zero and the reflection is complete. The facts are that for angles of incidence less than this critical angle there is partial reflection as well as refraction, and for increasing values of the angle of incidence the reflected fraction increases at the expense of the refracted portion until at the critical angle, and beyond, the reflection is total. $\sin i_c = \frac{n_2}{n_1}$ or $\sin i_c = \frac{1}{n_1}$, if n_2 refers to air. (n_2 = 1.0002921 for yellow light.) *Recall* that n_1 always refers to the *first* medium and n_2 refers to the *second* medium.

The principle of total internal reflection is made use of in reflecting prisms. Reflection by this method is more nearly complete than from any silvered surface. For glass $n = 1.5$ approx. $\therefore i_c = 42°$ approx., whence a ray of light parallel to one side of an isosceles right-angled 45° prism will be totally reflected internally from the hypotenuse and will emerge parallel to the other side, having been changed in direction by 90°.

Review Questions

(1) What evidence is there for a wave theory of light?
(2) Is there any evidence at all for a corpuscular theory?
(3) Comment upon the function of a theory.
(4) What is Huygens' principle of wave propagation?
(5) Distinguish between candle power, brightness, and illuminance.
(6) What is the law of reflection? The law of refraction?
(7) What is meant by total internal reflection? Under what circumstances is it produced? What is the critical angle of incidence?

18: Geometric Optics: Mirrors, Lenses, and Other Optical Instruments

REFRACTION AND REFLECTION AT THE BOUNDARY OF A SINGLE SPHERICAL SURFACE

The known facts concerning the propagation of light are summarized in the following postulates: (1) that a ray of light travels in a straight line in a homogeneous medium; (2) that two rays may exist separately unaffected by intersecting one another; (3) that the law of regular reflection holds, i.e., $i = r$; (4) that the law of refraction holds, i.e., $n_1 \sin i = n_2 \sin r'$. It can be shown that the behavior of a beam of light upon striking the boundary of a spherical surface can be predicted. To accomplish this in an unambiguous and analytical manner, certain conventions regarding mathematical signs and directions must be agreed upon and diagrams must be drawn in such a manner as to be consistent with these conventions.

The following conventions are followed:

(1) In drawing diagrams of light rays incident upon boundary surfaces, always assume the light to be traveling from left to right.

(2) Assume the object distance, that distance from the object to the point of intersection between the axis and the surface (sometimes called the vertex), to be a positive quantity when the object lies to the left of the surface. Indicate it by u.

(3) Indicate the image distance, that distance from the vertex of the surface to the image, by v, and consider it a positive quantity if the image lies to the right of the vertex.

(4) Consider the radius of curvature (R) of a surface to be a positive quantity if the center of the curvature lies to the right of the vertex, and a negative quantity if the center of curvature lies to the left of the vertex.

(5) Measure all angles in a counterclockwise manner with respect to the axis (or the radius of curvature, as the case may be). Consider clockwise angles to be negative.

(6) Designate the size of an object (⊥ to the axis) by y, and consider upward directions as positive. Designate similarly the size of an image by y′.

Then for rays making very small angles θ, θ', i, and r′ (Fig. 108) (such that $\sin \theta = \theta$ approximately, and similarly $\sin \theta' = \theta'$, $\sin i = i$, $\sin r' = r'$), the following relations give the location, the nature, and the magnification of whatever image may be

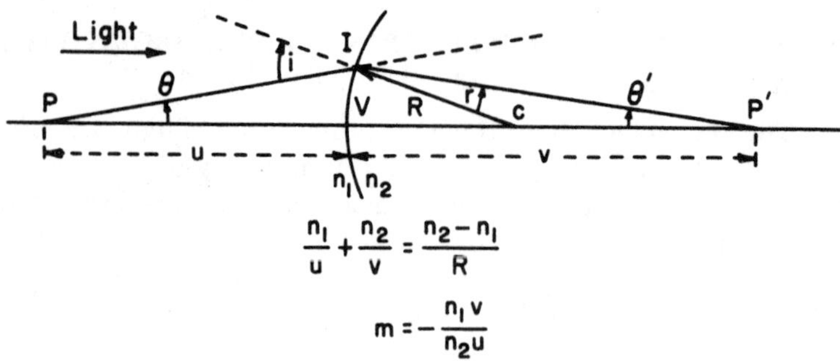

(These relations also hold for reflection if $n_2 = -n_1$)

Fig. 108—Refraction and reflection at a single spherical surface

formed as a result of rays emanating from a point in the object, being bent by refraction or reflection, and coming together again to form an image:

$$\frac{n_1}{u} + \frac{n_2}{v} = \frac{n_2 - n_1}{R}, \text{ magnification } m = \frac{y'}{y} = -\frac{n_1 v}{n_2 u},$$

where n_1 refers to the refractive index of the first medium (to the left), n_2 is the refractive index of the second medium (to the right of the surface being considered), u is the object distance along the axis of the surface, v is the image distance, R is the radius of curvature of the spherical surface, y is the size of the object, and v′ is the size of the image. When a single surface is considered, a positive answer for m indicates an erect image, and a negative value of m indicates an inverted image. It will be shown later that an inverted image is real and an erect image is virtual. In using this formula, then, it is the sign of m that determines the nature of the image.

These formulae work for any spherical surface if only rays nearly parallel to the axis are considered. Furthermore, if a plane surface is assumed to be a spherical surface of infinite radius of curvature $\left(R = \infty. \therefore \frac{1}{R} = 0.\right)$, they also hold for plane surfaces.

If the somewhat artificial assumption is made that upon reflection from a mirror the medium in which the ray is reflected has a refractive index equal to the negative of that for the medium in which the incident ray arrives, i.e., $n_2 = -n_1$ (of course, actually the reflected ray is reflected back into the same medium), then these same formulae hold for reflection as well as refraction at a single spherical surface, i.e.,

$$\frac{1}{u} - \frac{1}{v} = -\frac{2}{R}$$

REFRACTION AND REFLECTION FOR A SUCCESSION OF SPHERICAL SURFACES

The foregoing applies to a single surface. If the path of a ray through a number of surfaces separating different media is desired it is merely necessary to apply the above formulae repeatedly, each time remembering that the medium that was designated as medium No. 2 for a given surface becomes medium No. 1 for the next surface to the right of it. The process can be repeated for any number of surfaces.

The case of two spherical refracting surfaces close together, forming a *thin lens* bounded on each side by air, is very important. The same relation above applied twice (two boundary surfaces) leads to the following special result (where $u_2 = -v_1$):

$$\frac{1}{u} + \frac{1}{v} = (n - 1)\left(\frac{1}{R_1} - \frac{1}{R_2}\right) = \frac{1}{f},$$

where u is the object distance measured to the lens (*supposed to be very thin and in air*), v is the image distance, n is the refractive index of the medium of which the lens is made, R_1 refers to the first surface (to the left), R_2 refers to the second surface (to the right), and f is called the *focal length* of the lens.

The focal length of a *converging* lens is that distance from the lens to the point *at which* originally parallel light rays converge (Fig. 109-A, p. 164), and is positive.

The focal lenght of a *diverging* lens is that distance from the lens (behind), *from which* light originally parallel to the principal axis *appears* to come (diverge) (Fig. 109-B), and is negative.

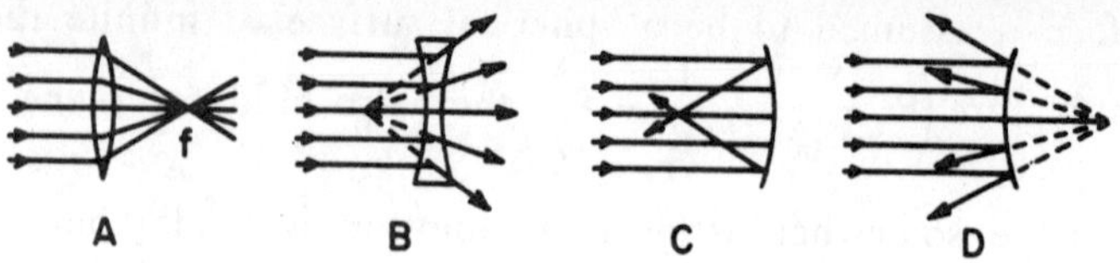

Fig. 109—Illustrating focal length of (A) Converging lens; (B) Diverging lens; (C) Converging mirror; (D) Diverging mirror

Graphical Methods of Locating Images Formed by Spherical Mirrors and Thin Lenses. For *mirrors,* recognition of the facts that the law of reflection and the nature of the focal point of a mirror so definitely restrict two particular rays emanating from an object, and that the point of intersection of these rays after reflection is definitely located, leads to a simple graphical method of locating the image of an object.

Assuming the object to be located on the axis of the mirror, draw from the head end of the object (which for purposes of discussion can be represented by an arrow drawn transversely with respect to the axis) the ray which runs parallel to the axis and reflect it from the mirror so as to make it pass through the focus if the mirror is concave. (Fig. 110.) If it is a convex mirror the ray will have to be reflected *as if* if had originated at the focus, which in this case will be on the far side of the mirror.

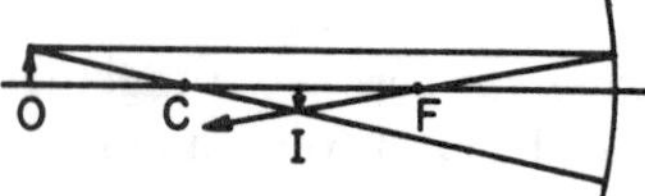

Fig. 110—Ray diagram (mirror)

Note: It can be shown that for a spherical mirror (for a small portion of it at least) the focal length is half the radius of curvature.

Of the remaining infinite number of rays supposedly emanating from the head end of the object, pick out the one which passes through the center of curvature of the mirror. Obviously this one will be reflected straight back upon itself.

The point of intersection of these two reflected rays must be the image of the head end of the object. If the rays intersect in space (i.e., in front of the mirror) the image is said to be real. As such, it can be localized upon a screen and is always *inverted* with respect to the object. If the rays do not intersect in the space in front of the mirror, but their extensions appear to intersect behind the mirror (where, of course, there really is no light at all), then the image is said to be *virtual,* and as such cannot be located on a screen and is always *erect.*

In the case of *thin lenses* in air, of which two general types are recognized, *converging* (such as a double convex lens), and *diverging* (such as a double concave lens), a somewhat similar procedure may be followed.

From the head end of the object draw the ray parallel to the axis and bend it as it passes through the lens so that upon emerging it passes through the focus on the far side, if the lens is converging. (Fig. 111.) If the lens is diverging, the emerging ray,

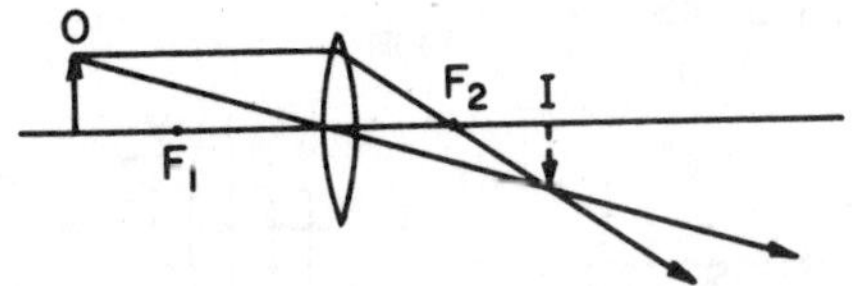

Fig. 111—Ray diagram (lens)

instead of having been converged, will have been diverged as if it had originated at the focus on the near side of the lens. *Note:* A lens has two focal points.

Draw the ray through the center of the lens straight on through upon the assumption that at the center the surfaces of the lens are essentially parallel and, consequently, the emerging ray must be parallel with the incident ray and displaced from it by a negligible amount if the lens is thin.

The intersection of the two emerging rays is the image of the head end of the object. If the intersection takes place on the far side of the lens, a real (inverted) image is located. If the rays do not actually intersect on the far side but appear to intersect (or their extensions appear to intersect) on the near side, a virtual (erect) image is located. A diverging lens *always* produces a virtual image on the same side of the lens as itself. A converging lens produces a real image on the far side, *except* when the object is located within the focal length of the lens, in which case a virtual image is formed on the near side.

In all cases (lenses and mirrors) the ratio of the image size to the object size is the same as the ratio of image distance to object distance, i.e., $\frac{I}{O} = \frac{v}{u}$.

Lens Aberrations. Lenses are subject to two general types of aberrations which must not be considered as due to faulty construction but are inherent by virtue of the laws of optics.

Spherical aberrations (axial, coma, astigmatism, curvature of field, distortion) are indicated by diagrams. (Fig. 112.) They are

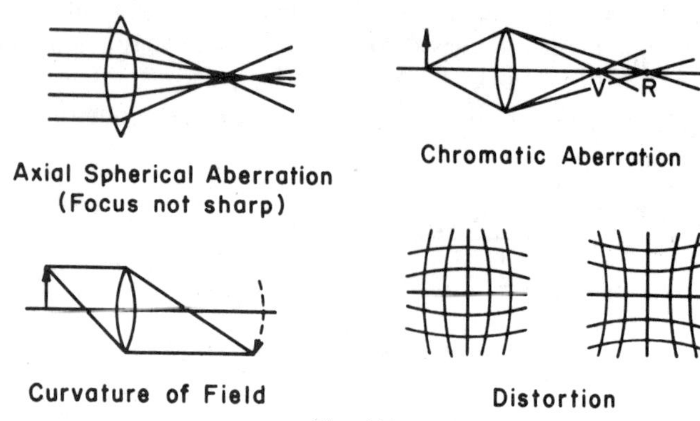

Fig. 112

all minimized by the use of a diaphragm which allows the light rays to pass only through the very center portion of the lens.

Chromatic aberration is due to the fact that different colors are focussed at different points. This can be offset by the use of compound lenses made of glass of different refractive indices for the different colors.

OPTICAL INSTRUMENTS

The laws of geometric optics are applied in the design and operation of many optical instruments, of which the following is a partially complete list.

The Simple Microscope. The magnifying glass is often referred to as a *simple microscope.* It is a converging lens which in normal use is placed nearer than its focal length from an object so that a virtual (erect) image is formed on the same side of the lens. (Fig. 113.) The power of a lens is given in *diopters* when the reciprocal is taken of the focal length expressed in meters. (A diverging

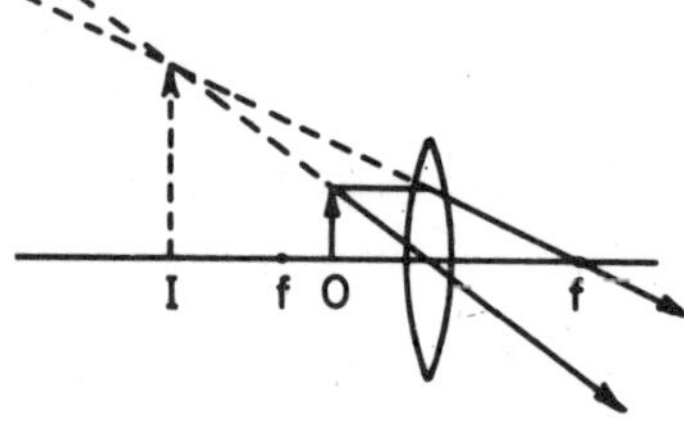

Fig. 113—Simple microscope

lens is said to have a negative power.) The *magnifying power* of a simple microscope (not to be confused with the magnification of the lens) is given by the expression $m = \frac{25}{f} + 1$ when f is expressed in centimeters. It is the ratio of the angle subtended at the lens by the image to the angle subtended by the object at 25 cm. away from the lens.

The Eye. Probably one of the most important optical instruments is the human eye, which has a rather complicated optical system. (Fig. 114.) The formation upon the retina of the eye of

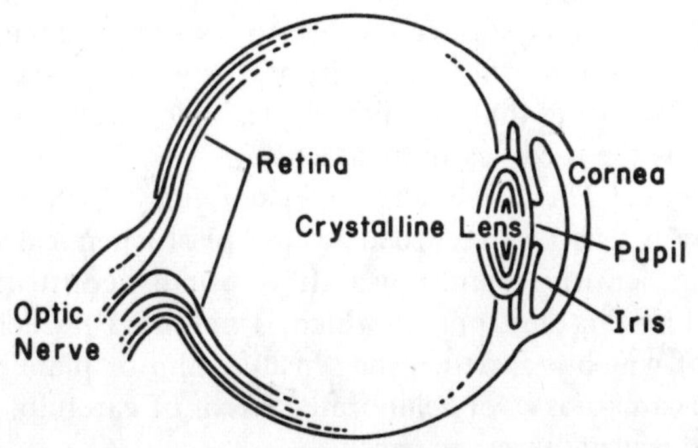

Fig. 114—The eye

an image must not be confused with the physiological sensation of seeing, which, of course, involves an interpretation of the image by the brain. Human eyes may be defective in many ways, but the study of optics has shown that many of these defects can be corrected by the use of spectacle lenses worn in front of the eyes. Some of the commonest of these defects are described here.

Myopia (nearsightedness) is a condition resulting from the fact that the eyeball is too long, because of which objects farther away than a short distance cannot be focussed on the retina but are focussed in front of it. The so-called *far-point* (the farthest point at which the eye can focus objects) is rather close instead of being at infinity as it is for the normal eye. Also the *near-point* (the nearest point at which the eye can focus objects) is rather closer then for the normal eye. Myopia is corrected by the use of a negative lens which forms a virtual image of the object at such a distance away that it can be easily seen.

Hypermetropia (farsightedenss) is a condition resulting from an abnormally short eyeball, because of which objects nearer than a certain distance are not focussed on the retina but behind it. Hypermetropia is corrected by the use of a positive lens.

Presbyopia is the name given to the loss of accommodation with age. *Accommodation* is the property of dilating or contracting the lens muscles of the eye to make it possible for the eye to first focus upon a near object and later upon a far object. The near-point of an eye ordinarily recedes with age; thus it is often observed that age alone corrects a condition of slight myopia.

Astigmatism is the name given to another very common eye defect. It is the result of an unequal curvature of the surface of the cornea, the outer surface on the front of the eyeball. It gives rise to a condition wherein horizontal lines are focussed in a different plane from that in which vertical lines are focussed. It is corrected by the use of cylindrical lenses.

The Camera. The camera is a device with which images are formed by a lens and recorded by the photochemical effects of light upon sensitive emulsions. It is usually constructed as a light-tight box in the front of which is mounted the lens and in the rear of which is fastened the sensitive film or plate. The lens of a good camera is a very elaborate system of carefully corrected lenses and is usually very expensive.

The Projection Lantern. This is a device by which an intense light beam is condensed by lenses upon a transparent object placed in front of an objective lens which focuses an image of this object upon a distant screen. (Fig. 115.)

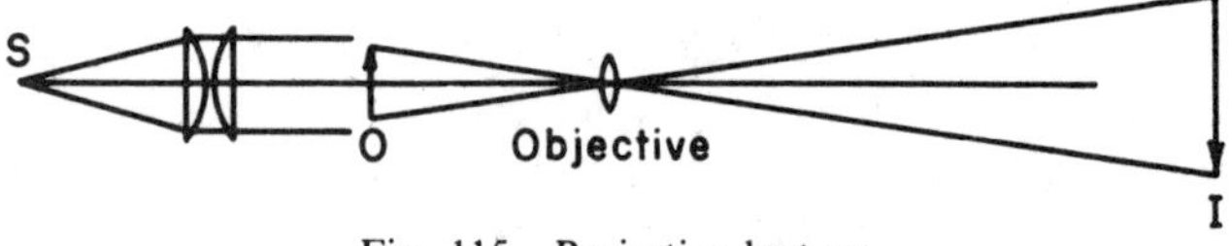

Fig. 115—Projection lantern

The Compound Microscope. The compound microscope is a combination of converging lenses designed to produce large magnification. This is accomplished by placing a very short-focus (high-powered) lens near the object, thereby producing a real (inverted) and magnified image which is viewed by an eyepiece used in the manner of a simple magnifier to further magnify this inverted and already magnified image. The magnifying power is given by the expression $M = m_1 \times m_2$, where m_1 and m_2 refer to the magnifying powers of the objective and the eyepiece (ocular) respectively. This can also be expressed by $M = -\frac{18}{f_1} \times \frac{25}{f_2}$ (where f_1 and f_2 refer to the focal lengths in centimeters of the objective and ocular respectively) since it is customary to separate the two by 18 cm. and to form the final image 25 cm. away from the eye.

The Astronomical Telescope. The astronomical telescope functions in a manner quite similar to that of the compound microscope. The outstanding difference is that the objective lens has a much larger focal length, whence the instrument is suited for distance work. (Fig. 116.) The magnification is

$$M = -\frac{f\text{ (objective)}}{f\text{ (ocular)}}.$$

The negative sign indicates an inverted image. In the largest telescopes the objective lens is replaced by a large converging mirror.

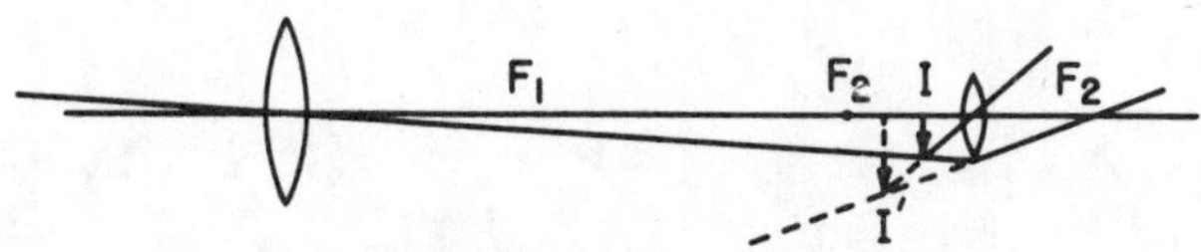

Fig. 116—Astronomical telescope

The Terrestrial Telescope or Spyglass. This incorporates a third lens in the optical system for the purpose of re-inverting the image to make it erect. This requires a longer telescope tube than would otherwise be necessary. The *prism binoculars* accomplish this same result in less space by the use of reflecting prisms mounted between the lenses.

The Opera Glass or the Galilean Telescope. This, the common field glass, utilizes a diverging ocular lens by which a virtual magnified image is formed of an object. (Fig. 117.)

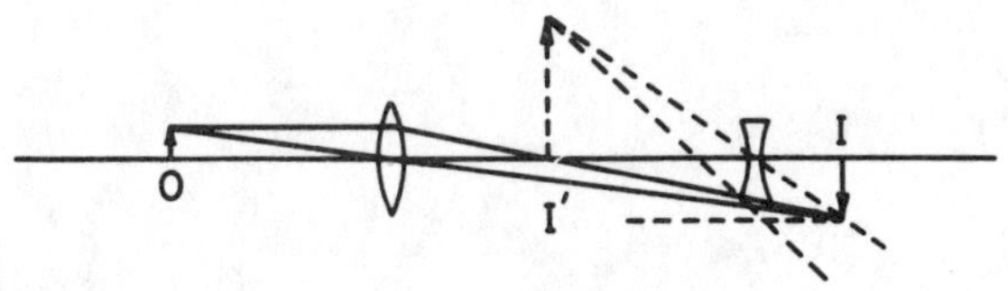

Fig. 117—Opera glass

Review Questions

(1) What conventions must be established for the following laws of reflection and refraction at a single surface to hold: $\frac{n_1}{u} + \frac{n_2}{v} = \frac{n_2 - n_1}{R}$ and $m = -\frac{n_1 v}{n_2 u}$?
(2) Distinguish between real and virtual images.
(3) What is the thin lens formula?
(4) What is meant by focal length of a convex lens? of a convex mirror?
(5) How can ray diagrams be traced to locate the image formed by a convex lens when the object is interposed between the lens and its focus?
(6) Distinguish between curvature of field and distortion of a lens.
(7) Describe how chromatic aberration is reduced.
(8) If the lens and the various liquids of the eye have approximately the same refractive index as water, how can a person "see' under water?
(9) Diagram a compound microscope.
(10) How can one tell from a person's spectacles whether or not that person is myopic or hypermetropic?

19: Optical Phenomena: Physical Optics

DISPERSION AND SPECTRA

When a beam of sunlight is passed through a glass prism it is not only bent in direction, but is spread out into an array of colors. This indicates that white light is a composite of all colors (all visible wave lengths) and that the refractive index of the prism differs for different wave lengths, being ordinarily greater for violet light than for red light. (Fig. 118.) This spreading of light out into its component colors, or the variation of refractive index with wave length, is known as *dispersion.* The array of colors is called a *spectrum.* The instrument which spreads out these colors is called a *spectroscope* if used visually, or a *spectrograph* if designed for photographic recording. The nature of the spectrum produced by a given source of light is characteristic of the chemical constitution and condition of the light source.

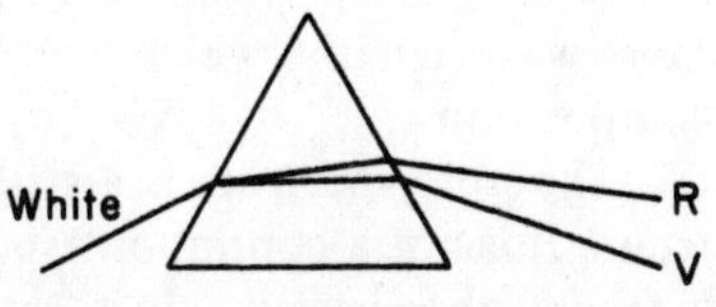

Fig. 118—Refraction and dispersion by a prism

Four distinct types of spectra have been classified and are here listed along with the general conditions under which they are produced:

Continuous Spectrum. When the light from an incandescent solid or liquid is analyzed by a spectroscope it is found that the visible spectrum is a continuous array of colors extending from red through orange, yellow, green, blue, to and including violet.

Bright-Line Spectrum. When the source of light is a hot gas or a hot vapor, however, the resulting spectrum is characterized by a certain discreteness. The spectrum is not a continuous array of colors in this case but consists of certain colors only, separated by broad dark regions. As a matter of practical convenience a narrow slit is ordinarily incorporated into the spectroscope to serve as an object to be illuminated by the various light sources to be analyzed. The resulting spectrum is then an overlapping pattern of bright-line images of this slit, and the hot vapor spectrum under consideration is a pattern of discrete bright lines. Furthermore, the line patterns are characteristic of the chemical constitution of the light source, the bright-line spectrum of a sodium flame being, for example, merely a single orange-yellow line. (Upon close examination this line is actually found to be a double line.) The spectroscope thus affords a method of analyzing the chemical content of unknown substances.

Dark-Line Spectrum. If light from an incandescent substance is passed through a hot vapor before being analyzed, it is found that the resulting spectrum is a spectrum continuous for the most part, but crossed by dark lines which constitute gaps in it, and these dark lines fall at exactly the places where bright lines would have been found had the hot vapor been analyzed alone. Such a spectrum is called an *absorption specturm* in that it appears that the hot vapor has the property of absorbing from the original light those wave lengths which are characteristic of its own chemical composition.

The solar spectrum is a striking example of this type of spectrum. It is not a continuous spectrum, as might be inferred from a casual observation. It is crossed by an extraordinarily large number of dark lines, some very fine but others quite coarse, called *Fraunhofer lines*. It has been found that for every dark line in this spectrum some chemical substance is known to exist on the earth which gives a corresponding bright line when properly analyzed. The interpretation of these lines is that the corresponding chemical substances exist in the layers of hot vapor which surround the more incandescent central regions of the sun. The element, helium, was discovered on the earth as a result of a study of the spectrum of the sun.

Band Spectra. The flame spectra of many substances, notably the rare earths, are found to be broad bands. Such spectra constitute the fourth type in the most general classifications of spectra. It has been found that band spectra result when the particles in the source are molecules, whereas line spectra are produced by vibrating atoms. Upon close examination most band spectra have been resolved into series of lines very close together.

Spectroscopy and Atomic Structure. It is through the study of spectroscopy that most of the advances have been made in connection with the present knowledge of the structure of matter, particularly the atom. Very briefly, it might be pointed out that the spectral lines form series extending throughout the electromagnetic spectrum from the X-ray region to the infrared and even beyond, and that the arrangement of the lines in these series is definitely related to the electronic structure and energy states of the atoms concerned. By the aid of the quantum theory, previously discussed, these spectroscopic facts have shed considerable light upon the electronic origin of light. In short, spectroscopy has been one of the most fruitful fields of modern research, both experimental and theoretical.

Color. Until very recently the subject of color had been studied only qualitatively. Consequently, this phase of physics is not capable of the analytical treatment so characteristic of the subject in general. Color is a sensation associated with the wave length of light. For example, red is a name given to light occupying the spectral range in the vicinity of wave lengths .00006 to .00008 cm.

Colors can be added and subtracted. Not only can white light be broken up into component colors, but all the components can be recombined to form white light.

By proper combinations, any color can be reproduced by three colors called *primary* colors. It is customary to think of red, green, and blue as the primary colors, although any three can be taken if subtractive as well as additive processes of combination are allowed.

A careful distinction has to be drawn between the color of a beam of light transmitted by a surface and the color of the light reflected by the same surface. A thin sheet of gold is yellow by reflected light, but green by transmitted light.

Color blindness is more common that is generally supposed. The accepted theory of *color vision* is that the normal eye is sensitive to three primary colors, red, green, blue, and that color blindness is the result of a lack of sensitivity for one or more of these colors. This is the Young-Helmholtz theory.

INTERFERENCE

Classical Experiments. It was shown by Young that two beams of light could be made to annul or re-enforce one another's effects, depending upon circumstances. He caused a screen containing two pinholes to be placed a short distance behind another screen containing a single pinhole in such a manner that the single pinhole was equidistant from each of the other two. Then, upon placing a monochromatic source of light in front of the single pinhole, he obtained upon a third screen placed behind the double pinhole screen an interference pattern consisting of alternate bright and dark spots. (Fig. 119.) Using vertical slits in-

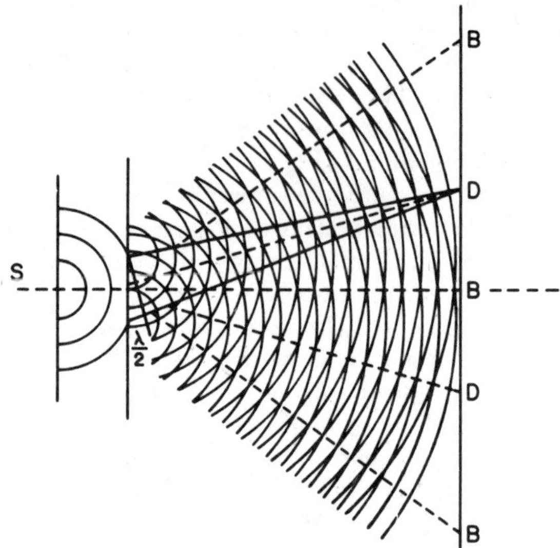

Fig. 119—Young's interference experiment

stead of pinholes the interference pattern consisted of alternate bright and dark vertical bands, or fringes. A white light source produced alternate bands, the bright ones of which were spread out into spectra. This experiment indicates the wave nature of light. By measuring the distance (BB) between two bright bands, the distance (d) between the two screens and the distance (ab) between the slits in the middle screen, the wave length of the light can be determined thus: $\lambda = \frac{(ab)\,(BB)}{d}$.

Fresnel obtained results similar to these by the use of a very small-angled biprism. A virtual image of a narrow light source is formed which acts as a second source from which light interferes with the light from the first. Lloyd accomplished the same result by the use of a single mirror very carefully arranged with respect to the source of light.

All of these experiments, and the many others by which interference effects have been since demonstrated, require a wave theory for explanation. Further conditions for complete destructive interference in accordance with wave theory are as follows.

The two sources must have the same frequency (meaning that interference can never be produced by two independent light sources, due to the heterogeneity of the electronic and molecular vibrations of light sources, but that the effects require a single source to be so modified as to produce two apparent sources from a single real source). There must be a fixed phase relation between the two sources (i.e., they must be 180° out of phase for destructive interference). For complete interference the amplitudes must be equal. Also the waves must be vibrating in the same manner (i.e., with the same polarization).

Colors of Thin Films. An interesting case of interference is encountered by the reflections of light from very thin films of semitransparent substances. So-called "irridescence" is a phenomenon of this sort. When a beam of light falls obliquely upon such a thin semitransparent film, part of it is reflected and part is transmitted to the back side of the film. At this back surface again part is reflected and part transmitted. If the film is very thin (of the order of a few wave lengths of light) the ray reflected from the second surface may be in a condition to partially interfere with the ray reflected from the front surface. Obviously the difference between the distances travelled by the two rays can be characterized by whether or not it comprises an integral number of wave lengths or half wave lengths of the light used. Knowing that destructive interference must result when these two rays are 180° out of phase, it is reasonable to suppose that the interference phenomenon depends upon the thickness of the film and the wave length of the light used.

It will be recalled from the study of reflected waves, however, that when a wave is reflected from a denser medium it undergoes a change in phase of 180°, or loses half a wave length. Optically, this corresponds to reflection from a medium of larger refractive index. Hence for destructive interference, the path difference $2t \cos \theta$ (t is the thickness of the film) between the divided portion of the light beam must be an even number of half wave lengths (not an odd number as would be expected except for the phase change due to reflection at one of the two surfaces). Therefore for *destructive interference* $2t \cos \theta = 2n \frac{\lambda}{2}$ where n is an integer 1, 2, 3, 4, etc. For *constructive interference* $2t \cos \theta =$

$(2n - 1)\frac{\lambda}{2}$. It will be noted that 2n is always an even number and (2n − 1) is always an odd number if n is 1, 2, 3, 4, 5, etc. For normal incidence, 2t cos θ becomes merely 2t.

For very thin films (.000 cm.) only certain wave lengths (colors) can be present in the reflected beams, thus accounting for the colors of thin films in white light. Also, for films of variable thickness (films of oil on water, etc.) the colors are changeable in position; i.e., the colored fringes are displaced.

When a convex lens is pressed against a plane surface a very thin air film of varying thickness is enclosed, and interference rings are produced. These are called Newton's rings and, curiously enough, it is the explanation of these Newton's rings which so urgently demands a wave theory of light, whereas Newton himself favored the corpuscular theory which he had to modify in a very artificial way to account for these rings.

A technique has been developed for coating glass surfaces with films approximately one-quarter of a wave length thick, which makes the surface invisible and eliminates glare.

The Interferometer. Obviously, the interference pattern produced by a thin transparent film makes possible the measurement of the thickness of the film in terms of the wave length of the light used. Also if the thickness is varied by moving one surface of the film, a count of the displaced interference fringes measures very accurately the actual displacement of the surface.

Michelson devised a clever arrangement of mirrors whereby a beam of light can be divided and the component beams can be so reflected as to artificially produce a film of air bounded on the one side by a silvered mirror surface and on the other side by the virtual image of another mirror. Also the thickness of this film is made variable by mounting one of the mirrors on a movable carriage. When the mirror is moved a small distance (d), a number (n) of interference fringes pass across the field of view of a telescope. Thus the displacement is measured by use of the relation $d = n\frac{\lambda}{2}$ if the wave length of the light is known. Such an instrument is known as an *interferometer,* and measurements of displacement can be made with it that are precise to a millionth part of an inch. (Fig. 120.)

Michelson devised this instrument for the purpose of measuring the velocity of the earth with respect to the ether, and his

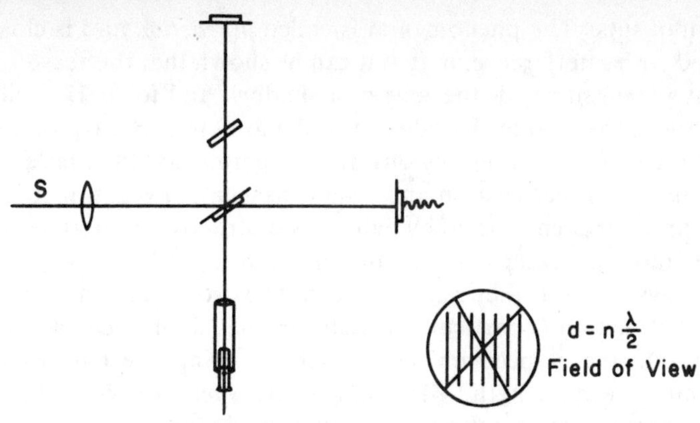

Fig. 120—Michelson interferometer

experiments led to the theory of relativity by Einstein. The experiment referred to is the classical Michelson-Morley ether-drift experiment.

Relativity. Einstein proposed that at speeds approaching the speed of light, and for masses on the atomic scale, Newtonian mechanics becomes inadequate. The laws of physics are the same in all inertial frames of reference, an inertial frame of reference being one in which Newton's laws of motion hold. The speed of light, however, is the same for all inertial frames. If it is assumed that lengths shrink and times dilate at high speeds, the Michelson-Morley observation that suggests no relative motion of the earth with respect to the luminiferous ether is explained. A consequence of this theory is that no real object can acquire a velocity greater than the velocity of light, whereupon it is necessary to postulate that the mass of a body increases with speed according to the relation $m = \frac{m_o}{\sqrt{1 - v^2/c^2}}$, where m_o is the so-called rest mass, and c is the velocity of light. This leads to the famous relation $e = m_o c^2$.

DIFFRACTION

Interference experiments and careful investigations on the nature of shadows show that light is bent around edges to a small but appreciable extent. Particularly conspicuous are these effects when light is passed through a narrow slit or a multiple arrangement of slits. The phenomenon is called *diffraction* and is closely allied with interference, in that it can be shown that the reason for light appearing inside the edge of a shadow, and for dark regions existing just outside the edge of a shadow, is that rays of light coming from adjoining regions of an illuminated slit interfere to produce both destruction and re-enforcement. In fact, if it were not for interference whereby light rays destructively interfere with one another, except in certain directions, nothing like sharp shadows, fuzzy as they really are, could be produced at all.

Diffraction is particularly useful in that it provides a means of producing a spectrum, because the bending effect is proportional to wave length. The *diffraction spectroscope* utilizes a transmission or a reflection grating made by ruling lines on optical surfaces (up to 30,000 or so per inch). When a beam of white light is passed normally through such a ruled grating, on either side of the transmitted beam a number of orders of the spectrum are observed, falling off rapidly in intensity the farther away they are from the central beam. Violet light is *diffracted less* than red light whereas violet light is *refracted more* than red light.

The law of the diffraction grating is $\sin \theta = \frac{n\lambda}{d}$ where n is the order of the spectrum and d is the grating space. The relative advantage of the grating spectroscope over the prism spectroscope is that the spectrum produced by the former is normal; i.e., if the incident angle is normal, the deviation is strictly proportional to wave length. This is not so for a prism, but the prism instrument has the advantage of wasting much less light.

Diffraction limits the resolving power of telescopes and microscopes. Due to the fact that light waves provide the means of "seeing," the impossibility of "seeing" things of dimensions smaller than optical wave lengths is obvious. Thus it is futile to attempt unlimited magnification with a microscope, because a definite limit is attained when diffraction rings appear around every point of an image. A magnification of greater than approximately one thousand times is a practical impossibility for an instrument to be used by the human eye. (A magnification of 375 times is considered a normal limit to the magnifying power of a microscope.)

POLARIZATION AND DOUBLE REFRACTION

When a wave results from a source vibrating in a particular

manner such as in a plane, circularly, or elliptically, the wave is said to be plane, circularly, or elliptically *polarized.* Light waves can be polarized in a number of ways, proving that light is a *transverse* wave phenomenon.

Polarizer and Analyzer. When light is passed through a tourmaline crystal it is plane polarized in such a way that it will not pass through a second crystal unless the latter is oriented in the same manner as the first one. The first tourmaline is called the *polarizer* and the second the *analyzer.*

Brewster's Law. The reflected and refracted components of a beam of light incident upon a transparent substance are partially polarized. When the incident angle made with the normal to a glass plate is approximately 57° the reflected component is practically completely polarized. This is the angle whose tangent is the refractive index of the glass used; and according to *Brewster's law* $\tan i = n$ corresponding to complete polarization by reflection.

Double Refraction. Some transparent substances are optically anisotropic in that they propagate light with different velocities in different directions. Calcite (Iceland spar) is one such substance which displays double refraction. An incident beam of light is split into two refracted beams for which there are different values of the refractive index. One ray is called the *ordinary ray,* in that it follows the laws of ordinary refraction, and the other is called the *extraordinary ray.* Each is polarized differently. The *Nicol prism* is frequently used to produce polarized light. (Fig. 121.) It is a crystal of calcite which has been cut in a definite manner with respect to the optic axis and cemented together again by a film of Canada balsam which has a refractive index lying between the two values for calcite. By this arrangement the ordinary ray is totally internally reflected out of the way so that only the extraordinary ray, which is, of course, polarized, is transmitted.

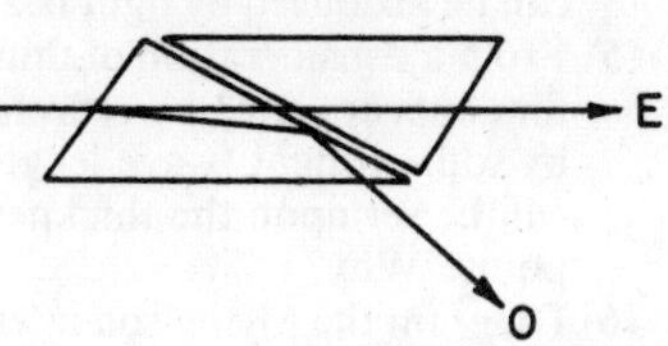

Fig. 121—Nicol prism for producing polarized light

Polarizing Material. Today a polarizing material is available that can be purchased readily. It polarizes by transmission and can be had in sheets of almost any desired size. Whereas, formerly, a beam of polarized light of more than a few centimeters in diameter could not be had at any price, it is now possible to obtain beams many times this size at a very modest cost.

Saccharimetry. Certain substances, notably sugar solutions, have the property of rotating the plane of plane polarized light. This property is utilized in the *saccharimeter* to determine the quality of sugar.

Photoelasticity. Many transparent substances, including glass, which are optically isotropic and singly refracting when free from strain, become strongly doubly refracting when subjected to stresses and strains. Under strain the double refraction produces highly colored interference patterns which have been utilized in a practical way to determine the existence of local strains in transparent substances. Models of machines are frequently constructed of glass or celluloid, and studied under strain in polarized light to help the machine designer to avoid disastrous results in the machine itself. Thus the practical machinist finds it worth while to know something about certain aspects of physics that only a short time ago were considered merely abstract and "theoretical." Who knows which of today's abstractions will become tomorrow's applications?

Review Questions

(1) Describe the action of a prism spectroscope that utilizes a vertical slit.
(2) What simple laws govern the elementary nature of spectrum lines?
(3) What are Fraunhofer lines?
(4) Describe the conditions under which destructive interference effects can be produced by light beams.
(5) From a consideration of thin films it is known that a shrinking soap film appears dark by reflected light just as it bursts. If it is viewed by sodium light (wave length .00005893 cm.), what maximum limit can be set upon the thickness of the film as it reaches the breaking point? Why?
(6) Diagram the Michelson interferometer and suggest how a short displacement can be accurately measured to within a millionth of an inch.
(7) What are the points of comparison between a prism spectroscope and a grating spectroscope?
(8) What limits the magnifying power of a microscope?
(9) How can the purity of sugar be tested?
(10) What is photoelasticity?

Appendixes

Appendix I: Glossary of Terms and Definitions

PART I. MECHANICS

Length is the distance between two points. It is a fundamental concept.

Mass is a measure of inertia. It is a fundamental concept.

Time is a measure of duration. It is a fundamental concept.

Force is a push or pull which tends to produce a change of motion. See Momentum.

Work is the product of force times the distance through which the point of application is moved in the direction in which the force acts. It is measured in foot-pounds or dyne-cms or newton-meters.

Power is the time-rate at which work is done. One horsepower is 550 foot-pounds per second.

Energy is the capacity to do work. Energy due to position is called **Potential energy.** Energy due to motion is called **Kinetic energy.**

Weight is the name given to the force of gravity on a body.

Coefficient of friction is the ratio between the tangential frictional force between two contact surfaces and the perpendicular force pressing them together. This coefficient is called static if the surfaces are not moving with respect to each other and kinetic if the surfaces are in relative motion.

Vector quantity is a quantity which requires direction and magnitude for its complete specification. A non-vector is a scalar quantity.

Component of a vector in a given direction is the projection of the vector in that direction. It is determined by drawing a line in the specified direction through the base of the vector and then dropping a perpendicular from the head of the vector to this line.

Rectangular components are perpendicular vector components such as those taken in the conventional x and y mathematical directions.

Concurrent forces are forces whose lines of action intersect at a point.

Coplanar forces are forces which lie in one plane.

Torque is defined as the product of a force times its **Lever arm,** the latter being the perpendicular distance from the axis, about which the force acts, to the line of action of the force.

Couple. Two equal and opposite parallel forces separated by a distance (l) constitute a couple. The product of the magnitude (f) of either force multiplied by the distance (l) is called the **Moment of the couple.**

Center of gravity of a body is that point through which the force of gravity can be considered to act upon the whole body.

Displacement is a vector quantity which indicates a change of position. It is not to be confused with the distance travelled.

Velocity is the time-rate of change of position; i.e., it is the rate of displacement. It may be constant or variable. If constant, it coincides with **Average velocity,** which is the ratio of the total displacement divided by the total time elapsed. **Instantaneous velocity** is the ratio of displacement to time for an infinitesimal interval of time. Velocity is a vector quantity.

Speed is the magnitude of a velocity.

Acceleration is the time-rate of change of velocity. It is a vector quantity.

Slug is the unit of mass in the British Engineering System of units. It is the amount of mass to which one pound of force will give an acceleration of one foot per second per second.

Dyne is the unit of force in the metric absolute system of units. It is the amount of force which will give one gram of mass an acceleration of one centimeter per second per second.

Newton is the force which will give one kilogram an acceleration of one meter per second per second.

Centripetal force is that force which gives the necessary central acceleration to a body rotating in a circular path with constant speed.

Centrifugal force is the reaction to a centripetal force.

Momentum is the product of mass times velocity. Force is the time-rate of change of momentum.

Impulse of a force is the product of a force by the time during which it acts. It is proportional to the time-rate of change of momentum.

Center of mass of a body is that point where all the mass of the body can be considered to be concentrated for purposes of translation.

Erg is a unit of energy equal to one dyne-cm.

Joule is a unit of energy equal to 10^7 ergs or one newton-meter.

A Machine is a device for transmitting and multiplying forces.

Mechanical advantage is the ratio of the force exerted by a machine to the force applied to the machine.

Efficiency of a machine is the ratio of the mechanical work done by the machine to the work done on the machine, the two quantities differing by the amount of work done in overcoming friction.

Angular displacement is a vector quantity which indicates a change of angular position. It is analogous to linear displacement.

Angular velocity is the time-rate of change of angular position. It is analogous to linear velocity and may be constant or variable.

Angular acceleration is the time-rate of change of angular velocity. It is analogous to linear acceleration.

Moment of inertia of a body is the sum of the products of every mass particle of a body multiplied by the square of its respective distance from the axis of rotation. It is also that property of a body by virtue of which its angular acceleration is proportional to the net torque acting upon it. It is analogous to mass, which is also defined as that property of a body by virtue of which its linear acceleration is proportional to the net force acting upon it.

Radius of gyration is that distance from the axis of rotation at which all the mass of a body can be considered concentrated for purposes of rotation. It is also the square root of the ratio of the moment of inertia divided by the mass, with respect to a given axis of rotation.

Angular momentum is the product of the moment of inertia of a body about a given axis times the angular velocity about the same axis.

Simple harmonic motion is a vibratory to-and-fro linear motion about an equilibrium position such that the acceleration is always proportional to the displacement from the equilibrium position and directed towards it. It is often referred to as the projection of uniform curvilinear motion upon a diameter of the circle of reference.

Frequency of S.H.M. is the number of vibrations per second.

Period of S.H.M. is the time required for one vibration.

Coefficient of stiffness is the proportionality factor by virtue of which the force which produces simple harmonic motion is proportional to the displacement.

Coefficient of torsional stiffness is the proportionality factor by virtue of which the torque which produces a rotary harmonic motion is proportional to the angular displacement.

Center of percussion of an oscillating body is the point at which the body may be struck without jar.

PART II. PROPERTIES OF MATTER AND SOUND

Strain is the fractional deformation that results when a body is deformed.

Stress is the restoring force per unit area of surface upon which it acts that is developed when a substance is strained.

Young's modulus is the ratio of stress to strain for a simple stretch or a longitudinal compression.

Bulk modulus is the ratio of stress to strain for the case of hydrostatic compression. It is the ratio of pressure to the fractional change in volume.

Shear modulus or the **Coefficient of rigidity** is the ratio of stress to strain for the case of a shear or a twist. It is the shearing stress divided by the fractional shear.

Density is mass per unit volume. It should not be confused with the concept of weight per unit volume, which is sometimes called weight density.

Specific gravity of a substance is the ratio of the density of the substance to the density of water.

Fluid pressure is the perpendicular force per unit area which a fluid exerts against a surface with which it is in contact.

Coefficient of surface tension is the magnitude of the perpendicular force per unit length which a surface exerts upon an adjacent surface.

Cohesive forces are molecular forces between similar substances or between parts of the same substance.

Adhesive forces are molecular forces between different substances.

Steady flow is that type of fluid motion such that the velocity of the fluid has a fixed magnitude and direction at every point; i.e., the velocity may differ from point to point within the fluid, but it does not change at a given point as time elapses.

Streamlines are the paths followed by moving particles of a fluid when the flow is steady.

Coefficient of viscosity of a fluid is the ratio of the tangential stress to the velocity gradient.

Wave motion is the propagation of deformation through a deformable medium or any motion which obeys the "wave equation."

Transverse waves are waves such that the vibration of the particles of the medium in which the waves travel is perpendicular to the direction of propagation.

Longitudinal waves are characterized by the fact that for such waves the vibrations of the medium take place along the direction of propagation.

Amplitude of a wave motion is the maximum displacement of the particles of the medium from the equilibrium position.

Wave length is the distance between two successive corresponding points on a wave.

Period of a wave motion is the time required for a complete wave to pass a given point. It is also the time required for one complete vibration of the medium.

Refraction of a wave is the change of velocity of the wave which results from the passage of a wave from one medium to another medium having different elastic properties.

Sound is a longitudinal wave phenomenon which may be capable of exciting the auditory nerve.

Pitch of a sound is measured by the number of vibrations per second.

Loudness of a sound depends upon the amplitude of the disturbance.

Quality of a sound is determined by the number of overtones present.

PART III. HEAT

Temperature is qualitatively that property which determines the direction of heat flow from one body to another in contact with it. Quantitatively, the temperature of a body is defined as the average kinetic energy of translation for molecules of its random molecular motion.

Brownian movement is the random agitation of particles of matter of molecular magnitude.

Linear coefficient of thermal expansion is the fractional change in length of a body per degree change in temperature.

Volume coefficient of thermal expansion is the fractional change in volume of a body per degree change in temperature.

Absolute zero is that temperature at which all molecular motion ceases. It is approximately 273 centigrade degrees below the freezing point of water.

Calorie, sometimes called the gram-calorie, is the amount of heat required to raise the temperature of one gram of water one degree centigrade. For refined work the water is specified to be initially at 15°C.

Large calorie is one thousand calories.

British thermal unit is the amount of heat required to raise the temperature of one pound of water one degree Fahrenheit.

Thermal capacity of a substance is the amount of heat required to raise by one unit the temperature of unit mass of the substance.

Thermal (or heat) capacity of a body is the amount of heat required to raise the temperature of the body one degree.

Water equivalent of a body is the same as Heat capacity of a body.

Specific heat of a substance is the ratio of the thermal (or heat) capacity of the substance to the thermal (or heat) capacity of water. It is numerically equal to the thermal capacity of the substance, and the distinction between the two concepts is often overlooked.

Heat of combustion of a substance is the amount of heat liberated when unit mass of the substance is completely burned.

Heat of vaporization of a substance is the amount of heat required to change unit mass of the substance in liquid form at a given temperature into vapor without changing the temperature. For water at 100°C. it is approximately 536 calories per gram.

Boiling point of a substance is defined as that temperature at which the saturated vapor pressure of the substance equals the atmospheric pressure upon its free surface. It is also that temperature at which for a given pressure the substance can exist either as a liquid or as a gas.

Critical temperature is that temperature above which pressure alone will not liquefy a gas.

Critical pressure is that pressure which corresponds to the critical temperature.

Heat of fusion of a substance is the amount of heat which must be withdrawn from unit mass of a substance in liquid form at a given temperature to change it into a solid without changing its temperature. For water it is approximately 80 cal./gram at 0°C.

Crystalline substances have definite melting points.

Amorphous substances do not have definite melting points.

Sublimation is the name applied to the direct change from the solid state to the gaseous state or vice versa.

Triple point is that pressure-temperature combination for which the solid, liquid, and gaseous states of a substance exist in equilibrium.

Absolute humidity is the mass of water vapor contained in unit volume of air.

Relative humidity is the ratio of the actual mass of water vapor present in unit volume of air to the mass that would produce saturation at that temperature.

Dew point is that temperature at which the relative humidity would correspond to 100% or saturation.

Ideal black body is a perfect absorber, and consequently a perfect radiator, of heat.

Isothermal process is a process in which temperature is maintained constant. It usually involves the addition or subtraction of heat.

Adiabatic process is a process during which no heat is allowed to enter or escape.

Reversible process is a process which can be made to take place in the opposite sense by an infinitesimal reversal in the conditions.

Entropy is a mathematical quantity which measures thermodynamic degeneration.

PART IV. ELECTRICITY AND MAGNETISM

Electrostatic unit of charge is defined as that amount of charge which will repel an exactly similar amount of like sign with a force of one dyne when the two are placed one centimeter apart in vacuum. It is often called a **Stat-coulomb.**

Electric field intensity at a certain place is the force per unit positive charge that would act upon a charge if it were placed there.

Electric lines of force are lines drawn to represent electric field intensity. Each line is the path that would be taken by a free unit positive charge. It is customary to draw one line per square centimeter of surface perpendicular to the direction of the field for each unit of field intensity.

Surface density of charge is the amount of charge located on a unit of surface area.

Electric induction is the separation of the positive from the negative charges in an uncharged conductor under the influence of an electric field.

Electrical potential at a point is the amount of work necessary to bring a unit positive charge from an infinite distance away (completely outside the field) up to the point in question.

Difference in potential between two points, A and B, is the amount of work per unit positive charge which must be done on a charge in moving it from position A to position B.

Electrical capacitance of a conductor is the ratio of the charge on the conductor to its potential. It is consequently the amount of charge necessary to increase the potential of a conductor by unit amount. It is *not* the total amount of charge which the conductor can hold.

Electrical condenser or **capacitor** is a device consisting of two conductors separated by a dielectric, by virtue of which capacitance is acquired.

Specific inductive capacitance of a substance is the ratio of the capacitance of a capacitor containing the substance as the dielectric to the capacitance of a similar capacitor having vacuum for the dielectric.

Dielectric constant of a substance is the reciprocal of the proportionality constant by virtue of which the attractive (or repulsive) force between two point charges located in the substance is proportional to the product of the two charges and inversely proportional to the square of the distance between them. By definition, it is unity for vacuum. It is also numerically equal to the specific inductive capacitance for a substance.

Intensity of electric current is the time-rate of flow of electric charge.

Electromotive force refers to the setting up of potential difference and is defined as the work required to drive a unit of electric charge completely around a closed circuit.

Anode is the electrode at which the conventional current enters an electrolyte.

Cathode is the electrode at which the conventional current leaves the electrolyte.

Electrochemical equivalent is the proportionality factor by which the mass of substance deposited on the cathode of a cell is proportional to the amount of charge transferred. It is also the ratio of the atomic weight of a substance divided by the product of the valence times 96,540.

Faraday is the quantity of electricity which will liberate one gram-equivalent of a substance. It is equal to 96,540 coulombs.

Resistance is the proportionality factor by virtue of which the rate of dissipation of energy (power) in heat is proportional to the square of the current. It is also the ratio of the electromotive force of a circuit to the steady current which it will maintain through the whole circuit.

Resistivity or **specific resistance** of a substance is the resistance of that portion of the substance having unit length and unit cross section.

Conductivity is the reciprocal of resistivity.

Circular mil is a unit of area. It is the unit in which the cross section of a circular wire is given if the diameter of the wire in mils (thousandths of an inch) is squared.

Temperature coefficient of resistance is the fractional change in resistance per degree change in temperature.

Seebeck effect is the effect by which an electromotive force is developed in a circuit consisting of dissimilar metals whose junction points are maintained at different temperatures.

Peltier effect is the effect by which a temperature difference is established between the junctions of a circuit consisting of dissimilar metals when a current is passed through the circuit.

Magnetic field is the region surrounding a magnet and in which magnetic forces act.

Unit magnetic pole is a pole which repels an exactly similar pole with a force of one dyne when it is separated from it in vacuum by a distance of one centimeter.

Magnetic field intensity at a point is the force per unit north pole that would act upon a magnetic pole if it were placed there.

Magnetic induction is a vector quantity which describes the magnetic field at a given point. It is the same as **Magnetic flux density.**

Magnetic moment of a bar magnet of length l and pole strength m is equal to the product ml.

Magnetic line of force is the path that would be taken by a free unit north pole. See Electric lines of force (p. 190).

Angle of declination is the angle between the magnetic meridian and the geographic meridian.

Angle of dip is that angle measured below the horizon which is made by a compass needle suspended freely in a vertical plane.

Magnetic permeability is the ratio of the magnetic induction to the magnetic field intensity.

Paramagnetic substance is one whose permeability is greater than unity. It is a substance which has the property of concentrating lines of flux.

Diamagnetic substance is one whose permeability is less than unity. It is a substance which has the property of dispersing lines of flux.

Magnetic susceptibility is a measure of the ease with which a substance is magnetized.

Absolute ampere (Electromagnetic absolute unit of current) is that intensity of current which will produce at the center of a circular conductor of one centimeter radius a magnetic field of strength 2π oersteds. It is also that unvarying current which, if present in each of two parallel conductors of infinite length and one meter apart in vacuum, causes each conductor to experience a force of 2×10^{-7} newton per meter of length.

International ampere (Legal unit of current) is that intensity of steady current which will deposit silver from a standard electrolytic cell at the rate of 0.001118 grams per second.

International ohm (Legal unit of resistance) is defined as the resistance offered to a steady current by a column of pure mercury 106.300 cm. long of constant cross section, of mass 14.4521 grams, at the temperature of melting ice.

International volt (Legal unit of potential) is that steady potential difference which will result in the flow of one international ampere through a resistance of one international ohm.

Absolute volt (Electromagnetic absolute unit of electromotive force) is that electromotive force induced when a conductor one centimeter long is moved perpendicularly across a uniform magnetic field of unit intensity (1 gauss) with a velocity of one centimeter per second.

Coefficient of self-inductance is the proportionality factor by which the induced electromotive force in a circuit is proportional to the time-rate of change of the current in the same circuit.

Coefficient of mutual inductance is the proportionality factor by which the electromotive force induced in a circuit is proportional to the time-rate of change of the current in a neighboring circuit.

Alternating current is a current that varies sinusoidally with time.

Impedance of a circuit is the factor by which the meter value of electromotive force is proportional to the meter value of the current for the circuit. For steady currents the impedance of a circuit is merely its resistance, but for alternating currents the impedance is the square root of the resistance squared plus the reactance squared.

Reactance of a circuit is a factor related to the inductance, the capacitance, and the frequency of the circuit. Inductive reactance is given by the relation $X_c = 2\pi\, nL$ where L is the inductance. Capacitive reactance is given by the relation $X_c = \dfrac{1}{2\pi nC}$ where C is the capacitance.

Power factor of an alternating current circuit is the factor by which the average power is proportional to the product of the meter value of the current and the meter value of the voltage. It is also equal to the cosine of the phase-lag angle.

Phase-lag angle is that fractional part of a complete oscillation by which an alternating current lags behind the alternating electromotive force which produces it. This lag is usually expressed in angular measure such that a complete oscillation is designated by 360 degrees.

Positive column is the name given to the positive end of an electrical discharge in a partially exhausted tube. It is characterized for a given gas in the tube by its color, its length, and the nature of its striations.

Negative glow is that violet glow around the negative electrode (cathode) of a discharge tube which appears shortly after the process of exhaustion is commenced.

Faraday dark space is the dark region in the discharge lying between the positive column and the negative glow.

Crookes' dark space is the dark region which appears in a discharge tube between the negative glow and the cathode when the exhaustion has reached a very high stage. It increases in size as the exhaustion is carried on until it completely fills the discharge tube when the pressure is reduced to the order of a thousandth of a millimeter of mercury.

Cathode rays are streams of negative electrons emitted from the cathode of a partially exhausted discharge tube.

Positrons are positively charged electrons.

Protons are positively charged particles which in part make up the nuclei of atoms. A proton is an ionized hydrogen atom.

X rays are radiations given off by matter when bombarded by cathode rays.

Photoelectric effect is the effect by virtue of which electrons are drawn out of a surface by the action of light.

Alpha particles are doubly ionized helium atoms, or helium nuclei.

Beta rays are streams of electrons.

Gamma rays are high frequency rays like X rays.

Positive rays are rays of positive ions emitted by the anode in discharge tubes.

Isotopes are substances which have the same atomic number but different mass numbers.

Atomic number Z is the number of protons in a nucleus. It therefore indicates the number of positive charges.

Mass number A is the nearest whole number to the atomic weight of a substance.

Heisenburg uncertainty principle states that the uncertainty in the measurement of the position of the electron multiplied by the uncertainty in the measurement of its momentum is approximately equal to Planck's constant h.

Cosmic rays are streams of protons penetrating the earth's atmosphere from outer space.

Neutron is a nuclear particle having the same mass as the proton but carrying no electrical charge.

Mesons are nuclear particles having masses ranging from several times to hundreds of times greater than the mass of the electron. They can have negative or positive charge.

Nuclear fission is the splitting of the nucleus of an atom with the release of radiation.

Nuclear fusion is the combining of nuclear components to form more massive nuclei with the release of radiation.

Pauli exclusion principle limits the number of electrons that can be in a given energy level of an atom.

Zero point energy is the amount of vibrational energy allowed by quantum mechanics to be associated with atomic particles at 0°K., whereas classical mechanics requires this to be zero.

Phonon is a bundle of vibrational waves, suggestive of the photon of electromagnetic radiation.

Donor impurity of a semiconductor is a material which provides additional electrons.

Acceptor impurity of a semiconductor is a material which produces an electron deficiency or a hole.

Transistor is a semiconductor device which behaves in much the manner of the vacuum tube in electronic circuits.

PART V. LIGHT

Photon is a corpuscle of light. At present it is thought to have a wave structure. It is a bundle of electromagnetic waves.

Candle power is a unit of intensity of a light source. It is usually defined as the intensity of a certain standard candle but recently it has become customary to define it as the intensity of a source which emits one lumen of light in one ster-radian.

Lumen is a unit of light flux. It is the amount of light which a source of one candle power emits in one ster-radian. It is a power unit, being the amount of light of wave length 0.0000555 cm. emitted by the dissipation rate of 0.00161 watts at maximum efficiency.

Ster-radian is a unit of solid angle. All space about a point is measured by 4π ster-radians.

Lambert is a unit of luminance, which is the amount of light per unit area emitted by an extended source. The lambert is one lumen per square centimeter. (One candle per square centimeter equals π lamberts.)

Illuminance is the amount of light per unit area incident upon a surface.

Foot-candle is a unit of illuminance equal to one lumen per square foot. It is the amount of light incident upon one square foot of spherical surface, whose radius of curvature is one foot, if a source of one candle is placed at the center of curvature.

Index of refraction of a substance with respect to light waves is the ratio of the velocity of light in vacuum to its velocity in the substance.

Critical angle of incidence is that angle of incidence when light passes from a denser toward an optically rarer medium such that all rays exceeding this angle are reflected back into the medium instead of being refracted out of it.

Focal length of a converging lens or a concave mirror is that distance from the lens or mirror to the point at which light originally parallel to the principal axis converges. Focal length of a diverging lens or a convex mirror is that distance behind the lens or mirror from which light originally parallel to the principal axis appears to diverge.

Real image is an image formed by the convergence of light rays in space. It is always inverted and can be localized upon a screen.

Virtual image is an image formed by the apparent convergence of rays or their extensions behind a lens or mirror. It is always erect.

Axial spherical abberation is that characteristic of a truly spherical surface by virtue of which axial rays passing through different parts of the surface do not come to a point focus.

Chromatic abberation is that characteristic of a lens by virtue of which rays of different colors are focussed at different points.

Diopter is a unit of lens power. The power is expressed in diopters by computing the reciprocal of the focal length in meters.

Myopia is the technical term for nearsightedness. Images are formed short of the retina.

Hypermetropia is farsightedness. Images are formed behind the retina.

Accommodation of the eye is that property of dilation and contraction of the lens muscles such that distant and near objects can be focussed consecutively.

Dispersion is the spreading of light out into its component colors, i.e., its spectrum.

Continuous spectra are formed by incandescent sources.

Bright-line spectra are formed by sources in a hot vapor or gaseous state.

Absorption (dark-line) spectra are formed when the light from an incandescent source passes through a hot vapor before being analyzed by the spectroscope.

Fraunhofer lines are the dark absorption lines in the solar spectrum.

Diffraction of light is that phenomenon in which light rays are bent as they pass around edges due to interference effects.

Polarization of light is accomplished by any agent capable of restricting the waves to special modes.

Saccharimetry is a manner of analyzing sugar solutions by means of polarized light.

Appendix II: Laws and Principles

Vector quantities. Vector quantities can be added by the parallelogram rule, i.e., the resultant of two vectors is given in magnitude and direction by the diagonal of a parallelogram of which the two vectors are adjacent sides.

Conservation of energy. Energy may be transformed but in no process, except perhaps in the realm of subatomic phenomena, can energy be created or destroyed.

Conditions of equilibrium. For a body to be in equilibrium:

(1) The vector sum of all forces acting upon the body must be equal to zero, i.e., $\Sigma F_x = 0$; $\Sigma F_y = 0$; $\Sigma F_z = 0$.

(2) The sum of all torques acting about any axis perpendicular to the plane in which the forces act must be equal to zero, i.e., $\Sigma L = 0$.

Newton's laws of motion.

(1) A body at rest or moving with uniform velocity continues so to move forever unless a force acts upon it.

(2) If a resultant force is applied to a body, the body acquires an acceleration in the direction in which the force acts and proportional in magnitude to it.

(3) To every force there is an equal and opposite reaction-force.

Conservation of momentum. In an isolated system the total momentum after a collision equals the total momentum before the collision.

Work-energy theorem. When the motion of a body is changed the gain in kinetic energy equals the work done on the body.

Kepler's laws of planetary motion.

(1) The planets move in ellipses, which are very nearly circular, with the sun at one focus.

(2) The radius vector from the sun to a planet sweeps out equal areas in equal times.

(3) The squares of the periods of revolution of the planets are proportional to the cubes of their greatest distances from the sun.

Newton's law of gravitation. Every mass particle in the universe attracts every other mass particle by a force proportional to the product of their masses and inversely as the square of their distance apart.

Hooke's law. Within the elastic limit, the ratio of stress to strain is constant.

Pascal's law of the transmissibility of pressure. Changes in pressure are transmitted equally throughout a liquid at a given level.

Archimedes' principle. A body wholly or partially immersed in a fluid is buoyed up by a force equal to the weight of the fluid displaced by it.

Boyle's law. If the temperature of a given mass of gas is maintained constant, an increase in pressure produces a decrease in volume such that the product of the pressure times volume is approximately constant.

Law of continuity. For the steady flow of an ideal incompressible fluid the discharge rate is constant; i.e., the product of the velocity of flow times the area of cross section is constant.

Bernoulli's principle. For the steady flow of an ideal frictionless incompressible fluid through a pipe of variable cross section, the total energy of unit volume of the fluid is constant, i.e., $\frac{1}{2} dv_1^2 + dgh_1 + p_1 = \frac{1}{2} dv_2^2 + dgh_2 + p_2$.

Doppler's principle. If there is a relative approach of a source of waves and an observer, the waves undergo an increase in frequency; and conversely, if there is relative recession of source and observer, the waves undergo a decrease in frequency.

$$n' = n \frac{v \pm v_o}{v \mp v_s}.$$

General gas laws. For a given mass of a given kind of gas the pressure multiplied by the volume and divided by the absolute temperature is a constant.

Dalton's law of partial pressures. In a confined mixture of liquids and their vapors, each vapor develops its own vapor-pressure independently of the others, such that the total pressure is equal to the sum of the pressures which each vapor would develop if it were alone.

Stefan's law of radiation. The rate at which energy is radiated from a hot body is proportional to the fourth power of the body's absolute temperature.

Wien's displacement law. If the energy in the radiation spectrum is plotted as a function of wave length for different temperatures, the product of the absolute temperature by the wave length corresponding to maximum energy is always constant.

First and second laws of thermodynamics.

(1) Mechanical energy is completely convertible into heat energy to the extent that 4.18 joules are equivalent to one calorie.

(2) Heat cannot pass directly from a cold body to a hot body of its own accord.

Coulomb's law of electric force. Like charges always repel and unlike charges always attract one another. The magnitude of the attractive or repulsive force between two point charges varies as the product of the charges and inversely as the square of the distance between them in a given medium, i.e.,

$$F = \frac{qq'}{Kr^2}.$$

Faraday's laws of electrolysis.

(1) For steady current the mass of a substance deposited at the cathode is proportional to the amount of electric charge carried; i.e., it is proportional to the intensity of the current multiplied by the time during which it flows.

(2) The proportionality factor in the above is called the electrochemical equivalent, and for a given substance it is equal to the ratio of the atomic weight of the substance to the product of the valence multiplied by 96,540.

Joule's law. When an electric current is established in a conductor heat is developed at a rate that is proportional to the square of the intensity of the current. The proportionality factor is known as resistance.

Ohm's law.

(1) For a portion of a circuit: The steady current through any portion of an electric circuit equals the potential difference across that portion of the circuit divided by the resistance of that portion of the circuit.

(2) For a complete circuit: The steady current through a complete electric circuit equals the electromotive force of the circuit divided by the over-all resistance of the circuit.

Kirchhoff's rules for steady current in an electric circuit.

(1) In any closed loop of a circuit the algebraic sum of all electromotive forces equals the algebraic sum of all potential drops, i.e., $\Sigma E = \Sigma IR$.

(2) At any branch point the sum of all currents entering the point must equal the sum of all currents leaving the point, i.e., $\Sigma I = 0$.

Coulomb's law of magnetic force. Like magnetic poles always repel and unlike magnetic poles always attract one another. The magnitude of the attractive or the repulsive force between two point-poles varies as the product of the pole strengths and inversely as the square of the distance between them in a given medium, i.e., $F = \dfrac{m m'}{\mu R^2}$.

Ampere-La Place rule: Law of Biot and Savart. When a steady electric current is passed through a conductor a magnetic field is established around the conductor in such a direction as would be indicated by the fingers of the right hand if the right hand were to grasp the conductor with the thumb pointing in the direction of the current. The magnitude of the field at a given point is proportional to the intensity of the current, the length of the conductor, and the position of the point, and inversely proportional to the square of the distance from the point to that segment of the current being considered.

Side thrust law. When a current-carrying conductor finds itself in a magnetic field, it experiences a side thrust due to the interaction of its own magnetic field and the field in which it finds itself.

Lenz's law of induced current. Whenever the intensity of a magnetic field is being changed an electromotive force is induced in any neighboring electric circuit. The current thereby induced in a closed circuit is always in such a direction as to oppose by its electromagnetic action the magnetic change responsible for the induction.

Huygens' principle. Every point on a wave front acts as a source of wavelets, the tangent to and envelope of which constitutes a new wave front.

Law of regular reflection. When a light ray is reflected regularly from a surface the angle of reflection (measured with respect to the normal to the surface) equals the angle of incidence (also measured with respect to the normal). The incident ray, the normal, and the reflected ray all lie in the same plane.

Snell's law of refraction. When a light ray strikes a surface making an angle i with its normal, the refracted ray lies in the same plane with the incident ray and the normal ray and makes an angle r′ with the normal in accordance with the relation: $n_1 \sin i = n_2 \sin r'$ where n_1 is the refractive index of the medium in which the ray originates, and n_2 is the refractive index of the medium into which the ray passes.

Inverse square law of illumination. The illumination of a surface by a point source of light varies with the intensity of the source and inversely as the square of the perpendicular distance from the source to the surface.

Ray method of locating images formed by spherical mirrors and thin lenses. Images formed by spherical mirrors and thin lenses can be located by tracing two rays from a point in the object by virtue of the following: Rays parallel to the principal axis of a spherical mirror, a converging lens, or a diverging lens are reflected through, refracted through, or diverged respectively from the principal focus. Furthermore all rays passing through the center of curvature of a mirror or through the actual center of a thin lens are undeviated. Wherever two rays emanating from the same point of an object later intersect, the intersection indicates an image of the given point.

Elementary laws of spectroscopy.

(1) Incandescent sources yield continuous spectra.

(2) Hot vapors or hot gaseous sources yield spectra consisting of discrete bright lines.

(3) If light from an incandescent source is passed through a hot vapor before being analyzed, the resulting spectrum is continuous for the most part but is crossed by dark discrete lines forming an absorption spectrum characteristic of the substance of which the hot vapor is composed.

(4) Many spectra are band spectra; i.e., they consist of series of bright lines very close together. Spectra of molecular origin are band spectra, whereas spectra of atomic origin are line spectra.

Brewster's law for polarized light. When a ray of light in air is reflected from a surface, such as glass, the reflected component is completely plane polarized if the tangent of the incident angle equals the refractive index of the substance of which the surface is composed. This angle is approximately 57° for glass in air.

Appendix III: Table of Analogies Between Translatory and Rotary Motion

Translatory	Rotary
Linear displacements	Angular displacement ϕ
Average velocity $\bar{v} = \frac{s}{t}$	Average angular velocity $\omega = \frac{\phi}{t}$; $(\bar{v} = r\omega)$
Acceleration $a = \frac{v - v_0}{t}$	Angular acceleration $\alpha = \frac{\omega - \omega_0}{t}$; $(a = r\alpha)$
For uniformly accelerated linear motion: $v = at + v_0$; $s = \frac{1}{2}at^2 + v_0 t$; $v^2 = 2as + v_0^2$	For uniformly accelerated angular motion: $\omega = \alpha t + \omega_0$; $\phi = \frac{1}{2}\alpha t^2 + \omega_0 t$; $\omega^2 = 2\alpha\phi + \omega_0^2$
For linear motion: net force (F) = ma	For angular motion: net torque (L) = $I\alpha$
Linear momentum (mv)	Angular momentum ($I\omega$)
Linear kinetic energy ($\frac{1}{2}mv^2$)	Rotary kinetic energy ($\frac{1}{2}I\omega^2$)
Simple harmonic motion: $F = -kx$	Rotary harmonic motion: $L = -k'\phi$

$$n = \frac{1}{2\pi}\sqrt{\frac{k}{m}} = \frac{1}{T} = \frac{1}{2\pi}\sqrt{-\frac{a}{x}};\ n' = \frac{1}{2\pi}\sqrt{\frac{k'}{I}} = \frac{1}{T'} = \frac{1}{2\pi}\sqrt{-\frac{\alpha}{\phi}}$$

Appendix IV: Supplementary Questions and Problems

CHAPTER 1—INTRODUCTION

Problems

(1) How many centimeters are there in one foot?

(2) Express 1000 grams in pounds.

(3) An elevator weighing one ton is hoisted up a 55-ft. vertical shaft. Neglecting friction, how much work is done? How long would it take for a man to accomplish this amount of work at the rate of $^1/_{10}$ H.P.?

(4) A one-ton granite block is dragged over a horizontal cement road on wooden skids by a tractor pulling with a horizontal force of 1600 lbs. Calculate the work done in 10 ft. if 2 seconds are required. What power is developed?

CHAPTER 2—STATICS

Questions

(1) What is meant by weight?

(2) What are concurrent forces?

(3) What is the moment of a couple?

(4) Is the coefficient of friction equal to the ratio of the tangential force between two surfaces, to the weight of a body resting upon one of the surfaces?

(5) How is the component of a vector determined in a specified direction?

(6) How are two vectors added? subtracted?

Problems

(1) Two forces, A and B, of 100 lbs. and 70 lbs. respectively, make an angle of 37° with each other. If **B** lies in the direction of the X-axis, calculate the X- and Y-component of each force, the magnitude, and the direction of the resultant force.

(2) A 50-lb. uniform boom 20 feet long is supported so as to make a 90° angle with a vertical mast. If a cord joining the tip end of the boom to the tip of the mast makes an angle of 60° with the boom, calculate the tension in the cord, and the vertical and horizontal thrust exerted by the mast on the boom.

(3) A boy hauls a cart up a 30° ramp, holding the handle of the cart parallel to the ramp's surface. With what force must he pull steadily if the cart weighs 50 lbs. and the frictional force is 5 lbs.?

(4) A uniform beam weighing 100 lbs. leans against a smooth wall making an angle of 30° with it. What must be the friction force between the floor and the beam if the beam does not slip?

(5) If a 200-lb. box is pushed steadily along a horizontal floor by a stick held so as to make an angle of 30° with the floor, calculate the push of the stick assuming a coefficient of friction between box and floor of 0.2. If the body were pulled by a cord making the same angle, what force would be necessary?

(6) If two similar uniform ladders 10 ft. long are fastened together at the top and made to stand on a smooth horizontal floor with their lower ends 12 ft. apart connected by a rope 3 ft. long, find the tension in the rope and the push of each ladder on the other, assuming each ladder weighs 20 lbs.

(7) What horizontal force will be required to hold a 10-lb. body, suspended from a 3-ft. cord, one foot away from the vertical? What will be the tension in the cord?

(8) Two parallel forces of 50 lbs. each act in opposite directions at the ends of a bar 10 ft. long, making an angle of 30° with the bar. What is the moment of this couple? What is the resultant torque about either end?

(9) The upper end of a 30-lb. uniform ladder is suspended by a rope hanging from a dock. The lower end of the ladder rests upon a light floating raft making an angle of 60° with the water, between which and the raft the friction is negligible. A man weighing 150 lbs. stands on the ladder one-third of its length from the bottom. What angle does the rope make with the water? What is the tension in the rope? How is the tension altered as the incoming tide decreases the angle made by the ladder with the water's surface?

CHAPTERS 3 AND 4—DYNAMICS OF TRANSLATORY MOTION, WORK AND ENERGY

Questions

(1) What is meant by the term "Kinematics"?

(2) Distinguish between displacement and distance.

(3) In view of the vector characteristic of acceleration, does the term deceleration refer to the magnitude or the direction of an acceleration, or to both?

(4) Distinguish between curvilinear and rotary motion.

(5) How is the proportionality constant in Newton's second law reduced to unity?

(6) Newton's second law justifies the setting of the net sum of all forces

acting *upon* a body equal to the product of the body's mass times its acceleration. Including zero as a special case, indicate how constant motion, uniformly accelerated linear motion, and uniform curvilinear motion are each treated.

(7) Distinguish between centripetal and centrifugal force.

(8) What is meant by center of mass?

(9) Distinguish between potential energy and energy of elevation.

(10) Under what conditions is the energy method of approach likely to be more profitable than the force analysis method in dealing with mechanics problems?

(11) Distinguish between theoretical mechanical advantage and efficiency of a machine.

(12) Diagram a block and tackle system with a theoretical mechanical advantage of *four* times.

(13) Does a jackscrew handle have to be turned through a complete revolution for the jackscrew to have a mechanical advantage?

(14) Derive the law of the lever from the principle of virtual work.

Problems

(1) A body which actually weighs 8 lbs. appears (when suspended from a spring balance in an elevator) to weigh 10 lbs. What is the acceleration of the elevator, assuming it to be constant? Is the elevator rising or falling? If the elevator cable should snap, what would the suspended body appear to weigh? Does this answer refer to the actual tension in the connecting unit between the body and the spring balance? What, then, is the acceleration of the body with respect to the elevator?

(2) A body is thrown vertically upward with an initial velocity of 200 ft. per second. How high does it rise? With what velocity does it return to earth? How long is it in the air?

(3) An airplane flying with a constant horizontal velocity of 90 miles per hour (132 ft./sec.) at a height of 1600 ft. drops a bomb when it is one-quarter of a mile (1320 ft.) from a point directly over a target which it is approaching. Neglecting air resistance, how near the target will the bomb strike? If the plane continues with its velocity unaltered where will it be when the bomb strikes?

(4) Two freight cars weighing 10 tons each are coupled together and the combination is pulled by a locomotive with a force of 4000 lbs. What acceleration is acquired if the frictional force on each car amounts to 500 lbs.? What is the pull on the last car?

(5) A rifle is fired horizontally at a height of 4 ft. above the ground. The bullet is observed to strike the ground at a distance of 600 ft. Calculate the initial velocity of the bullet (neglecting air resistance).

(6) A 9-lb. block is drawn along a horizontal table by a cord running parallel to the table and passing over a frictionless pulley to a freely

suspended weight of 7 lbs. Assuming a frictional resistance of 1 lb., calculate the acceleration of the block. What is the acceleration of the suspended body? What is the tension in the cord?

(7) A mass of $^1/_2$ slug is whirled in a horizontal circle at the end of a 5-foot chain capable of withstanding a tension of 400 lbs. How many revolutions per second are possible?

(8) A man in a balloon has a downward velocity of 4 ft. per second. How far will he descend in the succeeding 15 seconds, if a 10-lb. body weighs constantly 9.2 lbs. on his spring balance?

(9) Find the horizontal thrust on the rails when a 20-ton engine runs at 60 miles per hour on a curve of 2000 ft. radius.

(10) A 30-gram bullet is fired into a block of wood of mass 15 kilograms suspended by strings 2 meters long. If the block is moved through an angle of 37°, calculate the velocity of the bullet.

(11) A boy lifts a weight of 100 lbs. 10 ft. vertically in 3 minutes with a block and tackle. He pulls out 50 ft. of rope and exerts a force of 25 lbs. What is the actual mechanical advantage of his machine? What is the theoretical M.A.? What is the efficiency of the tackle? What horsepower is developed by the boy?

CHAPTER 5—DYNAMICS OF ROTARY MOTION

Questions

(1) Show that $v = r\omega$ and $a = r\alpha$.

(2) What is meant by a radian?

(3) To what concept in linear motion is moment of inertia analogous?

(4) Show that $I = I_0 + ma^2$ where I_0 is the moment of inertia of a body about an axis through its center of mass and a is the distance from the center of mass to an axis about which the moment of inertia of the body is I.

(5) What is meant by precession?

Problems

(1) A uniform homogeneous cylinder rolls along a horizontal level surface with a translational velocity of 20 cm. per sec. If its mass is 100 grams and its radius is 10 cm., what is its radius of gyration about its center? What is its total kinetic energy?

(2) How long will it take for a 640-lb. flywheel whose moment of inertia is 500 slug ft.^{2} to come to rest after the power has been shut off, if its velocity is 600 R.P.M. and the frictional torque amounts to 50 lb. ft.? What is the radius of gyration of the flywheel? What radius would a ring be required to have if its moment of inertia were to be the same?

(3) A 500-lb. flywheel is mounted on the same shaft with a pulley of 6 inch radius. The combined moment of inertia is 250 slug ft.^{2} What is the kinetic energy of the system when it revolves at 500 R.P.M.?

How much work will it do in coming to rest? If the excess tension on one side of a belt running over the pulley is 60 lbs., what is the resulting torque? If the belt is thrown off and the frictional torque has this same value, what angular acceleration results? How much time will elapse before the wheel stops? How many revolutions will the wheel make before coming to rest?

(4) A wheel and axle has a moment of inertia of 20 slug ft.^{2} and is rotating at 1200 R.P.M. If this speed changes uniformly to 600 R.P.M. in 5 minutes, what deceleration does it have? What is the amount of the decelerating torque?

(5) A solid homogeneous sphere $1/2$ ft. in radius, weighing 128 lbs., rolls along a floor with a translatory velocity of 10 ft. per second. What is its translatory kinetic energy? What is its rotational kinetic energy?

(6) A solid homogeneous cylinder rolls down a 30° inclined plane of length 5 meters. Show that the linear velocity at the bottom is given by the expression $v = \sqrt{4/3\, gh}$, if it starts from rest. Assuming the mass of the cylinder to be 2000 grams and the radius to be 10 cm., calculate: The linear velocity at the bottom, the average linear velocity on the incline, the time required to roll down the incline, the total kinetic energy at the instant it reaches the bottom, the linear acceleration at the same instant, and also the angular acceleration.

CHAPTER 6—SPECIAL DYNAMICAL CONSIDERATIONS

Questions

(1) Realizing that simple harmonic motion is a linear motion, what is the significance of the circle of reference?

(2) Distinguish between the velocity of a body undergoing simple harmonic motion and the velocity of a point on the circle of reference.

(3) Define coefficient of stiffness.

(4) What can be said of the acceleration of a simple harmonic motion at the instant when the velocity is zero?

(5) What length would a simple pendulum be required to have at a place where g has the standard value in order for the pendulum to beat seconds?

(6) What characterizes the center of oscillation?

(7) State Kepler's laws of planetary motion.

(8) What are the C.G.S. units in which G is equal to 6.66×10^{-8}?

Problems

(1) A particle performing S.H.M. has a velocity of 4 ft. per sec. when it passes through the midpoint of its path. If its period is π seconds, what is the amplitude of the vibration? What is the velocity when

the displacement is 1.5 ft. from the position of rest?

(2) A 4000-gram mass hung from a spring causes a stretch of the spring amounting to 2 cm. What is the coefficient of stiffness of the spring? If the mass is set into vertical vibration, calculate the period of the vibration.

(3) A steel ball weighing $\frac{1}{2}$ lb. is executing simple harmonic motion with an amplitude of 6 inches and a period of 2 seconds. What is the radius of the reference circle? What is the acceleration of a point on the reference circle? What is the maximum velocity of the ball? What is the acceleration of the ball when its displacement is 3 inches?

(4) Given a simple pendulum of length l, prove that its period of vibration is $2\pi\sqrt{l/g}$.

(5) Consider a long slender rod hanging from a hinge at its upper end. Show that it will vibrate like a simple pendulum of length equal to $\frac{4}{3}$ the half length of the pendulum.

CHAPTER 7—ELASTICITY AND FLUIDS

Questions

(1) Distinguish between solids and fluids.
(2) In what units are the elastic moduli expressed?
(3) Distinguish between density, and weight per unit volume.
(4) What is specific gravity? In what units is it expressed?
(5) Derive Archimedes' principle by force analysis.
(6) What is meant by steady flow?
(7) Discuss the effect of streamlined design as applied to bodies intended to travel at high speeds.

Problems

(1) If Young's modulus for steel is 20×10^{11} dynes per cm.^{2}, by how much will a steel rod 10 cm. long and 0.5 cm.^{2} in cross section be shortened if it is required to support a load of 100 killograms? What strain is developed in the rod?

(2) A canoe weighing 100 lbs. contains a boy who weighs 125 lbs. and a rock for an anchor which weighs 50 lbs. How much water does it displace? If the rock is thrown overboard but is attached to the canoe by a rope too short to reach the bottom, how much water will the canoe then displace? The volume of the stone is $\frac{1}{8}$ cubic foot.

(3) What use does the mercury barometer have? Is its reading affected by temperature? Is the reading affected sensibly by the area of the tube? What equations are involved?

(4) Assuming the volume of air in an automobile tire to be one cubic foot when under an absolute pressure of 50 lbs. per sq. inch (including atmospheric pressure), what volume will this air occupy at the same temperature if it is allowed to escape at atmospheric pressure?

(5) How big a load will a balloon lift if it weighs 250 kg. and contains 400 cubic meters of hydrogen? One cubic meter of hydrogen has a mass of 90 grams, and one cubic meter of air has a mass of 1200 grams.

(6) What is the total thrust on the bottom of a vertical cylindrical tank of water 10 ft. high and 6 ft. in diameter? What is the pressure at the bottom?

(7) What volume of wood of specific gravity 0.75 is required to support a boy who weighs 80 lbs. on a raft which is just barely submerged in fresh water?

(8) A rectangular cistern 6 ft. deep with a cross-sectional area of 6 ft. × 8 ft. is filled with alcohol of specific gravity 0.8. What is the weight per unit volume of the alcohol in lbs. per cubic ft.? What is the pressure at the bottom due to the liquid? What is the total force on one of the 6 × 8 sides due to the liquid? What is the density of alcohol in B.E. units?

(9) A cake of soap 2″ × 3″ × 6″ is placed in a tub of water. If the specific gravity of the soap is 0.9, what is its density in B.E. units? What buoyant force acts on the soap? If it is pushed and held beneath the surface, what buoyant force then acts on the soap and what force is required to just hold it there? What fractional part of the volume of the floating soap is to be found above the surface of water?

CHAPTER 8—WAVE MOTION AND SOUND

Questions

(1) Distinguish between wave pulse and wave train.

(2) How can a longitudinal wave be diagrammatically represented?

(3) What is the significance of the term "harmonic wave"?

(4) Distinguish between destructive and constructive interference.

(5) When a wave pulse is reflected from a surface, does it matter whether the surface is fixed or free?

(6) Describe Melde's experiment.

(7) Is Doppler's principle restricted to sound waves?

(8) Account for the difference in quality between middle "C" sounded on a piano and middle "C" sounded on a violin.

(9) Compare the number of harmonics emitted by a closed pipe with the number emitted by an open one.

Problems

(1) An echo is heard one second after a sound is produced. How far away is the reflecting surface? Assume a reasonable value for the velocity of sound.

(2) An oar slaps the water of a lake and an observer 2000 ft. away hears the sound through the air and also through the water. How

much time will elapse between the reception of the two sounds if the velocities are 4700 ft./sec. and 1100 ft./sec.? Which value refers to water?

(3) Assuming the hum of a certain automobile on the highway to have a pitch of 200 vibrations per second, calculate its apparent pitch to an observer toward whom it is approaching at a rate of 30 miles per hour.

(4) A beat note of frequency 10 vib./sec. is heard between two tuning forks. One fork is damped slightly by adding a bit of wax to one of its prongs and the beat note changes to 5 vibrations per second. If the frequency of the other fork is 256 vib. per sec. what wave length was emitted by the first fork before the wax was added?

(5) A closed pipe 2 ft. long is sounded alongside of an open pipe $4\frac{1}{2}$ ft. long. What is the frequency of the beat note between them?

CHAPTER 9—HEAT AND TEMPERATURE

Questions

(1) What is the coefficient of linear expansion of a substance?

(2) Distinguish between the volume-temperature coefficient and the pressure-temperature coefficient for a gas.

(3) Express absolute zero on the Fahrenheit scale.

(4) Distinguish between Boyle's law and Charles's law.

(5) What is meant by an "ideal" gas?

Problems

(1) Find the volume of air at 0° and 760 mm. Hg that will fill a one-liter container at 20°C. and 380 mm. Hg.

(2) If a rod one meter long increases one millimeter in length for a 75° rise in temperature, what is the coefficient of expansion over this temperature range?

(3) The volume of a gasoline storage tank is 500 gallons. Assuming a coefficient of volume expansion for gasoline of 1.1×10^{-3} per °C., calculate the shrinkage to a dealer who fills up this tank at 30° C. if the temperature drops to −20° before he disposes of it.

(4) Calculate the radius of a ring through which a solid copper sphere will pass at 100° C. if its radius at 0° is 10 cm. Make a similar calculation for a hollow copper sphere made of stock 1 mm. thick. The coefficient of volume expansion of air is very small in comparison with the value for copper.

(5) Show that the volume-temperature coefficient of expansion is approximately three times the linear-temperature coefficient.

CHAPTER 10—CALORIMETRY

Questions

(1) How many calories are equivalent to one B.T.U.?

(2) What is meant by the water equivalent of a body?
(3) What is meant by heat of combustion?
(4) What is meant by critical pressure?
(5) What is meant by critical temperature?
(6) Distinguish between regulation and sublimation.
(7) Distinguish between absolute and relative humidity.

Problems

(1) If 200 grams of copper of specific heat .09 at a temperature of 100° C. are dropped into 500 cc. of water at 0° C., find the resulting temperature.
(2) How much ice will be melted if 200 grams of copper at 100° C. are completely enclosed in ice? Specific heat of copper is .09.

CHAPTER 11—HEAT TRANSFER AND THERMODYNAMICS

Questions

(1) What is meant by temperature gradient?
(2) In what unit is the coefficient of thermal conductivity usually expressed?
(3) What are convection currents?
(4) Is it correct to speak of heat waves as electromagnetic waves located entirely in the infrared portion of the spectrum?
(5) Distinguish between Stefan's law and Wien's law.
(6) What are the virtues of the quantum theory?
(7) Is it correct to say that one calorie of heat is entirely equivalent to 4.18 joules of mechanical energy?
(8) Distinguish between an isothermal and an adiabatic process.
(9) Why is the second law of thermodynamics often compared to a "one way" traffic sign?
(10) Would an engine necessarily be 100% efficient if its exhaust temperature could be made equal to absolute zero?

Problems

(1) Assuming a coefficient of thermal conductivity for iron to be 0.11 cal. per sec. per cm. per °C., calculate the rate at which heat goes through an iron plate one cm. thick and 100 sq. cm. in area if one side is exposed to steam at 100°C. and the other side is maintained at 0° C. by ice.
(2) How much longer will it take for the temperature of the contents of a vacuum bottle to change by 5° C. if the contents are originally at 0° C. than if the contents are originally at 100° C. if the outside temperature is 30° C?
(3) By how much will the temperature of water in a waterfall be raised by striking a lower surface of water after a fall of 300 ft.?

(4) What is the theoretical efficiency of a steam engine whose boiler temperature is 150° C. and whose exhaust temperature is 60° C.?

CHAPTER 12—ELECTROSTATICS

Questions

(1) Distinguish between a conductor and an insulator.
(2) What is meant by dielectric constant of a substance?
(3) How does the mass of a proton compare with the mass of an electron?
(4) What is a neutron?
(5) What is a stat-coulomb?
(6) What is meant by electric induction?
(7) Are electric charges generated by friction machines?
(8) Discuss the action of the electrophorus in terms of the electron theory.
(9) What is a stat-volt? What is a stat-farad?
(10) How do capacitances add up in parallel? in series?

Problems

(1) It is desired to charge an isolated sphere negatively, but there is only a positively charged rod available. Can it be done and how?
(2) Two isolated positive charges of 200 E.S.U. each are placed 80 cm. apart. What is the direction and magnitude of the field intensity halfway between them? What is the absolute potential at this point? How much work must be done on a −10 E.S.U. charge to carry it from this point a distance of 30 cm. along the perpendicular bisector of the line joining the two charges?
(3) Two spheres having radii of 4 cm. and 8 cm. respectively, are joined by a long fine wire and charged together with +100 stat-coulombs of electricity. They are then separated to 50 cm. between centers. How much charge will each have? How much work would be required to move a charge of +10 stat-coulombs from a point A (10 cm. from the center of the 4 cm. sphere and 40 cm. from the 8 cm. sphere) to a point B (10 cm. from the center of the 8 cm. sphere and 40 cm. from the 4 cm. sphere)?
(4) An insulated air condenser is charged and the charge is indicated by the deflection of an electroscope connected to one of its plates. What happens to the leaves of the electroscope if the plates of the condenser are suddenly separated? What does this mean and why does it happen?
(5) If an insulated sphere of 10 cm. radius is charged in air to a potential of 1000 stat-volts with respect to the surroundings, how much charge does it have? If it is connected by a wire to an exactly similar uncharged insulated sphere and then is disconnected, what is the final potential of each sphere?

(6) An air condenser consisting of two plates of area 80 $cm.^2$ separated by .02 cm. is charged until it contains 2000 stat-coulombs. What is the difference in potential between the plates? How much work would be required to carry a charge of 10 E.S.U. from the negative to the positive plate? How would the potential difference between the plates be altered if the condenser were lowered into oil of dielectric constant equal to three?

(7) Two equally charged pith balls weighing 0.1 gram each are suspended from a point by threads 5.0 cm. long. If the balls separate to a distance of 6 cm., what is the charge on each?

CHAPTER 13—STEADY CURRENTS

Questions

(1) To how many electrons per second does one ampere correspond?
(2) Does a voltaic cell generate electricity?
(3) List several methods of establishing electromotive force.
(4) What is meant by dissociation?
(5) Describe the process of electroplating.
(6) State Faraday's laws of electrolysis.
(7) What is meant by electrical resistance?
(8) Distinguish between resistivity and conductivity.
(9) What is a circular mil?
(10) What substance displays a negative temperature coefficient of resistance?
(11) Discuss the phenomenon of superconductivity.
(12) Distinguish between the electromotive force of a battery and the potential drop across it.
(13) State Kirchhoff's rules for steady currents.
(14) Show how resistances combine in series and in parallel.
(15) Describe the use of the potentiometer for determining the electromotive force of a cell.
(16) Distinguish between the Seebeck effect and the Peltier effect.

Problems

(1) How long will a current of one ampere be obliged to flow in order to deposit 0.2236 grams of silver on a metal spoon? The electrochemical equivalent of silver is 0.001118 grams per coulomb.

(2) If the electrochemical equivalent of copper is .00033 grams per coulomb, how much copper will be deposited from an electrochemical cell in one hour by a current of 3 amperes?

(3) A circuit consists of a cell of E.M.F. 22 volts and internal resistance of 2 ohms in series with a combination of two resistances in parallel. If the current through the cell is 5 amperes and the current through one of the resistances of the parallel combination is 2 amperes, what are the resistance of each resistance, the current through

the second resistance, and the drop in potential across the parallel combination? What is the drop in potential across the cell?

(4) A milliammeter has a resistance of one ohm and a full scale reading of 100 milliamperes. Find the resistance of a shunt which must be used to make a full scale reading correspond to 10 amperes total circuit current.

(5) A circuit consists of a battery of electromotive force 16 volts and internal resistance of 1 ohm in series with a resistance of 5 ohms and a resistance combination made up of two parts in parallel. One part is a resistance of 4 ohms, and the other part is a resistance of 2 ohms in series with a parallel combination of 6 and 3 ohms respectively. Calculate the total external resistance of the circuit, the current through the battery, the potential drop across the 5 ohm coil, and the current through the 4 ohm coil.

(6) Consider twenty lamps of 400 ohms each connected in parallel on a 110 volt circuit. How much current is drawn? What is the power consumption? How many calories are developed per hour?

(7) A circuit consists of a battery of E.M.F. 13 volts and internal resistance of 0.7 ohm in series with a resistance of 9.9 ohms and a resistance combination consisting of three resistances in parallel of 10 ohms, 15 ohms, and 6 ohms respectively. Calculate the current through the battery, the potential difference across the resistance combination, and the rate of heating (cal/sec.) in the 9.9 ohm coil.

(8) A car heater operated on a 550 volt line draws 5 amperes. Find the resistance of the heater, the power drawn, the amount of heat developed per hour, and the cost per hour of operation at $.08 per kilowatt hour.

(9) A galvanometer whose resistance is 100 ohms gives a full scale deflection when 2×10^{-7} amps. passes through it. What shunt will make its full scale reading correspond to one ampere of current in a circuit into which it is connected? How can it be made to indicate one volt of potential difference across two points of a circuit?

(10) Compare the cost of operating two lamps in series and in parallel on a 100-volt line if each lamp has a resistance of 200 ohms.

CHAPTER 14—MAGNETISM AND MAGNETIC EFFECTS OF CURRENTS

Questions

(1) What is Coulomb's law of magnetic force?
(2) Distinguish between magnetic force and electrical force.
(3) Distinguish between angle of declination and angle of dip.
(4) What is a gauss?
(5) What is meant by magnetic induction?
(6) Indicate what is meant by magnetic permeability.

(7) Distinguish between magnetic permeability and magnetic susceptibility.
(8) Discuss magnetic hysteresis.
(9) Distinguish between residual magnetism and coercive force.
(10) What is permalloy?
(11) Describe the nature of the magnetic field associated with an electric current.
(12) How is the ab-ampere related to the legal ampere?
(13) What is meant by magnetic circuit?
(14) What is magnetomotive force? What is reluctance?
(15) What is a gilbert? What is a maxwell?
(16) What happens to a current-carrying conductor in a magnetic field?
(17) Describe the action of the D'Arsonval galvanometer.
(18) What is the function of the commutator in a D.C. motor?
(19) What is the left-hand motor rule?
(20) What significance is attached to the relationship between the statcoulomb and the ab-coulomb?

Problems

(1) How far from a north pole of strength 10 units must a south pole of strength 20 units be placed in air so that the relative attraction shall be 2 dynes? What is the magnitude and direction of the force that would act upon a unit north pole placed midway between these poles? What is the direction and intensity of the field intensity H at this point?
(2) A magnetic north pole of 40 units acts upon a south pole 5 cm. away (air) with a force of 32 dynes. How strong is the south pole? Suppose the south pole to be replaced by a north pole of the same strength. Would the intensity of the field midway between the poles be greater or less than before?
(3) What force in dynes is exerted upon a straight wire 15 cm. long carrying 20 amperes at right angles across a magnetic field of 5 E.M.U. intensity. Indicate by a diagram.
(4) A solenoid 31.4 cm. long and 5 square centimeters in sectional area has 1200 turns of wire and carries 5 amperes of current. Its core is iron of permeability 500. Calculate the field intensity H at the center of the solenoid and the flux density B at the center of the core. How many flux lines pass through the solenoid assuming a uniform distribution of lines within the solenoid?
(5) A ring solenoid of 500 turns is wound on an iron core whose mean radius is 5 cm. and whose cross section is 0.5 sq. cm. If a current of 0.25 amperes sets up 3750 maxwells, what is the permeability of the iron core?
(6) One of the wires of the drum armature of a motor is 20 cm. long and lies perpendicular to a magnetic field of intensity 2000 oersteds.

What side thrust is exerted upon the wire when it carries a current of 4 amperes?

(7) A small compass needle is placed 5 cm. above a long straight wire which runs north and south. Assuming the horizontal component of the earth's magnetic field to be 0.2 oersteds pointing north, calculate the field due to the current which will cause the needle to deflect 45° toward the east. What is the conventional direction of current? What is the intensity of the current in amperes?

(8) Consider two long straight parallel wires separated by a distance of 2 cm., carrying currents of 20 amperes and 10 amperes respectively in opposite directions. What is the force of attraction or repulsion (which?) between them per unit length of wire?

CHAPTER 15—ELECTROMAGNETIC INDUCTION, OSCILLATIONS, AND WAVES

Questions

(1) What is the right-hand generator rule?

(2) What is an ab-volt?

(3) What is meant by "cutting lines of force"?

(4) Describe Faraday's experiments for inducing electromotive force.

(5) How are eddy currents minimized by lamination?

(6) What is meant by back electromotive force?

(7) Discuss eddy current damping of vibrations.

(8) Distinguish between mutual and self induction.

(9) How is the ab-henry defined?

(10) Why is inductance sometimes referred to as electrical inertia?

(11) Why can an alternating current transformer not be used on direct current? Does not an induction coil work on direct current?

(12) What is meant by an alternating current?

(13) How is the R.M.S. value of an alternating E.M.F. related to the maximum value?

(14) What effect does resistance have in an A.C. circuit?

(15) Distinguish between resistance, reactance, and impedance.

(16) What is meant by compliance?

(17) Is average power equal to the average value of the current times the average value of the E.M.F. for an alternating current? Is it equal to the product of the R.M.S. values of current and E.M.F.?

(18) Describe the effect of resistance in an oscillating circuit.

(19) In what manner do electrical waves seem to be related to light waves?

(20) How is the dielectric constant of a transparent substance related to the optical refractive index of the same substance?

Problems

(1) What is the average value of the E.M.F. developed when a square

coil 20 cm. by 20 cm. with 50 turns is rotated from a position normal to a magnetic field of intensity 0.25 oersteds to a position parallel to this same field in 0.01 seconds? Express the answer in volts.

(2) What E.M.F. is induced in a circular coil of wire of 200 turns and of mean radius 1 cm. if it is withdrawn in 0.1 second from between the pole pieces of an electromagnet where the field intensity is 1500 oersteds perpendicular to the plane of the coil?

(3) Find the E.M.F. induced in an axle of a train travelling from north to south at 1500 cm./sec. if the length of the axle is 160 cm. The vertical component of the earth's field is .55 oersteds.

(4) When 100 volts D.C. are impressed across a coil, one ampere flows. When 100 volts A.C., 60 cycle are applied to the same coil, only 0.5 ampere flows. Calculate the resistance, the impedance, and the inductance of the coil.

(5) How much current is drawn by the primary of a transformer which steps 110 volts down to 11 volts to operate a device with an impedance of 220 ohms?

CHAPTER 16—GASEOUS CONDUCTION AND THE ELECTRON

Questions

(1) What is meant by the term "ionization of a gas")

(2) What is the negative glow?

(3) What is meant by the term "X-ray vacuum"?

(4) Describe an experiment by which it can be concluded that the direction of conventional current flow is opposite to the flow of the electrons which make up the flow.

(5) What property of the electron was measured by Millikan?

(6) What is the mass of an electron?

(7) Describe the Edison effect.

(8) What laws govern photoelectric emission?

(9) What is radioactivity?

(10) Distinguish between the negative electron, the positive electron (positron), the neutron, the proton, the alpha particle, and the beta particle.

CHAPTER 17—NATURE OF LIGHT: ITS PROPAGATION AND MEASUREMENT

Questions

(1) What contributions were made to the wave theory of light by the following: Young, Fresnel, Maxwell?

(2) What was Newton's influence upon the theory of light?

(3) Describe the electromagnetic spectrum.

(4) If a physical theory is superseded by another, does it necessarily follow that the original theory was wrong?
(5) What is meant by rectilinear propagation of light?
(6) Whose name is associated with the precise measurement of the velocity of light?
(7) Distinguish between ray and wave front.
(8) Distinguish between regular and diffuse reflection.
(9) What is Snell's law?
(10) How is the optical refractive index of a substance defined?
(11) How is the critical angle of incidence related to the refractive index of a substance?
(12) List several applications of the principle of total internal reflection.
(13) How is the lumen related to the candle power?
(14) What is a lambert?
(15) How is the ster-radian defined? How many ster-radians are there in all space?
(16) What is a foot-candle?

Problems

(1) What is the velocity of light in water of refractive index $^4/_3$?
(2) Derive a relation by which the candle power of an unknown lamp can be measured in terms of the candle power of a standard lamp and measurable quantities.
(3) If the refractive index of carbon bisulphide is 1.65 and that of glass is 1.45, what is the greatest angle of incidence for which a ray of light will pass from carbon bisulphide into glass?
(4) What is the shortest mirror in which a person 6 ft. tall can see his entire image? Indicate by a diagram how it should be placed.
(5) A 100-watt electric light which has an efficiency of 1.25 candle power per watt has how many candle power? What is the intensity of illuminance on a book 10 ft. away from this light if the book is held at right angles to the beam?
(6) What is the illuminance of a surface 8 ft. directly beneath a 100-C.P. light? What illuminance does this light produce at a point 8 ft. to the right of the preceding surface?

CHAPTER 18—MIRRORS, LENSES, AND OTHER OPTICAL INSTRUMENTS

Questions

(1) What simple relations give the behavior of a beam of light incident paraxially upon the boundary of a single spherical surface?
(2) What is the radius of curvature for a plane surface?
(3) State the relation which governs the location of an image produced by two spherical surfaces very close together in air, i.e., by a thin spherical lens.

(4) Through what point does a ray of light originally parallel to the axis of a converging spherical mirror pass after reflection?
(5) What is meant by axial spherical aberration?
(6) Distinguish between coma and astigmatism.
(7) What is meant by chromatic aberration?
(8) What is a diopter?
(9) Distinguish between myopia, hypermetropia, and presbyopia.
(10) How is the magnifying power of a simple microscope determined?
(11) Distinguish between the optical system of a compound microscope and an astronomical telescope.
(12) Distinguish between the opera glass and the field glass.

Problems

(1) Locate and determine the nature of the image of an object formed by a converging lens of 2-ft. focal length when object and lens are separated by a distance of 6 ft., using both graphical and analytical methods.
(2) Specify the radii of curvature of a symmetrical double convex lens having a focal length of one meter to be made of glass of refractive index 1.5. What is the power of this lens?
(3) A concavo-convex lens has radii of curvature of 30 cm. and 40 cm. respectively. Calculate its focal length if its refractive index is 1.5.
(4) Construct ray diagrams to show object, lens, and image relationships for a convex lens with the object placed such that (a) the object distance is greater than the image distance, (b) the object distance is equal to the image distance, (c) the object distance is less than the focal length.
(5) A double convex lens of glass ($\mu = 1.5$) has radii of 25 cm. and 50 cm. respectively. Calculate the focal length. Express the power of the lens in diopters with the correct sign. If an object is placed 66 cm. in front of this lens, calculate the image distance and check the result by a ray diagram.
(6) A nearsighted person cannot see clearly objects farther than 100 cm. What kind of spectacles, and of what power must they be, to enable him to see objects at a distance of 500 cm.?
(7) Calculate the kind and power of spectacles which will enable a person so farsighted as to not be able to see clearly objects closer than 50 cm. to see an object at a distance of 25 cm.

CHAPTER 19—OPTICAL PHENOMENA: PHYSICAL OPTICS

Questions

(1) Distinguish between a continuous spectrum, a bright-line spectrum, a dark-line spectrum, and a band spectrum.

(2) What connection is there between the optical spectrum and the atomic structure of a substance?
(3) What is the accepted explanation of color blindness?
(4) What are primary colors?
(5) Describe Young's interference experiment.
(6) Account for the colors produced when a beam of light is reflected from a film of oil.
(7) Distinguish between constructive and destructive interference, stating the conditions under which each phenomenon occurs.
(8) What role has the Michelson interferometer played in the development of the theory of relativity by Einstein?
(9) What is mean by diffraction?
(10) What is meant by polarization of light?
(11) Distinguish between ordinary and extraordinary rays in Iceland spar.
(12) What is Brewster's law?

ANSWERS TO THE PROBLEMS

Chapter 1

(1) 30.5 (2) 2.2 lbs. (3) 110,000 ft.-lbs.; 2000 sec. (4) 16,000 ft.-lbs.; 8000 ft.-lbs./sec.

Chapter 2

(1) 162 lbs.; 22° to horizontal (2) 29 lbs.; 25 lbs.; 14.5 lbs. (3) 30 lbs. (4) 28.8 lbs. (5) 52.2 lbs.; 41.4 lbs. (6) 30 lbs.; 30 lbs. (7) 3.54 lbs.; 10.6 lbs. (8) 250 lb.-ft.; 250 lb.-ft. (9) 90°; 65 lbs.; none

Chapters 3 and 4

(1) 8 ft./sec.^{2}; rising; zero; yes; zero (2) 622 ft.; 200 ft./sec.; 12.4 sec. (3) on target; over target (4) 2.4 ft./sec.^{2}; 1125 lbs. (5) 1200 ft./sec. (6) 12 ft./sec.^{2}; same; 4.4 lbs. (7) 2 R.P.S. (8) 348 ft. (9) 4840 lbs. (10) 140,000 cm./sec. (11) 4; 5; .80; .013 H.P.

Chapter 5

(1) 7 cm.; 30,000 ergs (2) 628 sec.; 5 ft.; 5 ft. (3) 348,000 ft.-lbs.; same; 30 lb.-ft.; .12 rad./sec.^{2}; 437 sec.; 1830 rev. (4) $\pi/15$ rad./sec.^{2}; $4/3\pi$ lb.-ft. (5) 280 ft.-lbs.; 80 ft.-lbs. (6) 572 cm./sec.; 286 cm./sec.; 1.75 sec.; 49×10^7 ergs; 327 cm./sec.^{2}; 32.7 rad./sec.^{2}

Chapter 6

(1) 2 ft.; 2.6 ft./sec. (2) 1,960,000 dynes/cm.; .285 sec. (3) 6 inches; 5 ft./sec.^{2}; 1.57 ft./sec.; 2.5 ft./sec.^{2} (4) and (5) consult index for discussion in text

Chapter 7

(1) .001 cm.; .0001 (2) 4.41 cu. ft.; 4.29 cu. ft. (3) consult index for discussion in text (4) 3.4 cu. ft. (5) 194 kg. (6) 17,650 lbs.; 624 lbs./ft.^{2} (7) 5.13 cu. ft. (8) 50 lbs./ft.^{3}; 300 lbs./ft.^{2}; 7200 lbs.; 1.55 slugs/ft.^{3} (9) 1.75 slugs/ft.^{3}; 1.17 lbs.; 1.3 lbs.; .1

Chapter 8

(1) 550 ft. (2) 1.4 sec.; .43 sec. (3) 208 vib./sec. (4) 4.13 ft. (5) 15.4 sec.

Chapter 9

(1) .465 liters (2) .0000133/°C. (3) 27.5 gal. (4) 10.018 cm.; 10.018 cm. (5) consult index for discussion in text

Chapter 10

(1) 3.48° C. (2) 22.5 grams

Chapter 11

(1) 1.1×10^3 cal./sec. (2) 3.82 times (3) .214° C. (4) 21.2%

Chapter 12

(1) consult index for discussion in text (2) zero; 10 E. S. U.; 20 ergs. (3) 33⅓ stat-coulombs; 66⅔ stat-coulombs; 25 ergs (4) consult index for discussion in text (5) 10,000 stat-coulombs; 500 stat-volts (6) 628 stat-volts; 62.8 ergs; 2.09 stat-volts (7) 51.5 stat-coulombs

Chapter 13

(1) 200 sec. (2) 3.57 grams (3) 6 ohms; 4 ohms; 3 amps.; 12 volts; 12 volts (4) .0101 ohms (5) 7 ohms; 2 amps.; 10 volts; 1 amp. (6) 5.5 amps.; 605 watts; 520,000 cal. (7) .958 amps.; 2.87 volts; 2.17 cal./sec. (8) 110 ohms; 2750 watts; 2.37×10^6 cal; $.22 (9) 2×10^{-5} ohms; 5×10^6 ohms (10) ¼

Chapter 14

(1) 10 cm.; 1.2 dynes to S; 1.2 oersteds S (2) 20 units; less (3) 150 dynes (4) 240 oersteds; 1.2×10^5 gauss; 6×10^5 lines (5) 1500 (6) 16,000 dynes (7) .2 oersteds; S-N; 5 amps. (8) 2×10^{-3} newton per meter repulsion

Chapter 15

(1) .005 volts (2) .094 volts (3) .0013 volts (4) 100 ohms; 200 ohms; .46 henry (5) .005 amp.

Chapter 17

(1) 2.25×10^{10} cm./sec. (2) consult index for discussion in text (3) 62° (4) 3 ft. (5) 125 C. P.; 1.25 ft.-candles (6) 1.56 ft.-candles; 1.11 ft.-candles.

Chapter 18

(1) 3 ft. beyond lens inverted and $\frac{1}{2}$ size (2) $R_1 = +100$ cm.; $R_2 = -100$ cm.; 1 D. O. (3) -240 cm. (4) consult index for discussion in text (5) 33.3 cm.; $+3$ D.O.; -194 cm. (6) $-\frac{4}{5}$ D.O. (7) $+2$ D.O.

Appendix V: Physical Constants

c	Velocity of light	2.9978×10^{10} cm./sec.
G	Gravitation constant	6.66×10^{-8} cm.^{3} gr.$^{-1}$ sec.$^{-3}$
		$= 6.67 \times 10^{-11} \dfrac{\text{newton-meter}^2}{\text{kilogram}^2}$
e	Electronic charge	4.803×10^{-10} stat-coulombs
		1.601×10^{-20} E.M.U. $=$ 1.601×10^{-19} coulombs
k	Proportionality constant	$\dfrac{1}{4\pi\epsilon_0} = 9 \times 10^9 \dfrac{\text{newton-meter}^2}{\text{coulomb}^2}$
		$\left(\epsilon_0 = 8.85 \times 10^{-12} \dfrac{\text{coulomb}^2}{\text{newton-meter}^2}\right)$
e/m_o	Electronic ratio	5.275×10^{17} E.S.U./gr.
		1.759×10^7 E.M.U./gr.
F	Faraday	9.6500×10^4 coulombs
v_o	Vol. of 1 gr. mol. at 0° C and 1 atm.	22.4115 liters/gr. mol.
h	Planck's constant	6.626×10^{-27} erg sec.
T_o	Ice point, abs.	273.1° A.
O	Atomic weight of oxygen	16.000
R	Gas constant	8.315×10^7 ergs/° C. gr. mol.
N_o	Avogadro's number	6.061×10^{23}/gr. mol.
M_H	Mass of hydrogen atom	1.663×10^{-24} gr.
m_o	Electronic mass	9.111×10^{-28} gr.
r_1	Radius of 1st Bohr orbit of hydrogen	0.5305×10^{-8} cm.
g_s	Standard gravity	980.665 cm./sec.^{2}.

1 Gram-calorie = 4.186 joules.

1 British thermal unit = 1054.8 joules.

RELATIONS BETWEEN COMMON UNITS

Length

1 in. = 2.540 cm.

1 ft. = 30.48 cm.

1 micron (μ) = 0.000001 m. = 0.001 mm. = 10^{-4} cm.

1 millionth micron ($\mu\mu$) = 10^{-10}.
1 Angstrom unit = 10^{-8} cm.

Volume

1 liter = 1000 cc. = 61.024 in.^{3} = 1.05671 qt.

Mass

1 lb. = 453.59 gr.
1 kg. = 2.2046 lb.

Angles

1 circumference = 360° = 2π radians.
1 radian = 57.2958°.

Density

1 gr./cm.^{3} = 62.4 lb./ft.^{3} = 1.94 slug/ft.^{3}

Pressure

1 atmosphere = 76 cm. of mercury = 14.697 lb./in.^{2}
= 1013200 dynes/cm.^{2}

Work or Energy

1 ft.-lb. = 1.356×10^7 ergs.
1 joule = 10^7ergs.
1 gr. cal. = 4.186×10^7 ergs.
1 B.T.U. = 777.8 ft.-lbs. = 252.2 gr. cal.

Power

1 H.P. = 33,000 ft.-lb./min. = 550 ft.-lb./sec. = 746 watts.
1 watt = 1 joule/sec.

Electrical Units

1 ampere = 10^{-1} ab-amps = 3×10^9 E.S.U.
1 volt = 10^8 E.M.U. = $\frac{1}{3} \times 10^{-2}$ E.S.U.
1 coulomb = 10^{-1} E.M.U. = 3×10^9 E.S.U.
1 ohm = 10^9 E.M.U. = $\frac{1}{9} \times 10^{-11}$ E.S.U.
1 farad = 10^{-9} E.M.U. = 9×10^{11} E.S.U.
1 henry = 10^9 E.M.U. = $\frac{1}{9} \times 10^{-11}$ E.S.U.

THE GREEK ALPHABET

Α	α	alpha	Ν	ν	nu
Β	β	beta	Ξ	ξ	xi
Γ	γ	gamma	Ο	o	omicron
Δ	δ	delta	Π	π	pi
Ε	ϵ	epsilon	Ρ	ρ	rho
Ζ	ζ	zeta	Σ	σ	sigma
Η	η	eta	Τ	τ	tau
Θ	θ	theta	Υ	υ	upsilon
Ι	ι	iota	Φ	ϕ	phi
Κ	κ	kappa	Χ	χ	chi
Λ	λ	lambda	Ψ	ψ	psi
Μ	μ	mu	Ω	ω	omega

Appendix VI: The Metric System

Length. 1 meter (1 m.) = 10 decimeters = 100 centimeters (100 cm.) = 1000 millimeters (1000 mm.).
1 kilometer = 1000 meters (1000 m.) = 0.6214 mile.
1 decimeter = 0.1 meter = 10 centimeters = 3.937 in.
1 meter = 1.094 yards = 3.286 ft. = 39.37 in.
Volume. 1 liter = 1000 cubic centimeters (1000 cc.) = a cube 10 cm. × 10 cm. × 10 cm.
1 liter = 0.03532 cu. ft. = 61.03 cu. in. = 1.057 quarts (U.S.) or 1.136 quarts (Brit.) = 34.1 fl. oz. (U.S.) = 35.3 oz. (Brit.)
1 fluid ounce (U.S.) = 29.57 cc. 1 ounce (Brit.) = 28.4 cc.
1 cu. ft. = 28.32 liters.
Mass. 1 gram (g) = mass of 1 cc. of water at 4° C. 1 kilogram = 1000 g. 1 gram = 10 decigrams = 100 centigrams (100 cgm.) = 1000 milligrams (100 mgm.).
1 kilogram = 2.205 lbs. avoird. (U.S. and Brit.)
1000 kilograms = 2205 lbs. = 1 metric ton.
1 lb. avoird. = 453.6 g.
1 oz. avoird. (U.S. and Brit.) = 28.35 g. 100 g. = 3.5 oz.

Appendix VII: Vapor Pressures of Water

Both the Fahrenheit (F), Centigrade (C) temperatures are given

Temperature.		Pressure, mm.	Temperature.		Pressure, mm.
F.	C.		F.	C.	
32°	0°	4.6	71.6°	22°	19.7
41	5	6.5	73.4	23	20.9
46.4	8	8.0	75.2	24	22.2
48.2	9	8.6	77.0	25	23.5
50.0	10	9.2	78.8	26	25.0
51.8	11	9.8	80.6	27	26.5
53.6	12	10.5	82.4	28	28.1
55.4	13	11.2	84.2	29	29.8
57.2	14	11.9	86.0	30	31.5
59.0	15	12.7	87.8	31	33.4
60.8	16	13.5	89.6	32	35.4
62.6	17	14.4	91.4	33	37.4
64.4	18	15.4	93.2	34	39.6
66.2	19	16.3	95.0	35	41.8
68.0	20	17.4			
69.8	21	18.5	212.0	100	760.0

Appendix VIII: Four-Place Logarithms

N	0	1	2	3	4	5	6	7	8	9	Proportional Parts 1	2	3	4	5
10	0000	0043	0086	0128	0170	0212	0253	0294	0334	0374	4	8	12	17	21
11	0414	0453	0492	0531	0569	0607	0645	0682	0719	0755	4	8	11	15	19
12	0792	0828	0864	0899	0934	0969	1004	1038	1072	1106	3	7	10	14	17
13	1139	1173	1206	1239	1271	1303	1335	1367	1399	1430	3	6	10	13	16
14	1461	1492	1523	1553	1584	1614	1644	1673	1703	1732	3	6	9	12	15
15	1761	1790	1818	1847	1875	1903	1931	1959	1987	2014	3	6	8	11	14
16	2041	2068	2095	2122	2148	2175	2201	2227	2253	2279	3	5	8	11	13
17	2304	2330	2355	2380	2405	2430	2455	2480	2504	2529	2	5	7	10	12
18	2553	2577	2601	2625	2648	2672	2695	2718	2742	2765	2	5	7	9	12
19	2788	2810	2833	2856	2878	2900	2923	2945	2967	2989	2	4	7	9	11
20	3010	3032	3054	3075	3096	3118	3139	3160	3181	3201	2	4	6	8	11
21	3222	3243	3263	3284	3304	3324	3345	3365	3385	3404	2	4	6	8	10
22	3424	3444	3464	3483	3502	3522	3541	3560	3579	3598	2	4	6	8	10
23	3617	3636	3655	3674	3692	3711	3729	3747	3766	3784	2	4	5	7	9
24	3802	3820	3838	3856	3874	3892	3909	3927	3945	3962	2	4	5	7	9
25	3979	3997	4014	4031	4048	4065	4082	4099	4116	4133	2	3	5	7	9
26	4150	4166	4183	4200	4216	4232	4249	4265	4281	4298	2	3	5	7	8
27	4314	4330	4346	4362	4378	4393	4409	4425	4440	4456	2	3	5	6	8
28	4472	4487	4502	4518	4533	4548	4564	4579	4594	4609	2	3	5	6	8
29	4624	4639	4654	4669	4683	4698	4713	4728	4742	4757	1	3	4	6	7
30	4771	4786	4800	4814	4829	4843	4857	4871	4886	4900	1	3	4	6	7
31	4914	4928	4942	4955	4969	4983	4997	5011	5024	5038	1	3	4	6	7
32	5051	5065	5079	5092	5105	5119	5132	5145	5159	5172	1	3	4	5	7
33	5185	5198	5211	5224	5237	5250	5263	5276	5289	5302	1	3	4	5	6
34	5315	5328	5340	5353	5366	5378	5391	5403	5416	5428	1	3	4	5	6
35	5441	5453	5465	5478	5490	5502	5514	5527	5539	5551	1	2	4	5	6
36	5563	5575	5587	5599	5611	5623	5635	5647	5658	5670	1	2	4	5	6
37	5682	5694	5705	5717	5729	5740	5752	5763	5775	5786	1	2	3	5	6
38	5798	5809	5821	5832	5843	5855	5866	5877	5888	5899	1	2	3	5	6
39	5911	5922	5933	5944	5955	5966	5977	5988	5999	6010	1	2	3	4	6
40	6021	6031	6042	6053	6064	6075	6085	6096	6107	6117	1	2	3	4	5
41	6128	6138	6149	6160	6170	6180	6191	6201	6212	6222	1	2	3	4	5
42	6232	6243	6253	6263	6274	6284	6294	6304	6314	6325	1	2	3	4	5
43	6335	6345	6355	6365	6375	6385	6395	6405	6415	6425	1	2	3	4	5
44	6435	6444	6454	6464	6474	6484	6493	6503	6513	6522	1	2	3	4	5
45	6532	6542	6551	6561	6571	6580	6590	6599	6609	6618	1	2	3	4	5
46	6628	6637	6646	6656	6665	6675	6684	6693	6702	6712	1	2	3	4	5
47	6721	6730	6739	6749	6758	6767	6776	6785	6794	6803	1	2	3	4	5
48	6812	6821	6830	6839	6848	6857	6866	6875	6884	6893	1	2	3	4	4
49	6902	6911	6920	6928	6937	6946	6955	6964	6972	6981	1	2	3	4	4
50	6990	6998	7007	7016	7024	7033	7042	7050	7059	7067	1	2	3	3	4
51	7076	7084	7093	7101	7110	7118	7126	7135	7143	7152	1	2	3	3	4
52	7160	7168	7177	7185	7193	7202	7210	7218	7226	7235	1	2	2	3	4
53	7243	7251	7259	7267	7275	7284	7292	7300	7308	7316	1	2	2	3	4
54	7324	7332	7340	7348	7356	7364	7372	7380	7388	7396	1	2	2	3	4
N	0	1	2	3	4	5	6	7	8	9	1	2	3	4	5

FOUR-PLACE LOGARITHMS (continued)

N	0	1	2	3	4	5	6	7	8	9	Proportional Parts 1	2	3	4	5
55	7404	7412	7419	7427	7435	7443	7451	7459	7466	7474	1	2	2	3	4
56	7482	7490	7497	7505	7513	7520	7528	7536	7543	7551	1	2	2	3	4
57	7559	7566	7574	7582	7589	7597	7604	7612	7619	7627	1	2	2	3	4
58	7634	7642	7649	7657	7664	7672	7679	7686	7694	7701	1	1	2	3	4
59	7709	7716	7723	7731	7738	7745	7752	7760	7767	7774	1	1	2	3	4
60	7782	7789	7796	7803	7810	7818	7825	7832	7839	7846	1	1	2	3	4
61	7853	7860	7868	7875	7882	7889	7896	7903	7910	7917	1	1	2	3	4
62	7924	7931	7938	7945	7952	7959	7966	7973	7980	7987	1	1	2	3	3
63	7993	8000	8007	8014	8021	8028	8035	8041	8048	8055	1	1	2	3	3
64	8062	8069	8075	8082	8089	8096	8102	8109	8116	8122	1	1	2	3	3
65	8129	8136	8142	8149	8156	8162	8169	8176	8182	8189	1	1	2	3	3
66	8195	8202	8209	8215	8222	8228	8235	8241	8248	8254	1	1	2	3	3
67	8261	8267	8274	8280	8287	8293	8299	8306	8312	8319	1	1	2	3	3
68	8325	8331	8338	8344	8351	8357	8363	8370	8376	8382	1	1	2	3	3
69	8388	8395	8401	8407	8414	8420	8426	8432	8439	8445	1	1	2	3	3
70	8451	8457	8463	8470	8476	8482	8488	8494	8500	8506	1	1	2	2	3
71	8513	8519	8525	8531	8537	8543	8549	8555	8561	8567	1	1	2	2	3
72	8573	8579	8585	8591	8597	8603	8609	8615	8621	8627	1	1	2	2	3
73	8633	8639	8645	8651	8657	8663	8669	8675	8681	8686	1	1	2	2	3
74	8692	8698	8704	8710	8716	8722	8727	8733	8739	8745	1	1	2	2	3
75	8751	8756	8762	8768	8774	8779	8785	8791	8797	8802	1	1	2	2	3
76	8808	8814	8820	8825	8831	8837	8842	8848	8854	8859	1	1	2	2	3
77	8865	8871	8876	8882	8887	8893	8899	8904	8910	8915	1	1	2	2	3
78	8921	8927	8932	8938	8943	8949	8954	8960	8965	8971	1	1	2	2	3
79	8976	8982	8987	8993	8998	9004	9009	9015	9020	9025	1	1	2	2	3
80	9031	9036	9042	9047	9053	9058	9063	9069	9074	9079	1	1	2	2	3
81	9085	9090	9096	9101	9106	9112	9117	9122	9128	9133	1	1	2	2	3
82	9138	9143	9149	9154	9159	9165	9170	9175	9180	9186	1	1	2	2	3
83	9191	9196	9201	9206	9212	9217	9222	9227	9232	9238	1	1	2	2	3
84	9243	9248	9253	9258	9263	9269	9274	9279	9284	9289	1	1	2	2	3
85	9294	9299	9304	9309	9315	9320	9325	9330	9335	9340	1	1	2	2	3
86	9345	9350	9355	9360	9365	9370	9375	9380	9385	9390	1	1	2	2	3
87	9395	9400	9405	9410	9415	9420	9425	9430	9435	9440	0	1	1	2	2
88	9445	9450	9455	9460	9465	9469	9474	9479	9484	9489	0	1	1	2	2
89	9494	9499	9504	9509	9513	9518	9523	9528	9533	9538	0	1	1	2	2
90	9542	9547	9552	9557	9562	9566	9571	9576	9581	9586	0	1	1	2	2
91	9590	9595	9600	9605	9609	9614	9619	9624	9628	9633	0	1	1	2	2
92	9638	9643	9647	9652	9657	9661	9666	9671	9675	9680	0	1	1	2	2
93	9685	9689	9694	9699	9703	9708	9713	9717	9722	9727	0	1	1	2	2
94	9731	9736	9741	9745	9750	9754	9759	9763	9768	9773	0	1	1	2	2
95	9777	9782	9786	9791	9795	9800	9805	9809	9814	9818	0	1	1	2	2
96	9823	9827	9832	9836	9841	9845	9850	9854	9859	9863	0	1	1	2	2
97	9868	9872	9877	9881	9886	9890	9894	9899	9903	9908	0	1	1	2	2
98	9912	9917	9921	9926	9930	9934	9939	9943	9948	9952	0	1	1	2	2
99	9956	9961	9965	9969	9974	9978	9983	9987	9991	9996	0	1	1	2	2
N	**0**	**1**	**2**	**3**	**4**	**5**	**6**	**7**	**8**	**9**	**1**	**2**	**3**	**4**	**5**

FOUR-PLACE ANTILOGARITHMS

FOUR-PLACE ANTILOGARITHMS

N	0	1	2	3	4	5	6	7	8	9	Proportional Parts 1	2	3	4	5
.00	1000	1002	1005	1007	1009	1012	1014	1016	1019	1021	0	0	1	1	1
.01	1023	1026	1028	1030	1033	1035	1038	1040	1042	1045	0	0	1	1	1
.02	1047	1050	1052	1054	1057	1059	1062	1064	1067	1069	0	0	1	1	1
.03	1072	1074	1076	1079	1081	1084	1086	1089	1091	1094	0	0	1	1	1
.04	1096	1099	1102	1104	1107	1109	1112	1114	1117	1119	0	1	1	1	1
.05	1122	1125	1127	1130	1132	1135	1138	1140	1143	1146	0	1	1	1	1
.06	1148	1151	1153	1156	1159	1161	1164	1167	1169	1172	0	1	1	1	1
.07	1175	1178	1180	1183	1186	1189	1191	1194	1197	1199	0	1	1	1	1
.08	1202	1205	1208	1211	1213	1216	1219	1222	1225	1227	0	1	1	1	1
.09	1230	1233	1236	1239	1242	1245	1247	1250	1253	1256	0	1	1	1	1
.10	1259	1262	1265	1268	1271	1274	1276	1279	1282	1285	0	1	1	1	1
.11	1288	1291	1294	1297	1300	1303	1306	1309	1312	1315	0	1	1	1	2
.12	1318	1321	1324	1327	1330	1334	1337	1340	1343	1346	0	1	1	1	2
.13	1349	1352	1355	1358	1361	1365	1368	1371	1374	1377	0	1	1	1	2
.14	1380	1384	1387	1390	1393	1396	1400	1403	1406	1409	0	1	1	1	2
.15	1413	1416	1419	1422	1426	1429	1432	1435	1439	1442	0	1	1	1	2
.16	1445	1449	1452	1455	1459	1462	1466	1469	1472	1476	0	1	1	1	2
.17	1479	1483	1486	1489	1493	1496	1500	1503	1507	1510	0	1	1	1	2
.18	1514	1517	1521	1524	1528	1531	1535	1538	1542	1545	0	1	1	1	2
.19	1549	1552	1556	1560	1563	1567	1570	1574	1578	1581	0	1	1	1	2
.20	1585	1589	1592	1596	1600	1603	1607	1611	1614	1618	0	1	1	1	2
.21	1622	1626	1629	1633	1637	1641	1644	1648	1652	1656	0	1	1	1	2
.22	1660	1663	1667	1671	1675	1679	1683	1687	1690	1694	0	1	1	2	2
.23	1698	1702	1706	1710	1714	1718	1722	1726	1730	1734	0	1	1	2	2
.24	1738	1742	1746	1750	1754	1758	1762	1766	1770	1774	0	1	1	2	2
.25	1778	1782	1786	1791	1795	1799	1803	1807	1811	1816	0	1	1	2	2
.26	1820	1824	1828	1832	1837	1841	1845	1849	1854	1858	0	1	1	2	2
.27	1862	1866	1871	1875	1879	1884	1888	1892	1897	1901	0	1	1	2	2
.28	1905	1910	1914	1919	1923	1928	1932	1936	1941	1945	0	1	1	2	2
.29	1950	1954	1959	1963	1968	1972	1977	1982	1986	1991	0	1	1	2	2
.30	1995	2000	2004	2009	2014	2018	2023	2028	2032	2037	0	1	1	2	2
.31	2042	2046	2051	2056	2061	2065	2070	2075	2080	2084	0	1	1	2	2
.32	2089	2094	2099	2104	2109	2113	2118	2123	2128	2133	0	1	1	2	2
.33	2138	2143	2148	2153	2158	2163	2168	2173	2178	2183	0	1	1	2	2
.34	2188	2193	2198	2203	2208	2213	2218	2223	2228	2234	1	1	2	2	3
.35	2239	2244	2249	2254	2259	2265	2270	2275	2280	2286	1	1	2	2	3
.36	2291	2296	2301	2307	2312	2317	2323	2328	2333	2339	1	1	2	2	3
.37	2344	2350	2355	2360	2366	2371	2377	2382	2388	2393	1	1	2	2	3
.38	2399	2404	2410	2415	2421	2427	2432	2438	2443	2449	1	1	2	2	3
.39	2455	2460	2466	2472	2477	2483	2489	2495	2500	2506	1	1	2	2	3
.40	2512	2518	2523	2529	2535	2541	2547	2553	2559	2564	1	1	2	2	3
.41	2570	2576	2582	2588	2594	2600	2606	2612	2618	2624	1	1	2	2	3
.42	2630	2636	2642	2649	2655	2661	2667	2673	2679	2685	1	1	2	2	3
.43	2692	2698	2704	2710	2716	2723	2729	2735	2742	2748	1	1	2	2	3
.44	2754	2761	2767	2773	2780	2786	2793	2799	2805	2812	1	1	2	3	3
.45	2818	2825	2831	2838	2844	2851	2858	2864	2871	2877	1	1	2	3	3
.46	2884	2891	2897	2904	2911	2917	2924	2931	2938	2944	1	1	2	3	3
.47	2951	2958	2965	2972	2979	2985	2992	2999	3006	3013	1	1	2	3	3
.48	3020	3027	3034	3041	3048	3055	3062	3069	3076	3083	1	1	2	3	3
.49	3090	3097	3105	3112	3119	3126	3133	3141	3148	3155	1	1	2	3	4
N	0	1	2	3	4	5	6	7	8	9	1	2	3	4	5

FOUR-PLACE ANTILOGARITHMS (continued)

N	0	1	2	3	4	5	6	7	8	9	Proportional Parts 1	2	3	4	5
.50	3162	3170	3177	3184	3192	3199	3206	3214	3221	3228	1	1	2	3	4
.51	3236	3243	3251	3258	3266	3273	3281	3289	3296	3304	1	1	2	3	4
.52	3311	3319	3327	3334	3342	3350	3357	3365	3373	3381	1	1	2	3	4
.53	3388	3396	3404	3412	3420	3428	3436	3443	3451	3459	1	2	2	3	4
.54	3467	3475	3483	3491	3499	3508	3516	3524	3532	3540	1	2	2	3	4
.55	3548	3556	3565	3573	3581	3589	3597	3606	3614	3622	1	2	2	3	4
.56	3631	3639	3648	3656	3664	3673	3681	3690	3698	3707	1	2	2	3	4
.57	3715	3724	3733	3741	3750	3758	3767	3776	3784	3793	1	2	3	3	4
.58	3802	3811	3819	3828	3837	3846	3855	3864	3873	3882	1	2	3	3	4
.59	3890	3899	3908	3917	3926	3936	3945	3954	3963	3972	1	2	3	4	5
.60	3981	3990	3999	4009	4018	4027	4036	4046	4055	4064	1	2	3	4	5
.61	4074	4083	4093	4102	4111	4121	4130	4140	4150	4159	1	2	3	4	5
.62	4169	4178	4188	4198	4207	4217	4227	4236	4246	4256	1	2	3	4	5
.63	4266	4276	4285	4295	4305	4315	4325	4335	4345	4355	1	2	3	4	5
.64	4365	4375	4385	4395	4406	4416	4426	4436	4446	4457	1	2	3	4	5
.65	4467	4477	4487	4498	4508	4519	4529	4539	4550	4560	1	2	3	4	5
.66	4571	4581	4592	4603	4613	4624	4634	4645	4656	4667	1	2	3	4	5
.67	4677	4688	4699	4710	4721	4732	4742	4753	4764	4775	1	2	3	4	5
.68	4786	4797	4808	4819	4831	4842	4853	4864	4875	4887	1	2	3	5	6
.69	4898	4909	4920	4932	4943	4955	4966	4977	4989	5000	1	2	3	5	6
.70	5012	5023	5035	5047	5058	5070	5082	5093	5105	5117	1	2	3	5	6
.71	5129	5140	5152	5164	5176	5188	5200	5212	5224	5236	1	2	4	5	6
.72	5248	5260	5272	5284	5297	5309	5321	5333	5346	5358	1	2	4	5	6
.73	5370	5383	5395	5408	5420	5433	5445	5458	5470	5483	1	3	4	5	6
.74	5495	5508	5521	5534	5546	5559	5572	5585	5598	5610	1	3	4	5	6
.75	5623	5636	5649	5662	5675	5689	5702	5715	5728	5741	1	3	4	5	7
.76	5754	5768	5781	5794	5808	5821	5834	5848	5861	5875	1	3	4	5	7
.77	5888	5902	5916	5929	5943	5957	5970	5984	5998	6012	1	3	4	5	7
.78	6026	6039	6053	6067	6081	6095	6109	6124	6138	6152	1	3	4	6	7
.79	6166	6180	6194	6209	6223	6237	6252	6266	6281	6295	1	3	4	6	7
.80	6310	6324	6339	6353	6368	6383	6397	6412	6427	6442	1	3	4	6	7
.81	6457	6471	6486	6501	6516	6531	6546	6561	6577	6592	2	3	5	6	8
.82	6607	6622	6637	6653	6668	6683	6699	6714	6730	6745	2	3	5	6	8
.83	6761	6776	6792	6808	6823	6839	6855	6871	6887	6902	2	3	5	6	8
.84	6918	6934	6950	6966	6982	6998	7015	7031	7047	7063	2	3	5	7	8
.85	7079	7096	7112	7129	7145	7161	7178	7194	7211	7228	2	3	5	7	8
.86	7244	7261	7278	7295	7311	7328	7345	7362	7379	7396	2	3	5	7	8
.87	7413	7430	7447	7464	7482	7499	7516	7534	7551	7568	2	4	5	7	9
.88	7586	7603	7621	7638	7656	7674	7691	7709	7727	7745	2	4	5	7	9
.89	7762	7780	7798	7816	7834	7852	7870	7889	7907	7925	2	4	6	7	9
.90	7943	7962	7980	7998	8017	8035	8054	8072	8091	8110	2	4	6	7	9
.91	8128	8147	8166	8185	8204	8222	8241	8260	8279	8299	2	4	6	8	9
.92	8318	8337	8356	8375	8395	8414	8433	8453	8472	8492	2	4	6	8	10
.93	8511	8531	8551	8570	8590	8610	8630	8650	8670	8690	2	4	6	8	10
.94	8710	8730	8750	8770	8790	8810	8831	8851	8872	8892	2	4	6	8	10
.95	8913	8933	8954	8974	8995	9016	9036	9057	9078	9099	2	4	6	8	10
.96	9120	9141	9162	9183	9204	9226	9247	9268	9290	9311	2	4	6	9	11
.97	9333	9354	9376	9397	9419	9441	9462	9484	9506	9528	2	4	6	9	11
.98	9550	9572	9594	9616	9638	9661	9683	9075	9727	9750	2	4	7	9	11
.99	9772	9795	9817	9840	9863	9886	9908	9931	9954	9977	2	5	7	9	11
N	0	1	2	3	4	5	6	7	8	9	1	2	3	4	5

Appendix IX: Natural Sines and Tangents

o	Sin	Tan	Cot	Cos	o
0	0.0000	0.0000		1.0000	90
1	0.0175	0.0175	57.2900	0.9998	89
2	0.0349	0.0349	28.6363	0.9994	88
3	0.0523	0.0524	19.0811	0.9986	87
4	0.0698	0.0699	14.3007	0.9976	86
5	0.0872	0.0875	11.4301	0.9962	85
6	0.1045	0.1051	9.5144	0.9945	84
7	0.1219	0.1228	8.1443	0.9925	83
8	0.1392	0.1405	7.1154	0.9903	82
9	0.1564	0.1584	6.3138	0.9877	81
10	0.1736	0.1763	5.6713	0.9848	80
11	0.1908	0.1944	5.1446	0.9816	79
12	0.2079	0.2126	4.7046	0.9781	78
13	0.2250	0.2309	4.3315	0.9744	77
14	0.2419	0.2493	4.0108	0.9703	76
15	0.2588	0.2679	3.7321	0.9659	75
16	0.2756	0.2867	3.4874	0.9613	74
17	0.2924	0.3057	3.2709	0.9563	73
18	0.3090	0.3249	3.0777	0.9511	72
19	0.3256	0.3443	2.9042	0.9455	71
20	0.3420	0.3640	2.7475	0.9397	70
21	0.3584	0.3839	2.6051	0.9336	69
22	0.3746	0.4040	2.4751	0.9272	68
23	0.3907	0.4245	2.3559	0.9205	67
24	0.4067	0.4452	2.2460	0.9135	66
25	0.4226	0.4663	2.1445	0.9063	65
26	0.4384	0.4877	2.0503	0.8988	64
27	0.4540	0.5095	1.9626	0.8910	63
28	0.4695	0.5317	1.8807	0.8829	62
29	0.4848	0.5543	1.8040	0.8746	61
30	0.5000	0.5774	1.7321	0.8660	60
31	0.5150	0.6009	1.6643	0.8572	59
32	0.5299	0.6249	1.6003	0.8480	58
33	0.5446	0.6494	1.5399	0.8387	57
34	0.5592	0.6745	1.4826	0.8290	56
35	0.5736	0.7002	1.4281	0.8192	55
36	0.5878	0.7265	1.3764	0.8090	54
37	0.6018	0.7536	1.3270	0.7986	53
38	0.6157	0.7813	1.2799	0.7880	52
39	0.6293	0.8098	1.2349	0.7771	51
40	0.6428	0.8391	1.1918	0.7660	50
41	0.6561	0.8693	1.1504	0.7547	49
42	0.6691	0.9004	1.1106	0.7431	48
43	0.6820	0.9325	1.0724	0.7314	47
44	0.6947	0.9657	1.0355	0.7193	46
45	0.7071	1.0000	1.0000	0.7071	45
o	Cos	Cot	Tan	Sin	o

Appendix X: Periodic Chart of the Elements

IA	IIA	IIIB	IVB	VB	VIB	VIIB	VIIIB			IB	IIB	IIIA	IVA	VA	VIA	VIIA	Inert Gases
1 **H** 1.00797																	2 **He** 4.0026
3 **Li** 6.939	4 **Be** 9.0122											5 **B** 10.811	6 **C** 12.01115	7 **N** 14.0067	8 **O** 15.9994	9 **F** 18.9984	10 **Ne** 20.183
11 **Na** 22.9898	12 **Mg** 24.312											13 **Al** 26.9815	14 **Si** 28.086	15 **P** 30.9738	16 **S** 32.064	17 **Cl** 35.453	18 **Ar** 39.948
19 **K** 39.102	20 **Ca** 40.08	21 **Sc** 44.956	22 **Ti** 47.90	23 **V** 50.942	24 **Cr** 51.996	25 **Mn** 54.9380	26 **Fe** 55.847	27 **Co** 58.9332	28 **Ni** 58.71	29 **Cu** 63.54	30 **Zn** 65.37	31 **Ga** 69.72	32 **Ge** 72.59	33 **As** 74.9216	34 **Se** 78.96	35 **Br** 79.909	36 **Kr** 83.80
37 **Rb** 85.47	38 **Sr** 87.62	39 **Y** 88.905	40 **Zr** 91.22	41 **Nb** 92.906	42 **Mo** 95.94	43 **Tc** (99)	44 **Ru** 101.07	45 **Rh** 102.905	46 **Pd** 106.4	47 **Ag** 107.870	48 **Cd** 112.40	49 **In** 114.82	50 **Sn** 118.69	51 **Sb** 121.75	52 **Te** 127.60	53 **I** 126.9044	54 **Xe** 131.30
55 **Cs** 132.905	56 **Ba** 137.34	57 ***La** 138.91	72 **Hf** 178.49	73 **Ta** 180.948	74 **W** 183.85	75 **Re** 186.2	76 **Os** 190.2	77 **Ir** 192.2	78 **Pt** 195.09	79 **Au** 196.967	80 **Hg** 200.59	81 **Tl** 204.37	82 **Pb** 207.19	83 **Bi** 208.980	84 **Po** (210)	85 **At** (210)	86 **Rn** (222)
87 **Fr** (223)	88 **Ra** (226)	89 **†Ac** (227)															

*Lanthanum Series	58 **Ce** 140.12	59 **Pr** 140.907	60 **Nd** 144.24	61 **Pm** (145)	62 **Sm** 150.35	63 **Eu** 151.96	64 **Gd** 157.25	65 **Tb** 158.924	66 **Dy** 162.50	67 **Ho** 164.930	68 **Er** 167.26	69 **Tm** 168.934	70 **Yb** 173.04	71 **Lu** 174.97
†Actinium Series	90 **Th** 232.038	91 **Pa** (231)	92 **U** 238.03	93 **Np** (237)	94 **Pu** (242)	95 **Am** (243)	96 **Cm** (247)	97 **Bk** (249)	98 **Cf** (251)	99 **Es** (254)	100 **Fm** (253)	101 **Md** (256)	102 **No** (253)	103 **Lw** (257)

The numbers in parentheses are the mass numbers of most stable or most common isotope.

Index

A

Ab-ampere, 117, 192
Aberrations, 166, 196
Ab-henry, 131
Absolute humidity, 78, 189
Absolute potential, 94
Absolute systems of units, 18
Absolute temperature scale, 72
Absolute unit of current, 117, 192
Absolute zero, 72, 188
Absorption spectrum, 172, 197
Ab-volt, 128, 192–193
Acceleration, 15, 184
  angular, 31, 185
  central, 16
  of gravity, 18
Acceptor, 149, 195
Accommodation, 168, 196
Addition of waves, 58
Adhesion, 51
Adhesive force, 51, 187
Adiabatic process, 81–82, 189
Advantage, mechanical, 27, 185
Alloys, Heusler, 125
Alpha particles, 143, 146, 194
Alternating current, 133, 193
Alternating electromotive force, 132–133
Ammeter shunts, 107
Amorphous substances, 77, 189
Ampere, 98–99, 121, 192, 226
  international, 102, 192
Ampere-La Place rule, 118–119, 201
Amplitude
  of simple harmonic motion, 36, 38
  of a wave, 57, 187
Analyzer, 179
Aneroid barometer, 49
Angle
  critical, 159, 160, 196
  of declination, 113, 192
  of dip, 113, 192
  phase-lag, 134, 193
Angular acceleration, 31, 185
Angular displacement, 30, 185
Angular momentum, 34, 185
Angular position, 30
Angular velocity, 30–31, 185
Anions, 101
Anode, 101, 191
Antilogarithms, tables of, 232–233
Antinodes, 59
Anti-particle, 145
Applications of induced electromotive force, 132
Archimedes' principle, 49, 199
Armature, 118
Artificial radioactivity, 147
Astigmatism
  eye, 168
  lens, 166
Astronomical telescope, 169
Atmospheric ionization, 138
Atmospheric moisture, 78
Atmospheric pressure, 48–49
Atom, 67, 143–145
Atom smashing devices, 145

Atomic mass, 146, 194
Atomic number, 146, 194
Audibility, 62
Average acceleration, 15
Average velocity, 3, 15, 184
Avogadro's number, 225
Avogadro's principle, 69
Axial spherical aberrations, 166, 196
Axis
instantaneous, 33
of rotation, 10

B

Back electromotive force, 130
Ball on jet, 53
Ballistic pendulum, 26
Band spectra, 172, 202
Barometer, 48–49
Barometric column, 48–49
Baseball, curved, 53
Battery, electric, 100
Beats, 58
Bernoulli's principle, 52–53, 199
Beta rays, 143, 194
B-H diagrams, 124–125
Binoculars, prism, 169
Biot and Savart's law, 118–120, 201
Blindness, color, 173
Body, black, ideal, 80, 189
Bohr atom, 144
Boiling point, 76, 188
Boyle's law, 50, 189
Brewster's law, 179, 202–203
Bridge, Wheatstone, 108–109
Bright-line spectrum, 171–172, 202
British engineering units, 19, 47
British thermal unit, 74, 188, 225
Brownian motion, 69, 188
Bubble chamber, 146
Bulk modulus, 46, 186
Buoyancy, 49

C

Calcite, 179
Calorie, 74, 188
Calorimetry, 74
Camera, 168
Candle, 157
Candle power, 157, 195
Capacitance, 95, 190
Capacitive reactance, 134, 193
Capacity
electric, 95
heat, 74, 188
Capillarity, 51
Carnot cycle, 82
Cathode, 101, 191
rays, 139–140, 194
Cations, 101
Cell
photoelectric, 142
voltaic, 99–100
Center
of gravity, 11, 184
of mass, 22–23, 185
of oscillation, 40
of percussion, 40, 186
of suspension, 40
Centigrade scale, 70
Centimeter, 2
Central acceleration, 16, 21
Centrifugal force, 20–21, 184
Centripetal force, 20–21, 184
Change of state, 75
Charge
density of, 91, 190
distribution of, 91
electric, 87, 189–190
on electron, 89, 140–141, 225
unit of, 87, 189–190
Charles's law, 73
Chemical effects of currents, 101–102
Chladni figures, 60
Choke coil, 132
Chromatic aberration, 166, 196

Circle of reference, 36–38
Circuit, magnetic, 125
Circular mil, 103, 191
Circulatory nature of current, 99
Clockwise torque, 10
Coefficient
compressibility, 46
of friction, 7, 8, 183
of linear expansion, 71, 188
of rigidity, 46–47, 186
of self-inductance, 131, 193
of stiffness, 38, 186
of surface tension, 51, 186
temperature, of resistance, 103, 191
of thermal conductivity, 79
of tortional stiffness, 38, 186
of viscosity, 53–54, 187
of volume expansion, 71, 188
Coercive force, 125
Cohesion, 51
Cohesive force, 51, 186
Coil
induction, 132
Tesla, 136
Color, 173
primary, 173
of thin films, 176
Color blindness, 173
Color vision, 173
Column, positive, 139, 193
Combinations of resistance, 106–107
Combustion, heat of, 75, 188
Commutator, 118
Compass, 112
Compliance, 134
Component
rectangular, 8–9, 183–184
of vector, 8–9, 183
Composition
of forces, 8
of vectors, 8
Compound microscope, 168–169
Compound pendulum, 40
Compressibility coefficient, 46
Compton effect, 155
Concurrent forces, 10, 184
Condensers, 95, 190
discharge of, 135
in parallel, 96
in series, 96
Conditions of equilibrium, 11–12, 198
Conductance, specific, 103, 191
Conduction
gaseous, 138–139
heat, 79
Conductivity, electric, 103, 191
Conductor, electric, 87
Conservation
of energy, 24–25, 81, 198
of momentum, 22, 198
Conservative force, 25
Constant
dielectric, 87–88, 190
gas, 73
Constructive interference, 58, 175–176
Continuity, 52, 199
Continuous spectrum, 171, 196
Convection, heat, 79
Conventions, optical, 161–162
Converging lens, 163–164
Coplanar forces, 10, 184
Cornea, 167
Corpuscular theory of light, 153
Cosmic rays, 145
Coulomb, 89, 121, 226
international, 102
Coulomb's law
of electrical force, 87–88, 200
of magnetic attraction, 112, 200
Counterclockwise torque, 10
Couple, moment of, 11, 184
Critical angle, 160, 196
Critical pressure, 76, 189
Critical temperature, 76, 189
Crookes' dark space, 139, 194
Crystalline lens of eye, 167

Crystalline substances, 77, 189
Current(s)
  alternating, 133, 193
  chemical effects of, 101–102
  eddy, 130
  effective, 133
  effects of, 99, 101–102, 114
  electric, 98
  heating effects of, 102–103
  induced, 127–128
  intensity of, 98, 190
  lagging, 134
  leading, 134
  magnetic effects of, 114–121
Current direction, conventional, 98
Curvature
  of field, 166
  radius of, 161
Curved baseball, 53
Cutting lines of force, 129
Cycle, Carnot, 82
Cyclic process, 82

D

Dalton's law, 76, 199
Dark space, Crookes', 139, 194
Dark space, Faraday, 139, 194
Dark-line spectrum, 172, 202
D'Arsonval galvanometer, 118
Day, mean solar, 3
Decibel, 62
Declination, angle of, 113, 192
Density, 47, 186
  magnetic induction, 114
  surface, of charge, 91, 190
Destructive interference, 58, 175
Deuteron, 145
Dew point, 78, 189
Diagrams
  B-H, 124–125
  ray, 164–165, 202
Diamagnetism, 122, 124, 192
Dielectric constant, 87–88, 190
Dielectric substance, 87
Difference in potential, 93–94, 190
Diffraction, 177–178, 197
  grating, 178
Diffraction spectroscope, 178
Diffraction spectrum, 178
Diopter, 166, 196
Dip, angle of, 113, 192
Direction of current, conventional, 100
Discharge
  of condenser, 135
  electrical, through gases, 138–139
Discharge rate, 52
Discovery of Oersted, 113–114
Disk paradox, 53
Dispersion, 171, 196
Displacement, 14, 184
  angular, 30, 185
  of simple harmonic motion, 36
Dissipative force, 25
Dissociation, 101
Distortion, 166
Distributive charge, 91
Diverging lens, 163, 165
Donor, 149, 195
Doppler's principle, 60–61, 199
Double refraction, 178–179
Drift
  of electrons, 98–99
  ether, 177
Drop in potential, 105
Dry ice, 77
Dynamical units, 17–18
Dynamics, 14
  rotational, 31
  translational, 17
Dyne, 18, 184
Dyne-centimeter, 3, 183

E

Earth as a magnet, 112–113
Edison effect, 141

Eddy currents, 54, 130
Effect
  Compton, 153
  Edison, 141
  Peltier, 110, 191
  Seebeck, 110, 191
  Zeeman, 175
Effective current, 133
Effects of currents, 99, 101–102, 114
  chemical, 101–102
  heating, 102–103
  magnetic, 114–121
Efficiency of machine, 28, 185
Efflux from a tank, 53
Elasticity, 45
Electric capacity, 95
Electric charge, 87, 189
Electric current, 98, 190
Electric eye, 143
Electric field intensity, 90, 190
Electric induction, 91–92, 190
Electric potential, 93–94, 190
Electric power, 102, 135
Electric resistance, 103, 191
Electric transformer, 132
Electrochemical equivalent, 102, 191
Electrolysis, 101
  Faraday's laws of, 102, 200
Electrolyte, 101
Electromagnetic induction, 127
Electromagnetic oscillations, 135
Electromagnetic radiation, 136
Electromagnetic spectrum, 80, 153–154
Electromotive force, 99–100, 191
  alternating, 132
  back, 130
  induced, 127
  thermal, 110
Electron(s), 68, 88, 140, 225
  drift of, 98–99
  thermionic emission of, 141
Electronic charge, 141
Electronic mass, 141
Electronics, 142–143
Electrophorus, 92
Electroplating, 101–102
Electroscope, 93
Electrostatics, 90
Emission of electrons, thermionic, 141
Energy, 4, 24–25, 39, 183
  conservation of, 24–25, 81, 198
  kinetic, 4, 25–26, 32, 39, 183
  in magnetic field, 132
  potential, 4, 25, 39, 183
Energy levels, 144
Engine, ideal, 82
Entropy, 83, 189
Equilibrium, conditions of, 11–12, 198
Equivalent
  electrochemical, 102, 191
  gram, 102
  mechanical, of heat, 81
Erg, 3, 185
Ether, 79, 153, 177
Ether drift, 177
Evaporation, 76
Exchange force, 148
Expansion
  of gases, 71
  thermal, 70–71, 188
Experiment(s)
  of Faraday on induction, 129
  Melde's, 60
  Young's interference, 173–174
Extraordinary ray, 179
Eye, 167
  electric, 143

F

Factor, power, 135, 193
Fahrenheit scale, 70
Farad, 96, 226
Faraday (unit), 102, 191
Faraday's dark space, 139, 194

Faraday's experiments on induction, 129
Faraday's laws of electrolysis, 102, 200
Far-point of eye, 167
Farsightedness, 167–168
Fermi level, 148
Field, curvature of, 166
Field glass, 169
Field intensity
electric, 90, 190
gravitational, 41
magnetic, 115, 123, 191
Figures, Chladni, 60
First law of thermodynamics, 81, 200
Fluid flow, 52, 187
Fluid friction, 53
Fluid pressure, 47–48, 186
Fluids
at rest, 47
in motion, 52
Fluorescence, 140
Flux
light, 156
magnetic, 115, 121, 125, 129
Focal length, 163, 196
Foot, 2
Foot-candle, 157, 195–196
Foot-pound, 183
Force(s), 3, 7
adhesive, 51, 187
centrifugal, 20–21, 184
centripetal, 20–21, 184
coercive, 125
cohesive, 51, 186
composition of, 8–9
concurrent, 10, 184
conservative, 25
contact, 7
coplanar, 10, 184
dissipative, 25
electric lines of, 90, 190
electromotive, 99–100, 191
field, 7
magnetic, 112
magnetic lines of, 113, 192
magnetomotive, 125
Formula(s)
for thin lenses, 163
for single spherical surface, 162
Foucault currents, 130
Fourier's theorem, 58
Fraunhofer lines, 172, 197
Freezing point, 76–77
Frequency
fundamental, 60
of simple harmonic motion, 38, 186
wave, 57
Friction, 7
coefficient of, 7, 186
fluid, 53
Front, wave, 156
Function of a theory, 154
Functions, trigonometric, tables of, 234
Fundamental concepts of physics, 2
Fundamental frequency, 60
Fusion, 76
heat of, 76, 189

G

Galilean telescope, 169
Galvanometer, D'Arsonval, 118
Gamma rays, 143, 194
Gas(es), 50
ideal, 50, 72–73
Gas constant, 73, 225
Gas expansion, 71–72
Gas laws, general, 72–73, 199
Gaseous conduction, 138–139
Gaseous discharge, electrical, 138–139
Gauss, 116
Gay-Lussac's laws, 73

Geissler tubes, 140
General gas laws, 72–73, 199
Geometric optics, 161
Glass
  field, 169
  magnifying, 166
  opera, 169
  spy-, 169
Glow, negative, 139, 193–194
Gradient
  potential, 90
  temperature, 79
Gram, 3, 18–19
Gram equivalent, 102
Grating, diffraction, 178
Gravitation, 41
Gravitational field intensity, 41
Gravitational potential, 41
Gravitational systems of units, 18
Gravity
  acceleration of, 18
  center of, 11, 184
  specific, 47, 186
Greek alphabet, 227
Gyration, radius of, 33, 185

H

Half life, 146
Harmonic motion
  rotary, 39
  simple, 36, 185–186
Harmonic waves, 57
Harmonics, 60
Heat, 67–69
  of combustion, 75, 188
  conduction of, 79
  convection of, 79
  of fusion, 76, 189
  measurement of, 74
  radiation of, 79–80
  specific, 74–75, 188
  transfer of, 79
  of vaporization, 76, 188
Heat capacity, 74, 188
  of gases, 75
Heating effects of currents, 102–103
Henry (unit), 131, 226
Heusler alloys, 125
Holes, 149
Hooke's law of elasticity, 45–46, 199
Horsepower, 4, 183, 226
Humidity, 78, 189
Huygens' principle, 155–156, 201
Hydraulics, 52
Hydrometer, 49
Hydrostatic pressure, 47–48, 186
Hydrostatics, 47
Hypermetropia, 167–168, 196
Hysteresis, magnetic, 124–125

I

Ice, 76
  dry, 77
Iceland spar, 179
Ideal black body, 80, 189
Ideal engine, 83
Ideal gas, 50, 72–73
Illuminance, 157, 195
Image
  real, 164–165, 196
  virtual, 164–165
Impedance, 134, 193
Impulse of force, 22, 184–185
Impurity semiconductor, 148
Inclined plane, 29
Index of refraction, 160, 196
Induced current, Lenz's law of, 130, 201
Induced electromotive force, 127
Inductance
  coefficient of self-, 131, 193
  of solenoid, 131–132
Induction
  electric, 91–92, 190
  electromagnetic, 127

Induction (*continued*)
magnetic, 114
mutual, 130, 193
self-, 130, 193
Induction coil, 132
Inductive reactance, 134, 193
Inertia, 3
moment of, 31–32, 185
Influence, electric, 91–92
Instantaneous axis, 34
Instantaneous velocity, 15, 184
Insulator, electric, 87
Intensity
of current, 98, 190
of electric field, 90, 190
of light source, 157
of magnetic field, 115, 123, 191
of magnetization, 124
Interference
constructive, 58, 175–176
destructive, 58, 175
of light, 173–175
of waves, 58
Interferometer, 176–177
Internal reflection, 159
International ampere, 102, 192
International coulomb, 102
International ohm, 104, 192
International volt, 105, 192
Inverse square law of illumination, 157, 202
Ion, 101
Ionization, atmospheric, 138
Irreversible process, 82
Isothermal process, 81, 189
Isotopes, 145, 194

J

Jet, ball on, 53
Joule (unit), 94, 102, 185
Joule's equivalent, 81, 102
Joule's law, 102, 200

K

Kepler's laws of planetary motion, 40–41
Kilogram, 3
Kinematics, 14
Kinetic energy, 4, 25, 32
Kinetic theory of gases, 67–69
Kirchhoff's rules, 105–106, 201

L

Lag angle, phase, 134, 193
Lagging current, 134
Lambert, 157, 195
Lamination, 130
Lantern projection, 168
Large calorie, 74, 188
Laser, 149
Law(s)
of Biot and Savart, 118–120, 201
of Boyle, 50, 199
of Brewster, 179, 202–203
of Charles, 73
of continuity, 52, 199
of Coulomb
electrical, 87–88, 200
magnetic, 112, 200
of Dalton, 76, 199
of electrolysis, 102, 200
of Faraday, 102, 200
of Gay-Lussac, 73
of gravity, 41, 199
of Hooke, 45–46, 199
of Joule, 102, 200
of Lenz, 130, 201
of machines, 27
of motion, 17, 198
of Newton, 17, 41, 198–199
of Ohm, 101, 200
of partial pressures, 76, 199
of Pascal, 48, 199
of reflection of light, 158, 201–202

Law(s) (*continued*)
of refraction of light, 158, 202
of Snell, 158, 202
of spectroscopy, 171–172, 202
of Stefan, 80, 200
of thermodynamics, 81, 83, 200
of Van der Waals, 50
of Wien, 80, 200
Leading current, 134
Left-hand rule, 116
Length, 2, 183, 225
focal, 163, 196
wave, 57, 187
Lens aberrations, 166
Lenses, 165
Lenz's law, 130, 201
Lever, 28
Lever arm, 10, 184
Light, 153
nature of, 153
propagation of, 155–156
velocity of, 155, 191
Light flux, 156
Light ray, 155
Linear expansion, 71, 188
Lines of force
cutting, 128
electric, 90, 190
magnetic, 113, 192
Lodestone, 112
Logarithms, tables of, 230–231
Longitudinal waves, 56, 187
Loops, 60
Loudness of sound, 62, 187
Lumen, 156, 195
Luminance of an extended source, 157

M

Machines, 27–29, 185
efficiency of, 28, 185
Magnetic effect of current, 114, 121
Magnetic field, 114–115, 191
near conductors, 113–114
intensity of, 115, 123, 191
Magnetic flux, 115, 121–122, 129
Magnetic force, 112
Magnetic hysteresis, 124–125
Magnetic induction, 114
Magnetic lines of force, 113, 192
Magnetic moment, 124, 192
Magnetic permeability, 121–122, 192
Magnetic pole(s), 112, 124
unit, 191
Magnetic reluctance, 125
Magnetic susceptibility, 124, 192
Magnetism, 112
residual, 125
Magnetization, 124
Magnetomotive force, 125
Magnifying glass, 166
Magnifying power, 167
Mass, 2, 17, 183, 186, 226
center of, 22–23, 185
of electron, 141, 225
Maxwell's law, 69
Mean free path, 138
Mean solar day, 3
Mean solar second, 3
Measurements, photometric, 157–158
Mechanical advantage, 27, 185
Mechanical equivalent of heat, 81
Melde's experiment, 60
Meson, 145, 194
Meteorology, 78
Meter, 2
Method of mixtures, 75
Metric system, 228
Michelson-Morley experiment, 177
Michelson's interferometer, 176–177
Micro-farad, 96
Micro-micro-farad, 96

Microscope
compound, 168–169
simple, 166
Mil
circular, 103, 191
square, 103
Milikan oil-drop experiment, 140–141
Millimeter, 2
Mirror formula, 163
Mixtures, method of, 75
M.K.S. units, 19
Modulus
bulk, 46, 186
shear, 46, 186
Young's, 46, 186
Moisture, atmospheric, 78
Molecules, 67
Moment
of couple, 11
of force, 10
of inertia, 31, 185
magnetic, 124, 192
Momentum, 22, 184
angular, 34–35, 185
conservation of, 22, 198
Morley: *see* Michelson-Morley experiment, 177
Motion
Brownian, 69, 188
Newton's laws of, 17, 41, 198–199
periodic, 36
planetary, 40–41
projectile, 21
rotary, 10, 31, 204
rotary harmonic, 39
simple harmonic, 36, 185–186
translatory, 10, 204
uniform, 15
uniform curvilinear, 16
uniformly accelerated, 15–16
wave, 55, 187
Motor electric, 118
Multipliers, voltage, 107
Muon, 145
Mutual induction, 130
coefficient of, 130, 193
Myopia, 167, 196

N

Natural sines and tangents, table of, 234
Nature of light, 153–154
Nature of a theory, 154
Near-point of eye, 167
Nearsightedness, 167
Negative charge, 87
Negative glow, 139, 193–194
Neutron, 68, 89, 145, 147, 194
Newton's law of gravity, 41, 199
Newton's laws of motion, 17, 31, 198–199
Newton's rings, 176
Nodes, 59
North poles, magnetic, 113
Nuclear binding energy, 147
Nuclear physics, 145–147
Nuclear reactions, 146
Nuclear transformations, 146

O

Oersted, 113–114
Ohm (unit), 102, 200
international, 104, 192
Ohm's law, 104, 200
Oil-drop experiment, Millikan's, 140–141
Opera glass, 169
Optical conventions, 161–162
Optical phenomena, 154–155
Optics
geometric, 161
physical, 171
Ordinary ray, 179
Organ pipes, 61–62

Oscillation, center of, 40
Oscillations, electromagnetic, 135
Overtones, harmonic, 62

P

Paradox, disk, 53
Parallel resistance, 106–107
Paramagnetism, 121–122, 192
Particles, alpha, 143, 146, 194
Pascal's law, 48, 199
Path, mean free, 138
Pauli exclusion principle, 148
Peltier effect, 110, 191
Pendulum
  ballistic, 26
  compound, 40
  simple, 26, 38
Percussion, center of, 40, 186
Period
  of simple harmonic motion, 38, 186
  wave, 57, 187
Periodic motion, 36
Permeability, magnetic, 121–122, 192
Phase change in reflection, 59
Phase-lag angle, 134, 193
Phenomena, optical, 154–155
Phonon, 148, 195
Phot, 157
Photoelasticity, 180
Photoelectric cell, 142
Photoelectric effect, 142, 194
Photometric measurements, 157–158
Photometry, 156
Photon, 154, 195
Physical constants, 225
Physical optics, 171
Piezoelectricity, 101
Pion, 145
Pipes, sounds in, 61–62
Pitch, 62, 187
Planck's constant, 142, 225
Planck's quantum theory, 80–81, 142
Planetary motion, 40–41, 198–199
Point
  boiling, 76, 188
  dew, 78, 189
  freezing, 76–77
  triple, 77, 189
Polarization, 178–179, 197
Polarized light, 178–180, 197, 202
Polarizer, 179
Polarizing material, 179
Poles, magnetic, 112, 124
Position, 14
  angular, 30
Positive charge, 87, 189–190
Positive column, 139, 193
Positron, 89, 145, 194
Potential
  absolute, 94
  drop in, 105
  electric, 93–94, 190
  gravitational, 41
Potential energy, 4, 25, 39, 183
Potential gradient, 90
Potentiometer, 109–110
Pound, 3, 19
Poundal, 19
Power, 4, 183, 226
  A.C., 133, 193
  electric, 102, 135
  resolving, 178
Power factor, 135, 193
Precession, 31, 35
Presbyopia, 167–168
Pressure(s)
  atmospheric, 48–49
  critical, 76, 189
  hydrostatic, 47–48, 186
  partial, 76, 199
  due to surface tension, 51
  transmissibility of, 48, 199
  vapor, 76

Pressure-temperature coefficient, 71
Primary colors, 173
Principle
of Bernoulli, 52–53, 199
of Doppler, 60–61, 199
of Huygens, 155–156, 201
of Torricelli, 48
of virtual work, 27
Prism binocular, 169
Problem procedures, 12, 19, 33, 49–50, 108
Process(es)
adiabatic, 81–82, 189
cyclic, 82
irreversible, 82, 189
isothermal, 81, 189
reversible, 82, 189
thermodynamic, 81–82
Projectile motion, 21
Projection lantern, 168
Propagation of light, rectilinear, 155
Proton, 68, 88
Pulley, 28
Pulse, wave, 55
Pupil of eye, 167
Pyroelectricity, 100

Q

Quality of sound, 63, 187
Quantum mechanics, 144
Quantum theory, 80–81, 142

R

Radar, 143
Radiation
electromagnetic, 136
of heat, 79–80
Radio, 143
Radio waves, 80
Radioactivity, 143
artificial, 147
Radius
of curvature, 161
of gyration, 33, 185
Range of a projectile, 21
Rate, discharge, 52
Ray(s)
alpha, 143, 146, 194
beta, 143, 194
cathode, 139–140, 194
extraordinary, 179
gamma, 143, 194
light, 156
ordinary, 179
X, 80, 143, 194
Ray diagrams, 164–165, 202
Reactance, 134, 193
capacitive, 134, 193
inductive, 134, 193
Real image, 164–165, 196
Rectangular components, 8–9, 183–184
Rectifiers, 143
Rectilinear propagation of light, 155
Reference circle, 36–38
Reflection
of light, 158, 201
and phase change, 59
of waves, 59
Refraction
double, 178–179
of light, 158, 202
of waves, 59, 187
Refractive index, 59, 160, 196
of light, 158, 196
Regelation, 77
Relative humidity, 78, 189
Relays, 143
Reluctance, magnetic, 125
Remanence, 125
Representation of waves, 56
Residual magnetism, 125
Resistance, electric, 103, 191
Resistance combinations, 106–107

Resistance-temperature coefficient, 103, 191
Resistivity, 103, 191
Resolution
of forces, 8
of vectors, 8
Resolving power, 178
Resonance, 60, 134
Resultant, vector, 8
Retina, 167
Reversible process, 82, 189
Right-hand rule, 127–128
Rigidity coefficient, 46–47, 186
Rings, Newton's, 176
Roentgen rays, 143
Root-mean-square value, 133
Rotary harmonic motion, 39
Rotary motion, 10, 31, 204
Rotational dynamics, 31
Rule(s)
of Ampere-La Place, 118–119, 201
Kirchhoff's, 105–106, 201
left-hand, 116
right-hand, 127–128

S

Saccharimeter, 180
Saccharimetry, 180, 197
Scalar quantity, 8
Scales, temperature, 70
Scattering of light, 175
Scintillation counter, 146
Screw, 29
Second, mean solar, 3
Second law of thermodynamics, 83, 200
Seebeck effect, 110, 191
Self-inductance, coefficient of, 131, 193
Self-induction, 113
Series resistance, 106
Shear modulus, 46, 186
Shunt, ammeter, 107
Side thrust, 116, 201
Simple harmonic motion, 36, 185–186
Simple microscope, 166
Simple pendulum, 26, 38
Sine waves, 57
Sines, table of, 234
Single spherical surface formulae, 162
Slug, 18, 184
Snell's law, 158, 202
Solid state physics, 148
Sound(s), 61–63
in pipes, 61–62
velocity of, 61
South poles, magnetic, 112, 124
Space
Crookes' dark, 139, 194
Faraday dark, 139, 194
Specific conductance, 103, 191
Specific gravity, 47, 186
Specific heat, 74–75, 188
Specific inductive capacity, 190
Spectrograph, 171
Spectroscope, 171
diffraction, 178
Spectroscopy, 171–172, 202
Spectrum
absorption, 172, 197
band, 172, 202
bright-line, 171–172, 202
continuous, 171, 196
dark-line, 172, 202
diffraction, 178
electromagnetic, 80, 153–154
optical, 171
Speed, 15, 184
Spherical aberration, 166, 196
Spherical angle, 156
Spyglass, 169
Square mil, 103
Standing waves, 59–60
Stat-coulomb, 89

State, change of, 75
Stat-farad, 95
Statics, 7
Stationary waves, 59–60
Stat-volt, 94
Steady flow, 52, 187
Steam, 76
Stefan's law of radiation, 80, 200
Ster-radian, 156, 195
Stiffness, coefficient of, 38, 186
Strain, 45, 186
Strange particle, 145
Streamlines, 52, 187
Stress, 45, 186
Striations, positive column, 193
Subdivisions of Physics, 1
Sublimation, 77, 189
Substance, dielectric, 87
Superconductivity, 104
Superheating, 77
Surface, vertex of, 161
Surface density of charge, 91, 190
Surface tension, 50–51, 186
Susceptibility, magnetic, 124, 192
Suspension, center of, 40
Systems of units, 18–19, 47

T

Table
  of antilogarithms, 232–233
  of logarithms, 230–231
  of natural sines and tangents, 234
Tangents, table of, 234
Telescope
  astronomical, 169
  Galilean, 169
  terrestrial, 169
Television, 143
Temperature, 67, 69, 187–188
  critical, 76, 189
  scales of, 70, 72
  thermodynamic, 83
Temperature gradient, 79
Temperature-pressure coefficient, 71
Temperature-resistance coefficient, 103, 191
Tension, surface, 50–51, 186
Tesla coil, 136
Theoretical mechanical advantage, 27
Theories of light, 153
Theory
  function of a, 154
  nature of a, 154
  quantum, 80–81, 144
Thermal capacity, 74, 188
Thermal conductivity, 79
Thermal electromotive force, 110
Thermal expansion, 70–71, 188
Thermionic emission, 141
Thermocouple, 110
Thermodynamic processes, 81–82
Thermodynamic temperature, 83
Thermodynamics, laws of, 81, 83, 200
Thermoelectricity, 110
Thermopiles, 110
Thin films, colors of, 175
Thin lens formula, 163
Threshold of audibility, 62
Thrust, side, 116, 201
Thyratrons, 143
Time, 2–3, 183
Torque, 10, 32, 184
Torricelli's principle, 48
Torsional stiffness, coefficient of, 38, 186
Torsional wave, 56
Total internal reflection, 159
Train, wave, 55
Transfer of heat, 79
Transformer, 132
Transistor, 142, 195
Translational dynamics, 47

Translatory motion, 10, 204
Transmissibility of pressure, 48, 199
Transverse wave, 56, 187
Trigonometric functions, table of, 234
Triode, 141
Triple point, 77, 189
Tubes, vacuum, 141, 143
Types of rotary motion, 31
Types of spectra, 171–172

U

Uncertainty principle, 144, 194
Undercooling, 77
Uniform curvilinear motion, 16
Uniform motion, 15
Uniform rotary motion, 31
Uniformly accelerated motion, 15
Uniformly accelerated rotary motion, 31
Unit(s)
  of charge, 87, 189–190
  British Engineering, 19, 47
  British thermal, 74, 188, 226
  C.G.S., 19, 47
  dynamical, 17–18
  electrostatic, 89
  metric, 228
  M.K.S., 19
Unit magnetic pole, 191
Unit positive charge, 89, 189–190

V

Vacuum tubes, 141, 143
Van der Waals law, 50
Vapor pressure(s), 76
  of water, 229
Vaporization, 76
  heat of, 76, 188
Vector(s), 8
Vector quantity, 8, 183
Velocity, 15
  angular, 30–31, 185
  average, 3, 15, 184
  instantaneous, 15, 184
  of light, 155, 191
  of sound, 61
  wave, 59
Venturi water meter, 53
Vertex of surface, 161
Virtual image, 164–165, 196
Virtual work, 27
Viscosity, 53, 187
Vision, color, 173
Volt, 94, 192, 226
  absolute electromagnetic, 128, 192–193
  international, 105, 192
  stat-, 94
Voltage multipliers, 107
Voltaic cell, 99–100
Volume, 2, 28
Volume expansion, 71–72, 188

W

Water, vapor pressure of, 229
Water equivalent, 74, 188
Watt (unit), 102, 226
Wave(s)
  amplitude of, 57, 187
  harmonic, 57
  longitudinal, 56, 187
  reflection of, 59
  refraction of, 59, 187
  representation of, 56
  torsional, 56
  stationary, 59
  transverse, 56, 187
  sine, 57
Wave front, 156
Wave length, 57, 187

Wave motion, 55, 187
  frequency of, 57
  period of, 57, 187
  velocity of, 59
Wave pulse, 55
Wave theory of light, 153
Wave train, 57
Wedge, 29
Weight, 3, 7, 17, 183
Weight density, 47, 186
Work, 3, 24, 34, 183, 198, 266
  virtual, 27
Wilson cloud chamber, 146
Wheatstone bridge, 108–109
Wheel and axle, 29
Wien's displacement law, 80, 200

X

X-component of vector, 9
X rays, 80, 143, 194

Y

Yard, 2
Y-component of vector, 9
Young's interference experiment, 173–174
Young's modulus, 46, 186

Z

Zeeman effect, 175
Zero, absolute, 72, 188
Zero point energy, 195